GCSE
Mathematics

At CGP, we're a bit obsessed with GCSE Maths... so we had a great time packing this book with everything you need for the Foundation Level exams. It's a Maths extravaganza.

As you'd expect, we've included unbeatably clear notes and examples, plus brilliant practice questions and realistic exam papers. And don't forget the amazing digital extras — there's a free Online Edition, interactive quizzes and step-by-step video solutions.

Once you've got through all that, you'll love GCSE Maths almost as much as we do.

Unlock your free online extras!

Just go to **cgpbooks.co.uk/extras** and enter this code or scan the QR codes in the book.

0647 7366 1740 9858

By the way, this code only works for one person. If somebody else has used this book before you, they might have already claimed the Online Edition.

Complete
Revision & Practice

Everything you need to pass the exams!

Contents

Throughout this book you'll see **grade stamps** like these:

You can use these to focus your revision on easier or harder work.
But remember — to get a top grade you have to know **everything**, not just the hardest topics.

You'll see **QR codes** throughout the book that you can scan with your smartphone.

A QR code next to an exam-style question takes you to a **video** that talks you through solving the question. You can access **all** the videos by scanning this code here.

A QR code on a 'Revision Questions' page takes you to a **Sudden Fail Quiz** for that topic. Fancy trying a quiz covering **every topic** in the book? Then scan this code right here!

You can also find the **full set of videos** at cgpbooks.co.uk/GCSEMathsVideos-Foundation and the **full set of quizzes** at cgpbooks.co.uk/GCSEMathsQuiz-Foundation

Published by CGP

From original material by Richard Parsons

Updated by: Martha Bozic, Eleanor Crabtree, Sammy El-Bahrawy, Sarah George,
          Ruth Greenhalgh, David Ryan, Caley Simpson

Contributor: Alastair Duncombe

With thanks to Simon Little and Michael Weynberg for the proofreading
With thanks to Jan Greenway for the copyright research

Printed by Elanders Ltd, Newcastle upon Tyne.
Clipart from Corel®

Types of Number and BODMAS

Ah, the glorious world of GCSE Maths. Get stuck into this first section and you'll be an expert in no time. Here are some handy definitions of different types of number, and a bit about what order to do things in.

Integers

An <u>integer</u> is another name for a <u>whole number</u> — either a positive or negative number, or zero.

Examples

Integers:	–365, 0, 1, 17, 989, 1 234 567 890
Not integers:	0.5, $\frac{2}{3}$, $\sqrt{7}$, $13\frac{3}{4}$, –1000.1, 66.66, π

Square and Cube Numbers

1) When you <u>multiply</u> a whole number by <u>itself</u>, you get a <u>square number</u>:

1^2	2^2	3^2	4^2	5^2	6^2	7^2	8^2	9^2	10^2	11^2	12^2	13^2	14^2	15^2
1	4	9	16	25	36	49	64	81	100	121	144	169	196	225
(1×1)	(2×2)	(3×3)	(4×4)	(5×5)	(6×6)	(7×7)	(8×8)	(9×9)	(10×10)	(11×11)	(12×12)	(13×13)	(14×14)	(15×15)

2) When you <u>multiply</u> a whole number by <u>itself</u>, then by itself <u>again</u>, you get a <u>cube number</u>:

1^3	2^3	3^3	4^3	5^3	10^3
1	8	27	64	125	1000
(1×1×1)	(2×2×2)	(3×3×3)	(4×4×4)	(5×5×5)	(10×10×10)

3) You should know these basic squares and cubes <u>by heart</u> — they could come up on a non-calculator paper, so it'll save you time if you already know what they are.

BODMAS — <u>B</u>rackets, <u>O</u>ther, <u>D</u>ivision, <u>M</u>ultiplication, <u>A</u>ddition, <u>S</u>ubtraction

<u>BODMAS</u> tells you the <u>ORDER</u> in which these operations should be done:
Work out <u>Brackets</u> first, then <u>Other</u> things like squaring, then <u>Divide</u> / <u>Multiply</u> groups of numbers before <u>Adding</u> or <u>Subtracting</u> them.

EXAMPLE **Find the reciprocal of $\sqrt{4 + 6 \times (12 - 2)}$.**

It's not obvious what to do inside the square root — so use BODMAS. <u>Brackets</u> first...

$$\sqrt{4 + 6 \times (12 - 2)} = \sqrt{4 + 6 \times 10}$$
$$= \sqrt{4 + 60}$$ ... then <u>multiply</u>...
$$= \sqrt{64}$$ ... then <u>add</u>.
$$= 8$$

<u>Take the square root</u>

The reciprocal of 8 is $\frac{1}{8}$.

Finally, take the <u>reciprocal</u> (the reciprocal of a number is just 1 ÷ the number).

Brackets, Other, Division, Multiplication, Addition, Subtraction

It's really important to check your working on BODMAS questions. You might be certain you did it right, but it's surprisingly easy to make a slip. Try this Exam Practice Question and see how you do:

Q1   Without using a calculator, find the value of $3 + 22 \times 3 - 14$. [2 marks]

Wordy Real-Life Problems

*Wordy questions can be a bit off-putting — for these you don't just have to do **the maths**, you've got to work out what the question's **asking you to do**. It's **really** important that you begin by reading through the question **really** carefully...*

Don't Be Scared of Wordy Questions

<u>Relax</u> and work through them <u>step by step</u>:

1) <u>READ</u> the question <u>carefully</u>. Work out <u>what bit of maths</u> you need to answer it.
2) <u>Underline</u> the <u>INFORMATION YOU NEED</u> to answer the question — you might not have to use <u>all</u> the numbers they give you.
3) Write out the question <u>IN MATHS</u> and answer it, showing all your <u>working</u> clearly.

 EXAMPLES

1. **A return car journey from Carlisle to Manchester uses $\frac{4}{7}$ of a tank of petrol. It costs <u>£56</u> for a <u>full tank</u> of petrol. How much does the journey cost?**

   You want to know $\frac{4}{7}$ of £56, so in maths: $\frac{4}{7}$ × £56 = £32

   See p.15-17 for more on using fractions.

   Don't forget the units in your final answer — this is a question about <u>cost in pounds</u>, so the units will be £.

2. **A water company has two different price plans for water usage:**

PLAN A	PLAN B
No fixed cost	**Fixed cost of £12**
23p per unit	**Plus 11p per unit**

   A household uses <u>102 units</u> of water in one month. Which price plan would be cheaper for this household in that particular month?

   Cost with plan A: 102 × £0.23 = £23.46
   Cost with plan B: £12 + (102 × £0.11) = £23.22

   So for this household in that particular month, plan B would be cheaper.

3. **Vashti buys dog food in boxes of <u>20 packets</u>. Each box costs <u>£12.50</u>. She has <u>3 dogs</u> which each eat <u>2 packets per day</u>. How much will it cost her to buy enough boxes of food for all of her dogs for <u>4 weeks</u>?**

   Number of packets for 3 dogs for 1 day = 3 × 2 = 6
   Number of packets for 3 dogs for 4 weeks = 6 × 7 × 4 = 168
   Number of boxes needed = 168 ÷ 20 = 8.4
   Vashti can't buy part of a box, so she needs to buy 9 boxes.
   9 × £12.50 = £112.50

Just because it's wordy doesn't mean it's difficult...

A lot of these wordy questions have a few stages to the working — if you take them one step at a time, they're really not bad at all. Have a go at breaking down this Exam Practice Question.

Q1   Hank owns a fruit stall. He sells <u>11 apples</u> and <u>5 oranges</u> for <u>£2.71</u>.
      One apple costs <u>16p</u>. How much does one orange cost?   [4 marks]

= 19p

Q1 Video Solution

Multiplying and Dividing by 10, 100, etc.

*You need to know the stuff on this page — it's quite simple and they're likely to **test you on it** in the exam.*

1) **Multiplying** and **Dividing** Any Number by **10**

Multiply — Move the decimal point <u>ONE</u> place <u>BIGGER</u> (↘) and if it's needed, <u>ADD A ZERO</u> on the end.

Divide — Move the decimal point <u>ONE</u> place <u>SMALLER</u> (↙) and if it's needed, <u>REMOVE ZEROS</u> after the decimal point.

E.g. 23.6 × 10 = 2 3 6

E.g. 23.6 ÷ 10 = 2 . 3 6

2) **Multiplying** and **Dividing** Any Number by **100**

Multiply — Move the decimal point <u>TWO</u> places <u>BIGGER</u> and <u>ADD ZEROS</u> if necessary.

Divide — Move the decimal point <u>TWO</u> places <u>SMALLER</u> and <u>REMOVE ZEROS</u> after the decimal point.

E.g. 34 × 100 = 3 4 0 0

E.g. 340 ÷ 100 = 3 . 4

3) **Multiplying** and **Dividing** by **1000** or **10 000**

Multiply — Move the decimal point so many places <u>BIGGER</u> and <u>ADD ZEROS</u> if necessary.

Divide — Move the decimal point so many places <u>SMALLER</u> and <u>REMOVE ZEROS</u> after the decimal point.

You always <u>move</u> the <u>decimal point</u> this much:
<u>1 place for 10</u>,   <u>2 places for 100</u>,
<u>3 places for 1000</u>,   <u>4 places for 10 000</u>, etc.

4) **Multiply** and **Divide** by Numbers like **20, 300,** etc.

<u>MULTIPLY</u> by <u>2</u> or <u>3</u> or <u>8</u> etc. <u>FIRST</u>, then move the decimal point so many places <u>BIGGER</u>, according to how many zeros there are.

<u>DIVIDE</u> by <u>4</u> or <u>3</u> or <u>7</u> etc. <u>FIRST</u>, then move the decimal point so many places <u>SMALLER</u>, according to how many zeros there are.

EXAMPLES

1. **Calculate 234 × 200.**
234 × 2 = 468
468 × 100 = 46800

2. **Calculate 960 ÷ 300.**
960 ÷ 3 = 320
320 ÷ 100 = 3.2

Multiplying — move the decimal point to the right

When dividing move the decimal point to the left. Seems easy, but still needs practice, so try these:

Q1   Work out   a) 12.3 × 100   b) 3.08 ÷ 1000   c) 360 ÷ 30   [3 marks]

Multiplying and Dividing Whole Numbers

*You need to be really happy doing multiplications and divisions **without** a calculator*
*— they're likely to come up in your **non-calculator** exam.*

Multiplying **Whole Numbers**

The Traditional Method:

1) Split it into <u>separate multiplications</u>.
2) Add up the results in <u>columns</u> (right to left).

EXAMPLES

1.   Work out 46 × 27

```
      4 6
    × 2 7
    3 2₄2  —— This is 7 × 46
    9,2 0  —— This is 20 × 46
    1 2 4 2 —— This is 322 + 920
```

2.   Work out 243 × 18

```
      2 4 3
    ×   1 8
  1 9₃4₂4 —— This is 8 × 243
  2 4 3 0 —— This is 10 × 243
  4₁3 7 4 —— This is 1944 + 2430
```

There are lots of other multiplication methods — make sure you're comfortable using whichever method you prefer.

Dividing **Whole Numbers**

EXAMPLE

What is 748 ÷ 22?

<u>Short Division Method</u>

1) Set out the division as shown.

number you're <u>dividing by</u>

number you're <u>dividing</u>

22 | 7 4 8

2) Look at the first digit under the line. 7 doesn't divide by 22, so <u>put a zero</u> above and look at the <u>next digit</u>.

22 | 7 4 8

3) 22 × 3 = 66, so 22 into 74 goes <u>3 times</u>, with a <u>remainder</u> of 74 – 66 = 8.

carry the remainder

22 | 7 4⁸8

4) 22 into 88 goes <u>4 times exactly</u>.

the top line has the final answer

22 | 7 4⁸8

So 748 ÷ 22 = 34

For questions like this, it's useful to write out the first few multiples of the number you're dividing by.
E.g $1 × 22 = 22$
        $2 × 22 = 44$
        $3 × 22 = 66$
        $4 × 22 = 88...$

The other common method for dividing is <u>long division</u> — if you prefer this method, make sure you know it <u>really</u> well, so you'll have no problems with any division in your exam.

Make sure you know how to multiply and divide without a calculator

Practice makes perfect when it comes to multiplication and division. Go through the worked examples on this page and make sure you can follow the methods, then try these practice questions... <u>without</u> a calculator.

Q1   Work out   a) 28 × 12   b) 56 × 11   c) 104 × 16   [6 marks]

Q2   Work out   a) 96 ÷ 8   b) 84 ÷ 7   c) 252 ÷ 12   [4 marks]

Q3   Joey has a plank of wood which is 220 cm long. He cuts it into 14 cm pieces. What length of wood will he have left over?   [2 marks]

Multiplying and Dividing with Decimals

You might get a scary non-calculator question on multiplying or dividing using decimals. Luckily, these aren't really any harder than the whole-number versions. You just need to know what to do in each case.

Multiplying **Decimals**

1) Start by <u>ignoring</u> the decimal points.
   Do the multiplication using <u>whole numbers</u>.

2) Count the <u>total</u> number of digits after the <u>decimal points</u> in the original numbers.

3) Make the answer have the <u>same number</u> of decimal places.

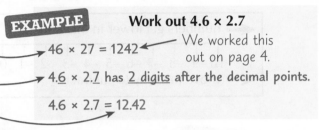

EXAMPLE   **Work out 4.6 × 2.7**

46 × 27 = 1242 ← We worked this out on page 4.

4.6 × 2.7 has <u>2 digits</u> after the decimal points.

4.6 × 2.7 = 12.42

Dividing a **Decimal** by a **Whole Number**

For these, you just set the question out like a whole-number division <u>but</u> put the <u>decimal point</u> in the answer <u>right above</u> the one in the question.

EXAMPLE   **What is 52.8 ÷ 3?**   Put the decimal point in the answer above the one in the question.

$$\begin{array}{r} 1\,. \\ 3\overline{)5\,^52.8} \end{array}$$

3 into 5 goes once, carry the remainder of 2.

$$\begin{array}{r} 1\,7\,. \\ 3\overline{)5\,^52.{}^18} \end{array}$$

3 into 22 goes 7 times, carry the remainder of 1.

$$\begin{array}{r} 1\,7.6 \\ 3\overline{)5\,^52.{}^18} \end{array}$$

3 into 18 goes 6 times exactly.

So 52.8 ÷ 3 = 17.6

Dividing a **Number** by a **Decimal**

Two-for-one here — this works if you're dividing a whole number by a decimal, or a decimal by a decimal.

EXAMPLE   **What is 36.6 ÷ 0.12?**

1) The trick here is to write it as a fraction:

2) Get rid of the decimals by multiplying top and bottom by 100 (see p.3):

3) It's now a decimal-free division that you know how to solve:

$$36.6 \div 0.12 = \frac{36.6}{0.12}$$
$$= \frac{3660}{12}$$

$$\begin{array}{r} 0 \\ 12\overline{)3\,^36\,6\,0} \end{array}$$

12 into 3 won't go so carry the 3

$$\begin{array}{r} 0\,3 \\ 12\overline{)3\,^36\,6\,0} \end{array}$$

12 into 36 goes 3 times exactly

$$\begin{array}{r} 0\,3\,0 \\ 12\overline{)3\,^36\,^66\,0} \end{array}$$

12 into 6 won't go so carry the 6

$$\begin{array}{r} 0\,3\,0\,5 \\ 12\overline{)3\,^36\,6\,^60} \end{array}$$

12 into 60 goes 5 times exactly

So 36.6 ÷ 0.12 = 305

To divide decimals by decimals, first turn them into whole numbers

Just be careful to multiply each decimal by the same amount when you do. Have a go at these questions:

Q1   Work out   a) 3.2 × 56   b) 0.6 × 10.2   c) 5.5 × 10.2   [6 marks]

Q2   Emma buys 14 packets of biscuits for a party. Each packet of biscuits costs £1.27.
How much does Emma spend on biscuits in total?   [2 marks]

Q3   Claire has £22.38. She wants to share it equally between her three nephews.
How much does each nephew receive?   [2 marks]

Q4   Find: a) 33.6 ÷ 0.6   b) 45 ÷ 1.5   c) 84.6 ÷ 0.12   [6 marks]

Q3 Video Solution

Negative Numbers

*Numbers less than zero are **negative**. You should be able to **add**, **subtract**, **multiply** and **divide** with them.*

Adding and Subtracting with Negative Numbers

Use the <u>number line</u> for <u>addition</u> and <u>subtraction</u> involving negative numbers:

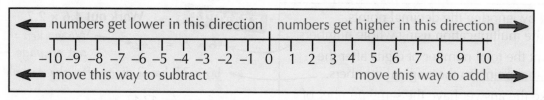

EXAMPLES

What is –4 + 7? Start at –4 and move 7 places in the positive direction:

So –4 + 7 = 3

Work out 5 – 8 Start at 5 and move 8 places in the negative direction:

So 5 – 8 = –3

Find –2 – 4 Start at –2 and move 4 places in the negative direction:

So –2 – 4 = –6

Use These Rules for Combining Signs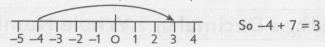

```
+  +  makes  +
+  –  makes  –
–  +  makes  –
–  –  makes  +
```

These rules are <u>ONLY TO BE USED WHEN</u>:

1) <u>Multiplying or dividing</u>

EXAMPLES

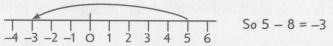

Find: a) –2 × 3   – + makes – so –2 × 3 = –6
      b) –8 ÷ –2   – – makes + so –8 ÷ –2 = 4

2) <u>Two signs appear next to each other</u>

EXAMPLES

Work out: a) 5 – –4   – – makes + so 5 – –4 = 5 + 4 = 9
          b) 4 + –6 – –7   + – makes – and – – makes +
                 so 4 + –6 – –7 = 4 – 6 + 7 = 5

Be careful when squaring or cubing. <u>Squaring</u> a negative number gives a <u>positive</u> number (e.g. –2 × –2 = 4) but <u>cubing</u> a negative number gives a <u>negative</u> number (e.g. –3 × –3 × –3 = –27).

Number lines are handy for adding or subtracting negative numbers

Don't just learn the rules in that burgundy box — make sure you know when you can use them too.

Q1 The temperature in Mathchester at 9 am on Monday was 4 °C.
At 9 am on Tuesday the temperature was –2 °C.
a) What was the change in temperature from Monday to Tuesday? [1 mark]
b) The temperature at 9 am on Wednesday was 3 °C lower than on Tuesday.
What was the temperature on Wednesday? [1 mark]

Warm-up and Worked Exam Questions

Doing maths without a calculator becomes easier the more you practise. These warm-up questions will help to get your brain in gear. Work through them without using your calculator.

Warm-up Questions

1) Without using a calculator, work out $7 + 15 - 6 \div 3$.

2) A ticket for entry to a funfair plus 3 rides costs £2.60. After that, each extra ride costs 95p. Roshani and Eve go on 8 rides each, how much do they pay altogether?

3) Work out: a) 0.957×1000 b) 2.4×20

4) Work out: a) $2.45 \div 10$ b) $4000 \div 800$

5) Work out the following:
   a) 43×9 b) 32×17 c) 5.8×21 d) 1.3×6.5

6) Work out the following:
   a) $91 \div 7$ b) $242 \div 2$ c) $24.8 \div 0.4$ d) $36 \div 1.2$

7) Work out: a) -4×-3 b) $-4 + -5 + 3$ c) $(3 + -2 - 4) \times (2 + -5)$ d) $120 \div -40$

Worked Exam Questions

These questions already have the answers filled in. Have a careful read through the working and handy hints before you have a go at the exam questions on the next page.

1   Yonas has a 500 ml bottle of a fizzy drink. Poppy has 216 ml of the same fizzy drink in a glass. Yonas gives Poppy some of his drink so that they each have the same amount.

 How much drink does Yonas give to Poppy?

Find how much fizzy drink there is in total.

Total amount of drink = 500 ml + 216 ml = 716 ml

$$2\overline{)7^1 1^1 6} = 358 \text{ ml each}$$

Divide this by 2 to find the amount they should each have.

500 ml − 358 ml = 142 ml,

so Yonas gives 142 ml of his drink to Poppy.

..........142....... ml
[2 marks]

2   Work out how many of each item below were sold if:

   a)   Tamera spent £14 on rulers that cost £0.70 each.

$$14 \div 0.7 = \frac{14}{0.7} = \frac{140}{7}$$

$$7\overline{)1^1 4 0} = 020$$

Multiply top and bottom by 10, then do the division as normal.

..........20.......
[2 marks]

   b)   Michael spent £2.76 on pencils that cost £0.12 each.

$$2.76 \div 0.12 = \frac{2.76}{0.12} = \frac{276}{12}$$

$$12\overline{)2^2 7^3 6} = 023$$

Don't worry if you have to keep carrying numbers — just continue like normal.

..........23.......
[2 marks]

Exam Questions

3   Write down the value of each of the following:

   a) 9^2

.........81.........
[1 mark]

   b) 4^3 (2)

$\begin{array}{r} \overset{2}{1}6 \\ \times\ 4 \\ \hline 64 \end{array}$ $4 \times 4 \times 4 = 16 \times 4 = 64$

.........64.........
[1 mark]

4   Three numbers multiply to give 288. Two of the numbers are –3 and 12.   (2)

   What is the third number?

$12 \times -3 = -36 \times 8 = 288$

$36\,\overline{)288}$

.........–8.........
[3 marks]

5   Alanna buys 15 tickets for a concert for herself and some friends.   (3)
   Each ticket is the same price. She pays with £200 and gets £5 change.

   How much does each ticket cost?

$=$ all tickets   cost £195

$195 \div 15 =$

$15\,\overline{)195}\ ^{1\ 3}$

£ ....13.........
[3 marks]

6   Georgie is a sales representative. She drives to
   different companies to sell air conditioning units.   (4)

   When she has to travel, her employer pays fuel expenses of 30p per mile.
   She drives to a job in the morning and drives home again later that day.
   She is also given £8 to cover any food expenses for each day that she is not in the office.

   The distances to her jobs for this
   week are shown on the right.

   Find Georgie's total expenses for this week.

| Monday: Buckshaw, 30 miles |
| Tuesday: in office |
| Wednesday: Wortham, 28 miles |
| Thursday: Harborough, 39 miles |
| Friday: Scotby, 40 miles |

Hint: think carefully
   about the total
   distance travelled.

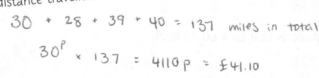

$30 + 28 + 39 + 40 = 137$ miles in total

$30^p \times 137 = 4110p = £41.10$

$8 \times 4 = £32$ →food

$41.10 = £73.10$

£ ....73.10.........
[4 marks]

Prime Numbers

There's no getting around it — prime numbers are as important as they sound. Luckily, they're not too difficult.

PRIME Numbers **Don't Divide** by Anything

Prime numbers are all the numbers that DON'T come up in times tables:

2 3 5 7 11 13 17 19 23 29 31 37 ...

The only way to get ANY PRIME NUMBER is: 1 × ITSELF

E.g. The only numbers that multiply to give 7 are 1 × 7
The only numbers that multiply to give 31 are 1 × 31

EXAMPLE **Show that 24 is not a prime number.**

Just find another way to make 24 other than 1 × 24: 2 × 12 = 24

24 divides by numbers other than 1 and 24, so it isn't a prime number.

Five **Important Facts**

1) 1 is NOT a prime number.
2) 2 is the ONLY even prime number.
3) The first four prime numbers are 2, 3, 5 and 7.
4) Prime numbers end in 1, 3, 7 or 9 (2 and 5 are the only exceptions to this rule).
5) But NOT ALL numbers ending in 1, 3, 7 or 9 are primes, as shown here:
(Only the circled ones are primes.)

②	③	⑤	⑦
⑪	⑬	⑰	⑲
21	㉓	27	㉙
㉛	33	㊲	39
㊶	㊸	㊼	49
51	(53)	57	(59)
(61)	63	(67)	69

How to **FIND** Prime Numbers — a very simple method

1) All primes (above 5) end in 1, 3, 7 or 9. So ignore any numbers that don't end in one of those.
2) Now, to find which of them ACTUALLY ARE primes you only need to divide each one by 3 and by 7. If it doesn't divide exactly by 3 or by 7 then it's a prime.

This simple rule using just 3 and 7 is true for checking primes up to 120.

EXAMPLE **Find all the prime numbers in this list: 71, 72, 73, 74, 75, 76, 77, 78**

1 First, get rid of anything that doesn't end in 1, 3, 7 or 9: **71, ~~72~~, 73, ~~74~~, ~~75~~, ~~76~~, 77, ~~78~~**

2 Now try dividing 71, 73 and 77 by 3 and 7:

71 ÷ 3 = 23.667 71 ÷ 7 = 10.143 so 71 is a prime number
73 ÷ 3 = 24.333 73 ÷ 7 = 10.429 so 73 is a prime number
77 ÷ 3 = 25.667 BUT: 77 ÷ 7 = 11 — 11 is a whole number,
so 77 is NOT a prime, because it divides by 7.

So the prime numbers in the list are 71 and 73.

Remember — prime numbers don't come up in times tables

Learn all three sections above, then cover the page and try this Exam Practice Question without looking:

Q1 Below is a list of numbers. Write down all the prime numbers from the list.
39, 51, 46, 35, 61, 53, 42, 47 [2 marks]

Multiples, Factors and Prime Factors

You might get asked to list multiples or find factors in the exam. This page will teach you how.

Multiples and Factors

The MULTIPLES of a number are just its <u>times table</u>.

 EXAMPLE **Find the first 8 multiples of 13.**

You just need to find the first 8 numbers in the 13 times table:

13   26   39   52   65   78   91   104

The FACTORS of a number are all the numbers that <u>divide into it</u>.

There's a method that guarantees you'll find them all:

1) Start off with 1 × the number itself, then try 2 ×, then 3 × and so on, listing the pairs in rows.

2) Try each one in turn. Cross out the row if it doesn't divide exactly.

3) Eventually, when you get a number <u>repeated</u>, <u>stop</u>.

4) The numbers in the rows you haven't crossed out make up the list of factors.

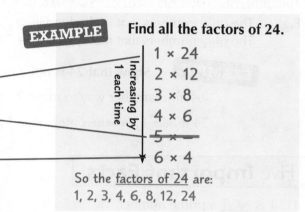

EXAMPLE **Find all the factors of 24.**

Increasing by 1 each time

1 × 24
2 × 12
3 × 8
4 × 6
5 ×
6 × 4

So the <u>factors of 24</u> are:
1, 2, 3, 4, 6, 8, 12, 24

Finding Prime Factors — The Factor Tree

<u>Any number</u> can be broken down into a string of prime numbers all multiplied together — this is called '<u>expressing it as a product of prime factors</u>', or its '<u>prime factorisation</u>'.

EXAMPLE **Express 420 as a product of prime factors.**

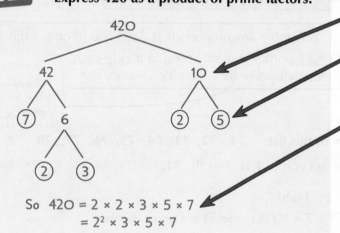

So 420 = 2 × 2 × 3 × 5 × 7
= $2^2 × 3 × 5 × 7$

To write a number as a product of its prime factors, use the <u>Factor Tree</u> method:

1) Start with the number at the top, and <u>split</u> it into <u>factors</u> as shown.

2) Every time you get a prime, <u>ring it</u>.

3) Keep going until you can't go further (i.e. you're just left with primes), then write the primes out <u>in order</u>. If there's more than one of the <u>same factor</u>, you can write them as <u>powers</u>.

No matter which numbers you choose at each step, you'll find that the prime factorisation is exactly the same. Each number has a <u>unique</u> set of prime factors.

Follow the methods above to find factors and prime factors

Make sure you know the Factor Tree method inside out, then give these Exam Practice Questions a go...

Q1   Use the following list of numbers to answer the questions below.   4, 6, 10, 14, 15, 17, 24, 30
    a) Find one number that's a multiple of 2, a multiple of 3 and a multiple of 4.   [1 mark]
    b) Find one number that's a multiple of 3 and a factor of 36.   [2 marks]

Q2   What number should replace the ☐ to make 14 × 30 = 7 × ☐ true?   [1 mark]

Q3   Express 990 as a product of its prime factors.   [2 marks]

Q3 Video Solution

LCM and HCF

*Two big fancy names but don't be put off — they're both **real easy**. There are two methods for finding each — this page starts you off with the **nice, straightforward** methods.*

LCM — 'Lowest Common Multiple'

'Lowest Common Multiple' — sure, it sounds kind of complicated, but all it means is this:

The SMALLEST number that will DIVIDE BY ALL the numbers in question.

METHOD:
1) LIST the MULTIPLES of ALL the numbers.
2) Find the SMALLEST one that's in ALL the lists.

The LCM is sometimes called the Least (instead of 'Lowest') Common Multiple.

EXAMPLE   **Find the lowest common multiple (LCM) of 12 and 15.**

Multiples of 12 are: 12, 24, 36, 48, (60,) 72, 84, 96, ...

Multiples of 15 are: 15, 30, 45, (60,) 75, 90, 105, ...

So the lowest common multiple (LCM) of 12 and 15 is 60.

HCF — 'Highest Common Factor'

'Highest Common Factor' — all it means is this:

The BIGGEST number that will DIVIDE INTO ALL the numbers in question.

METHOD:
1) LIST the FACTORS of ALL the numbers.
2) Find the BIGGEST one that's in ALL the lists.

EXAMPLE   **Find the highest common factor (HCF) of 36, 54, and 72.**

Factors of 36 are: 1, 2, 3, 4, 6, 9, 12, (18,) 36

Factors of 54 are: 1, 2, 3, 6, 9, (18,) 27, 54

Factors of 72 are: 1, 2, 3, 4, 6, 8, 9, 12, (18,) 24, 36, 72

So the highest common factor (HCF) of 36, 54 and 72 is 18.

Just take care listing the factors — make sure you use the proper method (as shown on the previous page) or you'll miss one and blow the whole thing out of the water.

LCM and HCF — learn what the names mean

LCM and HCF questions shouldn't be too bad as long as you know exactly what's meant by each of the terms. Now, it's time to make sure you're happy with this stuff by trying out some lovely exam practice questions...

Q1   Find the lowest common multiple (LCM) of 12, 14 and 21.   [2 marks]   (3)

Q2   Find the highest common factor (HCF) of 36 and 84.   [2 marks]   (3)

LCM and HCF

*The two **methods** on this page are a **little trickier** — but you might have to use them in your exam.*

LCM — Alternative Method

If you already know the <u>prime factors</u> of the numbers, you can use this method instead:

1) List all the <u>PRIME FACTORS</u> that appear in <u>EITHER</u> number.

2) If a factor appears <u>MORE THAN ONCE</u> in one of the numbers, list it <u>THAT MANY TIMES</u>.

3) <u>MULTIPLY</u> these together to give the <u>LCM</u>.

EXAMPLE $18 = 2 \times 3^2$ **and** $30 = 2 \times 3 \times 5$. **Find the LCM of 18 and 30.**

$$18 = 2 \times 3 \times 3 \qquad 30 = 2 \times 3 \times 5$$

So the prime factors that appear in either number are: 2, 3, 3, 5

$$LCM = 2 \times 3 \times 3 \times 5 = 90$$

List 3 twice as it appears twice in 18.

HCF — Alternative Method

Again, there's a different method you can use if you already know the <u>prime factors</u> of the numbers:

1) List all the <u>PRIME FACTORS</u> that appear in <u>BOTH</u> numbers.

2) <u>MULTIPLY</u> these together to find the HCF.

EXAMPLE $180 = 2^2 \times 3^2 \times 5$ **and** $84 = 2^2 \times 3 \times 7$. **Use this to find the HCF of 180 and 84.**

$$180 = ②\times②\times③\times 3 \times 5 \qquad 84 = ②\times②\times③\times 7$$

2, 2 and 3 are prime factors of both numbers, so

$$HCF = 2 \times 2 \times 3 = 12$$

Real-Life LCM and HCF Questions

You might be asked a wordy real-life LCM or HCF question in your exam — these can be <u>tricky</u> to spot at first, but once you have done, the method's <u>just the same</u>.

EXAMPLE Maggie is making party bags. She has 60 balloons, 48 lollipops and 84 stickers. She wants to use them all. Each type of item must be distributed equally between the party bags. What is the maximum number of party bags she can make?

Factors of 60 are: 1, 2, 3, 4, 5, 6, 10, ⑫ 15, 20, 30, 60

Factors of 48 are: 1, 2, 3, 4, 6, 8, ⑫ 16, 24, 48

Factors of 84 are: 1, 2, 3, 4, 6, 7, ⑫ 14, 21, 28, 42, 84

The <u>highest common factor</u> (HCF) of 60, 48 and 84 is 12, so the maximum number of party bags Maggie can make is 12.

You could use the <u>prime factorisation</u> method here if you wanted — use whichever method's <u>easier</u> for you.

In each bag there will be 60 ÷ 12 = 5 balloons, 48 ÷ 12 = 4 lollipops and 84 ÷ 12 = 7 stickers.

You might need to use these alternative methods in the exam

Have a go at these Exam Practice Questions to see if you've got the hang of this LCM and HCF business.

Q1 $112 = 2^4 \times 7$ and $140 = 2^2 \times 5 \times 7$. Use this to find the HCF of 112 and 140. [1 mark]

Q2 A café sells different cakes each day. It sells banana cake every 8 days, and raspberry cake every 22 days. If the café is selling the two cakes today, how many days will it be until the cakes are both sold on the same day again? [3 marks]

Warm-Up and Worked Exam Questions

These warm-up questions will test whether you've learned the facts from the last few pages.
Keep practising any you get stuck on, before moving on.

Warm-up Questions

1) Which of the following numbers are prime? 30, 31, 32, 33, 34, 35, 36, 37, 38, 39, 40.
2) Explain why 27 is not a prime number.
3) Find all the factors of 40.
4) Find the prime factors of 40.
5) Find the lowest common multiple of 4 and 5.
6) Find the highest common factor of 32 and 88.

Worked Exam Questions

Time for more exam questions with the answers filled in. Understanding these solutions will help
you with the exam questions that follow and in the exam itself.

1   Write down: (3)

a)   all the factors of 28,   *Think of pairs of factors, for example 1 and 28, 2 and 14....*

1, 2, 4, 7, 14, 28

[2 marks]

b)   all the multiples of 8 which appear in the list below.

55   56   57   58   59   60   61   62   63   64   65

56, 64

[1 mark]

2   Dev is making jam. (5)

He needs to buy mini jam jars which come in packs of 12, lids which come in packs
of 16 and labels which come in packs of 36. He doesn't want to have any items left over.

Find the smallest number of packs of each item he can buy.

Multiples of 12 are: 12, 24, 36, 48, 60, 72, 84, 96, 108, 120, 132, 144, 156, ...

Multiples of 16 are: 16, 32, 48, 64, 80, 96, 112, 128, 144, 160, ...

Multiples of 36 are: 36, 72, 108, 144, 180, ...

The LCM of 12, 16 and 36 is 144, which is the minimum number of each item he needs.

The minimum number of packs of jars he needs is 144 ÷ 12 = 12 packs

The minimum number of packs of lids he needs is 144 ÷ 16 = 9 packs

The minimum number of packs of labels he needs is 144 ÷ 36 = 4 packs

12 .... packs of jars, ...9............ packs of lids and ....4.......... packs of labels

[3 marks]

Exam Questions

3   Jasmine says, "there are no prime numbers between 100 and 110."
Is she correct? Give evidence for your answer. **(3)**

[2 marks]

4   Mei thinks of a prime number. The sum of its digits is one more than a square number. **(3)**
Write down one number Mei could be thinking of.

[2 marks]

5   Write 72 as a product of its prime factors. **(4)**

Make sure your answer only uses prime numbers. Multiply them all together to check you get the number you started with.

[2 marks]

6    $P = 3^7 \times 11^2$ and $Q = 3^4 \times 7^3 \times 11$. **(5)**

Write as the product of prime factors:
a)   the LCM of P and Q,

[1 mark]

b)   the HCF of P and Q.

[1 mark]

Fractions without a Calculator

*These pages show you how to cope with fraction calculations without your **beloved calculator**.*

1) Cancelling down

To <u>cancel down</u> or <u>simplify</u> a fraction, <u>divide top and bottom by the same number</u>, till they won't go further:

EXAMPLE   Simplify $\frac{18}{24}$.

Cancel down in a series of <u>easy steps</u> — keep going till the top and bottom don't have <u>any</u> common factors.

$$\frac{18}{24} \xrightarrow{\div 3} \frac{6}{8} \xrightarrow{\div 2} \frac{3}{4}$$

> The number on the top of the fraction is the <u>numerator</u>, and the number on the bottom is the <u>denominator</u>.

2) Mixed numbers

<u>Mixed numbers</u> are things like $3\frac{1}{3}$, with an integer part and a fraction part.

<u>Improper fractions</u> are ones where the top number is larger than the bottom number.

You need to be able to convert between the two.

EXAMPLES   1.   **Write $4\frac{2}{3}$ as an improper fraction.**

1)   Think of the <u>mixed number</u> as an <u>addition</u>:
$$4\frac{2}{3} = 4 + \frac{2}{3}$$

2)   Turn the <u>integer part</u> into a <u>fraction</u>:
$$4 + \frac{2}{3} = \frac{12}{3} + \frac{2}{3} = \frac{12 + 2}{3} = \frac{14}{3}$$

2.   **Write $\frac{31}{4}$ as a mixed number.**

<u>Divide</u> the top number by the bottom.

1)   The <u>answer</u> gives the <u>whole number part</u>.

2)   The <u>remainder</u> goes <u>on top</u> of the fraction.
$$31 \div 4 = 7 \text{ remainder } 3 \quad \text{so} \quad \frac{31}{4} = 7\frac{3}{4}$$

3) Multiplying

Multiply top and bottom <u>separately</u>. Then <u>simplify</u> your fraction as far as possible.

EXAMPLE   Find $\frac{8}{5} \times \frac{7}{12}$.

Multiply the top and bottom <u>separately</u>:
$$\frac{8}{5} \times \frac{7}{12} = \frac{8 \times 7}{5 \times 12}$$

Then <u>simplify</u> — top and bottom both <u>divide by 4</u>.
$$= \frac{56}{60} = \frac{14}{15}$$

You have to know how to handle mixed numbers

Mixed numbers look difficult, but they're OK once you've converted them into normal fractions.
If you keep on practising working with fractions, you'll bag some easy marks in the exam.

Fractions without a Calculator

Here are some more tricks for dealing with fractions.

4) Dividing

Turn the 2nd fraction <u>UPSIDE DOWN</u> and then <u>multiply</u>:

> When you're multiplying or dividing with <u>mixed numbers</u>, <u>always</u> turn them into improper fractions first.

EXAMPLE   **Find $2\frac{1}{3} \div 3\frac{1}{2}$.**

Rewrite the <u>mixed numbers</u> as improper <u>fractions</u>: $2\frac{1}{3} \div 3\frac{1}{2} = \frac{7}{3} \div \frac{7}{2}$

Turn $\frac{7}{2}$ <u>upside down</u> and <u>multiply</u>: $= \frac{7}{3} \times \frac{2}{7} = \frac{7 \times 2}{3 \times 7}$

<u>Simplify</u> — top and bottom both <u>divide by 7</u>. $= \frac{14}{21} = \frac{2}{3}$

5) Common denominators

This comes in handy for <u>ordering fractions</u> by size, and for <u>adding</u> or <u>subtracting</u> fractions.

You need to find a number that <u>all</u> the denominators <u>divide into</u> — this will be your <u>common denominator</u>. The simplest way is to find the <u>lowest common multiple</u> of the denominators:

EXAMPLE

Put these fractions in ascending order of size:

$$\frac{8}{3} \qquad \frac{5}{4} \qquad \frac{12}{5}$$

The <u>LCM</u> of 3, 4 and 5 is 60, so make 60 the <u>common denominator</u>:

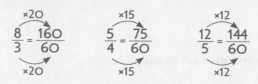

So the correct order is $\frac{75}{60}, \frac{144}{60}, \frac{160}{60}$ i.e. $\frac{5}{4}, \frac{12}{5}, \frac{8}{3}$

> Don't forget to use the original fractions in the final answer.

Common denominators are really handy

You need to find a common denominator to order, add or subtract fractions (see next page). If you're ordering fractions, don't forget to turn them back into their original forms when you give your answers.

Fractions without a Calculator

6) Adding, subtracting — sort the denominators first

If you're adding or subtracting <u>mixed numbers</u>, it usually helps to convert them to improper fractions first.

> Make sure the denominators are <u>the same</u> (see previous page).
> Add (or subtract) the top lines <u>only</u>.

EXAMPLE Calculate $2\frac{1}{5} - 1\frac{1}{2}$.

Rewrite the <u>mixed numbers</u> as improper <u>fractions</u>: $\quad 2\frac{1}{5} - 1\frac{1}{2} = \frac{11}{5} - \frac{3}{2}$

Find a <u>common denominator</u>: $\qquad\qquad\qquad = \frac{22}{10} - \frac{15}{10}$

Combine the <u>top lines</u>: $\qquad\qquad\qquad = \frac{22-15}{10} = \frac{7}{10}$

7) Fractions of something

EXAMPLE What is $\frac{9}{20}$ of £360?

'$\frac{9}{20}$ of £360' means '$\frac{9}{20} \times$ £360'.

<u>Multiply</u> by the top of the fraction and <u>divide</u> by the bottom.

$\frac{9}{20} \times £360 = (£360 \div 20) \times 9$
$\qquad\qquad = £18 \times 9 = £162$

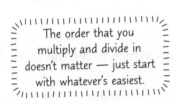
The order that you multiply and divide in doesn't matter — just start with whatever's easiest.

8) Expressing as a Fraction

EXAMPLE Write 180 as a fraction of 80.

Write the first number over the second and <u>cancel down</u>. $\qquad \frac{180}{80} = \frac{9}{4}$

You have to learn how to handle fractions in these 8 situations

When you think you've got the hang of it all, try these Exam Practice Questions without a calculator.

Q1 Calculate: a) $\frac{5}{8} \times 1\frac{5}{6}$ [3 marks] b) $\frac{10}{7} \div \frac{8}{3}$ [2 marks]

c) $\frac{8}{9} + \frac{19}{27}$ [2 marks] d) $5\frac{2}{3} - 9\frac{1}{4}$ [3 marks]

Q2 Dean has made 30 sandwiches. $\frac{7}{15}$ of the sandwiches he has made are vegetarian, and $\frac{3}{7}$ of the vegetarian sandwiches are cheese sandwiches. How many cheese sandwiches has he made? [2 marks]

Q2 Video Solution

Fraction Problems

*The previous three pages gave you all the tools you'll need to tackle these more **pesky fraction questions**. All these questions could come up on the **non-calculator** paper so put your calculators away.*

Use the **Methods** You've **Already Learnt**

 EXAMPLES

1. **Rachel is making cupcakes. Each cupcake needs $\frac{2}{25}$ of a pack of butter. How many packs of butter will Rachel need to buy to make 30 cupcakes?**

Once you've done the <u>multiplication</u>, convert $\frac{60}{25}$ to a <u>mixed number</u> to see how many packs she'll need — careful though, she can only buy a <u>whole number</u> of packs.

1 cupcake needs $\frac{2}{25}$ of a pack of butter,

so 30 cupcakes need: $30 \times \frac{2}{25} = \frac{60}{25} = \frac{12}{5} = 2\frac{2}{5}$ packs

2 packs won't be enough, so Rachel will need to buy 3 packs.

2. **The diamond to the right is made up of two identical equilateral triangles. The equilateral triangle at the top is split into three equal triangles. The equilateral triangle at the bottom is split into two equal triangles. Find the fraction of the diamond that is shaded.**

$\frac{2}{3}$ of the top triangle is shaded. This is $\frac{2}{3} \times \frac{1}{2} = \frac{2}{6} = \frac{1}{3}$ of the diamond.

$\frac{1}{2}$ of the bottom triangle is shaded. This is $\frac{1}{2} \times \frac{1}{2} = \frac{1}{4}$ of the diamond.

Remember to <u>multiply by a half</u> because each equilateral triangle makes up <u>half the diamond</u>.

Find a <u>common denominator</u> to add the fractions. $\frac{1}{3} + \frac{1}{4} = \frac{4}{12} + \frac{3}{12} = \frac{7}{12}$

3. **Which of the fractions, $\frac{2}{3}$ or $\frac{9}{7}$, is closer to 1?**

1) Give the fractions a <u>common denominator</u>. $\quad \frac{2}{3} = \frac{2 \times 7}{3 \times 7} = \frac{14}{21} \qquad \frac{9}{7} = \frac{9 \times 3}{7 \times 3} = \frac{27}{21}$

2) Convert 1 into a fraction and <u>subtract</u> to see which fraction is <u>closer</u> to 1.
$\quad \frac{21}{21} - \frac{14}{21} = \frac{7}{21} \qquad \frac{27}{21} - \frac{21}{21} = \frac{6}{21} \qquad$ So $\frac{9}{7}$ is closer to 1.

4. **At the Prism School, year 10 is split into two classes, each with the same number of pupils in total. $\frac{3}{5}$ of one class are girls, and $\frac{4}{7}$ of the other class are girls. What fraction of year 10 students are girls?**

1) <u>Divide</u> each fraction by 2 to find the number of girls in each class as a fraction of <u>total year 10 pupils</u>.

Class 1 girls are: $\frac{3}{5} \div 2 = \frac{3}{10}$ of the total pupils in year 10.

Class 2 girls are: $\frac{4}{7} \div 2 = \frac{4}{14}$ of the total pupils in year 10.

2) Find a <u>common denominator</u>, then <u>add</u> the fractions.

So $\frac{3}{10} + \frac{4}{14} = \frac{21}{70} + \frac{20}{70} = \frac{41}{70}$ of year 10 pupils are girls.

Practise using the different fraction rules

A lot of questions require you to find a common denominator, so make sure you're comfortable with that.

Q1 Bill has some books. They're all fiction books, biographies or history books. $\frac{3}{14}$ of the books are biographies and $\frac{1}{6}$ are history books. What fraction of Bill's books are fiction books? Give your answer as a fraction in its simplest form. **[4 marks]**

Fractions, Decimals and Percentages

*Fractions, decimals and percentages are **three different ways** of describing when you've got **part** of a **whole thing**. They're **closely related** and you can **convert between them**. These tables show some really common conversions which you should know straight off without having to work them out:*

Fraction	Decimal	Percentage
$\frac{1}{2}$	0.5	50%
$\frac{1}{4}$	0.25	25%
$\frac{3}{4}$	0.75	75%
$\frac{1}{3}$	0.333333...	$33\frac{1}{3}\%$
$\frac{2}{3}$	0.666666...	$66\frac{2}{3}\%$
$\frac{5}{2}$	2.5	250%

Fraction	Decimal	Percentage
$\frac{1}{10}$	0.1	10%
$\frac{2}{10}$	0.2	20%
$\frac{1}{5}$	0.2	20%
$\frac{2}{5}$	0.4	40%
$\frac{1}{8}$	0.125	12.5%
$\frac{3}{8}$	0.375	37.5%

The more of those conversions you learn, the better — but for those that you <u>don't know</u>, you must <u>also learn</u> how to <u>convert</u> between the three types. These are the methods:

$$\text{Fraction} \xrightarrow{\text{Divide}} \text{Decimal} \xrightarrow{\times \text{ by 100}} \text{Percentage}$$

E.g. $\frac{7}{20}$ is $7 \div 20$ = 0.35   e.g. 0.35 × 100   = 35%

$$\text{Fraction} \xleftarrow[\text{The awkward one}]{} \text{Decimal} \xleftarrow[\div \text{ by 100}]{} \text{Percentage}$$

<u>Converting decimals to fractions</u> is awkward. To convert terminating decimals to fractions:

The digits after the decimal point go on the top, and a <u>10, 100, 1000, etc.</u> on the bottom — so you have the same number of zeros as there were decimal places.

$$0.6 = \frac{6}{10} \qquad 0.78 = \frac{78}{100} \qquad 0.024 = \frac{24}{1000} \quad \text{etc.}$$

These can often be <u>cancelled down</u> — see p.15.

Recurring Decimals have Repeating Digits

1) Recurring decimals have a <u>pattern of numbers</u> which <u>repeats forever</u>, e.g. 0.333333... which is $\frac{1}{3}$.
2) The <u>repeating part</u> is usually marked with <u>dots</u> on top of the number.
3) If there's <u>one dot</u>, only <u>one digit</u> is repeated. If there are <u>two dots</u>, <u>everything from the first dot to the second dot</u> is the repeating bit.
4) You can <u>convert</u> a fraction to a recurring decimal:

E.g. $0.2\dot{5} = 0.2555555...$,
$0.\dot{2}\dot{5} = 0.25252525...$,
$0.\dot{2}6\dot{5} = 0.265265265...$

EXAMPLE   **Write $\frac{5}{11}$ as a recurring decimal.**

Just do the division, and look for the <u>repeating pattern</u>. $5 \div 11 = 0.454545...$ so $\frac{5}{11} = 0.\dot{4}\dot{5}$

Fractions, decimals and percentages are interchangeable

You just need to remember how to switch between them. Give it a go with these Exam Practice Questions.

Q1   Which is greater: a) 57% or $\frac{5}{9}$,   b) 0.2 or $\frac{6}{25}$,   c) $\frac{7}{8}$ or 90%?   [3 marks]

Q2   a) Write 0.555 as a fraction in its simplest form.   [2 marks]

     b) Write $\frac{1}{6}$ as a recurring decimal.   [2 marks]

Warm-up and Worked Exam Questions

Here's a set of warm-up questions for this section. Work through them to check you've got the hang of fractions and to limber up for the exam questions that follow.

Warm-up Questions

1) Simplify $\frac{48}{64}$ as far as possible.

2) Which of these fractions are equivalent to $\frac{1}{3}$? $\frac{2}{6}, \frac{5}{15}, \frac{9}{36}, \frac{6}{20}$

3) Work these out, then simplify your answers where possible:

   a) $\frac{2}{5} \times \frac{2}{3}$ b) $\frac{2}{5} \div \frac{2}{3}$ c) $\frac{2}{5} + \frac{2}{3}$ d) $\frac{2}{3} - \frac{2}{5}$

4) What decimal is the same as $\frac{7}{10}$?

5) What percentage is the same as $\frac{2}{3}$?

6) What fraction is the same as 0.4?

7) Write $\frac{2}{7}$ as a recurring decimal.

Worked Exam Questions

Make sure you understand what's going on in these questions before trying the next page for yourself.

1   Sarah and her 4 friends eat $\frac{5}{6}$ of a pizza each. Pizzas cost £4.50 each, or 2 for £7.
   What is the minimum amount they will have to spend on pizzas?

$$5 \times \frac{5}{6} = \frac{25}{6}$$

$$= 4\frac{1}{6}, \text{ so they will need 5 pizzas in total.}$$

Cost = (2 × £7) + £4.50

= £14 + £4.50   *They can get 4 pizzas*
                        in the 2 for £7 offer.
= £18.50

£ ....18.50.......
[3 marks]

2   *ABC* is an equilateral triangle. It has been divided
   into smaller equilateral triangles as shown below.

   Find the shaded areas as
   separate fractions of the whole
   triangle, then add them up.

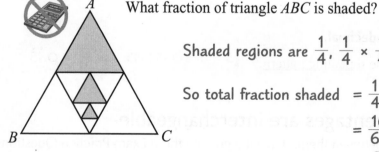

What fraction of triangle *ABC* is shaded?

Shaded regions are $\frac{1}{4}$, $\frac{1}{4} \times \frac{1}{4} = \frac{1}{16}$ and $\frac{1}{4} \times \frac{1}{4} \times \frac{1}{4} = \frac{1}{64}$

So total fraction shaded $= \frac{1}{4} + \frac{1}{16} + \frac{1}{64}$

$$= \frac{16}{64} + \frac{4}{64} + \frac{1}{64}$$

$$= \frac{21}{64}$$

$\frac{21}{64}$
....
[3 marks]

Exam Questions

3   The number of people at last Saturday's Norchester City game was 12 400. **(3)**
     Season ticket holders made up $\frac{3}{8}$ of the crowd. How many season ticket holders were there?

....

[2 marks]

4   Write the following in order of size, starting with the smallest. **(3)**

Start by writing all the numbers as decimals.   65% $\frac{2}{3}$ 0.065 $\frac{33}{50}$

.... , ... , ... , ...

[2 marks]

5   Work out the following, giving your answers as mixed numbers in their simplest form: **(4)**

    a) $1\frac{1}{8} \times 2\frac{2}{5}$

....

[3 marks]

     b) $1\frac{3}{4} \div \frac{7}{9}$

....

[3 marks]

6   Bilal, Eli, Ruth and Jenny split the bill at a restaurant. Bilal pays $\frac{1}{4}$ of the bill **(4)**
     and Eli and Ruth each pay 20% of the bill. Jenny pays £17.50.

    How much was the bill in total?

£ ....

[4 marks]

Rounding Numbers

*You need to be able to use **3 different rounding methods**.*
We'll do decimal places first, but there's the same basic idea behind all three.

Decimal Places (d.p.)

To round to a given number of <u>decimal places</u>:

> 1) <u>Identify</u> the position of the '<u>last digit</u>' from the number of decimal places.
> 2) Then look at the next digit to the <u>right</u> — called <u>the decider</u>.
> 3) If the <u>decider</u> is <u>5 or more</u>, then <u>round up</u> the <u>last digit</u>.
>   If the <u>decider</u> is <u>4 or less</u>, then leave the <u>last digit</u> as it is.
> 4) There must be <u>no more digits</u> after the last digit (not even zeros).

If you're rounding to 2 d.p. the last digit is the <u>second</u> digit after the decimal point.

EXAMPLES

1. **What is 13.72 correct to <u>1 decimal place</u>?**

$$13.\widehat{72} = 13.7$$

<u>LAST DIGIT</u> to be written (1st decimal place because we're rounding to 1 d.p.)

<u>DECIDER</u>

The <u>LAST DIGIT</u> stays the <u>same</u> because the <u>DECIDER</u> is <u>4 or less</u>.

2. **What is 7.45839 to <u>2 decimal places</u>?**

$$7.4\widehat{58}39 = 7.46$$

<u>LAST DIGIT</u> to be written (2nd decimal place because we're rounding to 2 d.p.)

<u>DECIDER</u>

The <u>LAST DIGIT</u> rounds <u>UP</u> because the <u>DECIDER</u> is <u>5 or more</u>.

Watch Out for **Pesky Nines**

If you have to <u>round up</u> a <u>9</u> (to 10), replace the 9 with 0, and <u>add 1</u> to the digit on the <u>left</u>.

E.g. Round 45.698 to 2 d.p: 45.6<u>9</u>8 ⟶ 45.6̸9̸ ⟶ 45.70 to 2 d.p.

decider

last digit — round up

The question asks for 2 d.p. so you <u>must</u> put 45.<u>70</u> not 45.7.

You might be asked to round off your answers in the exam

This is important stuff, so learn the steps of the basic method and then have a go at these:

Q1 a) Give 21.435 correct to 1 decimal place
   b) Give 0.0581 correct to 2 d.p.
   c) Round 4.968 to 1 d.p.   [3 marks]

Q2 Calculate $\dfrac{25.49 - 16.73}{2.82}$
   and give your answer to 2 d.p.   [2 marks]

Rounding Numbers

Significant Figures (s.f.)

The <u>1st significant figure</u> of any number is <u>the first digit which isn't a zero</u>.

The <u>2nd, 3rd, 4th, etc. significant figures</u> follow immediately after the 1st — they're allowed to be zeros.

0.002309   506.07

SIG. FIGS: 1st 2nd 3rd 4th   1st 2nd 3rd 4th

To <u>round</u> to a given number of significant figures:

1) Find the <u>last digit</u> — if you're rounding to, say 3 s.f., then the <u>3rd significant figure</u> is the last digit.
2) Use the digit to the right of it as the <u>decider</u>, just like for d.p.
3) Once you've rounded, <u>fill up</u> with <u>zeros</u>, up to but <u>not beyond</u> the decimal point.

EXAMPLE   **Round 506.07 to 2 significant figures.**

Last digit is the <u>2nd sig. fig.</u>

Need one <u>zero</u> to fill up to decimal point.

506.07 = 510

<u>DECIDER is 5 or more</u> ⟶ Last digit <u>rounds UP</u>

To the **Nearest Whole Number, Ten, Hundred** etc.

You might be asked to round to the <u>nearest whole number</u>, <u>ten</u>, <u>hundred</u>, <u>thousand</u>, or <u>million</u>:

1) <u>Identify the last digit</u>, e.g. for the nearest <u>whole number</u> it's the <u>units</u> position, and for the '<u>nearest ten</u>' it's the <u>tens</u> position, etc.
2) <u>Round the last digit</u> and <u>fill in with zeros</u> up to the decimal point, just like for significant figures.

EXAMPLE   **Round 6751 to the nearest hundred.**

Last digit is in the '<u>hundreds</u>' position

Fill in <u>2 zeros</u> up to decimal point.

6751 = 6800

<u>DECIDER is 5 or more</u> ⟶ Last digit <u>rounds UP</u>.

Significant figures can be a bit tricky to get your head round

Learn the method on this page for identifying them, and make sure you really understand the example.

Q1 a) Round 653 to 1 s.f.   b) Round 14.6 to 2 s.f.

   c) Give 168.7 to the nearest whole number.

   d) Give 82 430 to the nearest thousand. [4 marks]

Q2 Calculate $\frac{8.43 + 12.72}{5.63 - 1.21}$.

   Give your answer to 2 s.f.

   [2 marks]

Q2 Video Solution

Estimating

*'**Estimate**' doesn't mean 'take a wild guess', it means 'look at the numbers, make them a bit easier, then do the calculation'. Your answer won't be as **accurate** as the real thing but it's easier on your brain.*

Estimating **Calculations**

1) <u>Round everything off</u> to <u>1 significant figure</u>.
2) Then <u>work out the answer</u> using these nice easy numbers.
3) <u>Show all your working</u> or you won't get the marks.

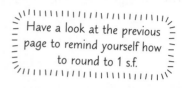
Have a look at the previous page to remind yourself how to round to 1 s.f.

EXAMPLES   1.   **Estimate the value of 42.6 × 12.1.**

$\approx$ means '<u>approximately equal to</u>'.

1) <u>Round</u> each number to <u>1 s.f.</u> $42.6 \times 12.1 \approx 40 \times 10$
2) Do the <u>calculation</u> with $= 400$
   the rounded numbers.

You might have to say if it's an <u>underestimate</u> or an <u>overestimate</u>. Here, you rounded both numbers <u>down</u>, so it's an <u>underestimate</u>.

2.   **Estimate the value of** $\dfrac{\sqrt{6242 \div 57}}{9.8 - 4.7}$.

Don't be put off by the <u>square root</u>, just <u>round</u> each number to <u>1 s.f.</u> and do the <u>calculation</u>.

$$\frac{\sqrt{6242 \div 57}}{9.8 - 4.7} \approx \frac{\sqrt{6000 \div 60}}{10 - 5} = \frac{\sqrt{100}}{5} = \frac{10}{5} = 2$$

3.   **Jo has a cake-making business. She spent £984.69 on flour last year. A bag of flour costs £1.89, and she makes an average of 5 cakes from each bag of flour. Work out an estimate of how many cakes she made last year.**

Don't panic if you get a '<u>real-life</u>' estimating question — just round everything to 1 s.f. as before.

1) Estimate number of bags of flour — <u>round</u> numbers to <u>1 s.f.</u>

$$\text{Number of bags of flour} = \frac{984.69}{1.89}$$
$$\approx \frac{1000}{2} = 500$$

2) Multiply to find the number of cakes.

$$\text{Number of cakes} \approx 500 \times 5 = 2500$$

You Might Need to Estimate **Height**

Use <u>1.8 m</u> as an estimate for the <u>height of a man</u>.

EXAMPLE   **Estimate the height of the giraffe in the picture.**

In the picture the giraffe's about <u>two and a half times</u> as tall as the man.

Height of a man is about 1.8 m
Rough height of giraffe = 2.5 × height of man
$= 2.5 \times 1.8 = 4.5$ m

Round the numbers first, then do the calculation like normal

If you're asked to estimate something in the exam, make sure you show all your steps (including what each number is rounded to) to prove that you didn't just use a calculator. Hassle, but it'll pay off.

Q1   Estimate the value of: a) $\dfrac{22.3 \times 11.4}{0.532}$ [2 marks] **(4)**   b) $\sqrt{\dfrac{18.79 \times 5.22}{1.23 + 3.21}}$ [2 marks] **(4)**

Q2   Padma buys 17 kg of turnips at a cost of £1.93 per kg. Estimate the total cost.   [2 marks]

Rounding Errors

*Whenever a number is **rounded** or **truncated** it will have some amount of **error**.*
*The error tells you how far the **actual value** could be away from the **rounded value**.*

Rounded Measurements Can Be Out By Half A Unit

> Whenever a measurement is <u>rounded off</u> to a <u>given UNIT</u> the
> <u>actual measurement</u> can be anything up to <u>HALF A UNIT bigger or smaller</u>.

If you're asked for the <u>error interval</u>, you can use <u>inequalities</u>
to find the <u>range of values</u> that the <u>actual measurement</u> could be:

EXAMPLE **The mass of a cake is given as 2.4 kg to the nearest 0.1 kg.**
Find the interval within which *m*, the actual mass of the cake, lies.

It's measured to the nearest 0.1 kg, so the actual mass could be 0.1 ÷ 2 = 0.05 kg bigger or smaller.

Minimum mass = 2.4 − 0.05 = <u>2.35 kg</u>
Maximum mass = 2.4 + 0.05 = <u>2.45 kg</u>

So the interval is 2.35 kg ≤ m < 2.45 kg

The actual maximum mass is 2.44999... kg, but it's OK to say 2.45 kg instead.

The actual value is <u>greater than or equal to</u> the <u>minimum</u> but <u>strictly less than</u> the <u>maximum</u>.
The actual mass of the cake could be <u>exactly</u> 2.35 kg,
but if it was exactly 2.45 kg it would <u>round up</u> to 2.5 kg instead.

If a question involves <u>more than one</u> rounded value,
you need to think about the range of <u>possible values</u> for <u>each one</u>.

EXAMPLE **The length of rope A is 120 cm to the nearest 10 cm.**
The length of rope B is 200 cm to the nearest 50 cm.
Work out the maximum total length of the two ropes.

Find the <u>maximum</u>
length of <u>each</u> rope.

Maximum length of rope A = 120 + 5 = 125 cm
Maximum length of rope B = 200 + 25 = 225 cm

So the maximum total length is 125 cm + 225 cm = 350 cm

Truncated Measurements Can Be A Whole Unit Out

You truncate a number by <u>chopping off</u> decimal places. E.g. 25.765674 truncated to 1 d.p. would be 25.7

> When a measurement is <u>TRUNCATED</u> to a <u>given UNIT</u>, the
> <u>actual measurement</u> can be up to <u>A WHOLE UNIT bigger but no smaller</u>.

If the mass of the cake in the first example above was 2.4 kg <u>truncated</u> to 1 d.p.,
the error interval would be 2.4 kg ≤ m < 2.5 kg.
So even if the mass was 2.499999 kg, it would still truncate to 2.4 kg.

Learn the difference between rounding and truncating

You need to be comfortable with rounding before you tackle this topic — so if you're feeling a bit unsure,
take a look back at those pages. Feeling confident? Then have a go at these questions now.

Q1   The following numbers have been rounded to 2 significant figures.
       Give the error interval for each: a) 380 [2 marks]   b) 0.46   [2 marks]

Q2   A bag of apples weighs 800 g to the nearest 100 g.
       A bag of potatoes weighs 1.5 kg to the nearest 500 g.
       What is the minimum possible total weight of the apples and potatoes?   [3 marks]

Q2 Video Solution

Warm-up and Worked Exam Questions

Before you dive into the exam questions on the next page, have a paddle in these friendly-looking warm-up questions. If you're not sure about any of them, go back and look at the topic again.

Warm-up Questions

1) Round these numbers off to 1 decimal place:
   a) 3.24   b) 1.78   c) 2.31   d) 0.46   e) 9.76

2) Round these off to the nearest whole number:
   a) 3.4   b) 5.2   c) 1.84   d) 6.9   e) 3.26

3) Round these numbers to the stated number of significant figures:
   a) 352 to 2 s.f.   b) 465 to 1 s.f.   c) 12.38 to 3 s.f.   d) 0.03567 to 2 s.f.

4) Round these numbers off to the nearest hundred:
   a) 2865   b) 450   c) 123

5) a) Estimate (29.5 − 9.6) × 4.87   b) Is your answer an underestimate or an overestimate?

6) A bottle contains 568 ml of milk to the nearest ml.
   What is the minimum possible volume of milk in the bottle?

7) The following numbers have been rounded as shown.
   Give the error interval for each: a) 0.915 (to 3 d.p.)   b) 1120 (to 3 s.f.)

8) Truncate: a) 37.919 to 1 d.p.   b) 2.1503 to 1 d.p.

Worked Exam Question

Look at that — an exam question with all the answers filled in. How unexpected.

1   Round the following to the given degree of accuracy.

a)   Kudzai has 123 people coming to his party.
      Write this number to the nearest 10.

   1②3 ——— Last digit is in the 'tens' position
   12③ ——— Decider is less than 5
   120 ——— 1 space to fill before the decimal point

                                                         120
                                                         ....
                                                         [1 mark]

b)   The attendance at a football match was 2568 people.
      What is this to the nearest hundred?

   Last digit   Decider
   2⑤68
   2600 ——— 2 spaces to fill

                                                         2600
                                                         ....
                                                         [1 mark]

c)   The population of Ulverpool is 452 529.
      Round this to the nearest 100 000.

   Last digit   Decider
   ④52 529
   500 000 ——— 5 spaces to fill

                                                         500 000
                                                         ....
                                                         [1 mark]

Exam Questions

2   The distance between two stars is 428.6237 light years. ③

    a)   Round this distance to one decimal place.

                                        .... light years
                                                     [1 mark]

    b)   Round this distance to 2 significant figures.

                                          .... light years
                                                     [1 mark]

3   A stall sells paperback and hardback books. Paperback books cost £4.95 and hardback books cost £11. One Saturday, the stall sells 28 paperback and 19 hardback books. ④

    a)   Find an estimate for the amount of money the stall made that day.
         Show all your working.

                                    £ ....
                                                     [2 marks]

    b)   The actual amount the stall made was £347.60.
         Do you think your estimate was sensible? Explain your answer.

         ....

         ....
                                                                         [1 mark]

4   Estimate the value of $\dfrac{12.2 \times 1.86}{0.19}$ ④
                                        You should start by rounding each number to an easier one.

                                          ....
                                                     [2 marks]

5   Joseph is weighing himself. His scales give his weight to the nearest kilogram. ⑤

    According to his scales, Joseph is 57 kg.
    What are the minimum and maximum weights that he could be?

                             Minimum weight: .... kg

                             Maximum weight: .... kg
                                                     [2 marks]

6   Given that a = 3.8 to 1 decimal place, ⑤
    write down the error interval for a.

                                          ....
                                                     [2 marks]

Powers

You've already seen 'to the power 2' and 'to the power 3' — they're just 'squared' and 'cubed'.
They're just the tip of the iceberg — any number can be a power if it puts its mind to it...

Powers are a very Useful Shorthand

1) Powers are 'numbers <u>multiplied by themselves</u> so many times':

   $2 \times 2 \times 2 \times 2 \times 2 \times 2 \times 2 = 2^7$ ('two to the power 7')

2) The <u>powers of ten</u> are really easy — the power tells you the number of zeros:

   > to the power of 6

   $$10^1 = 10 \qquad 10^2 = 100 \qquad 10^3 = 1000 \qquad 10^6 = 1\,000\,000$$

   > 6 zeros

3) Use the $x^\blacksquare$ or y^x button on your calculator to find powers,
   e.g. press $3 \cdot 7 \; x^\blacksquare \; 3 \; =$ to get $3.7^3 = 50.653$.

4) Anything to the <u>power 1</u> is just <u>itself</u>, e.g. $4^1 = 4$.

5) <u>1 to any power</u> is <u>still 1</u>, e.g. $1^{457} = 1$.

6) <u>Anything</u> to the <u>power 0</u> is just <u>1</u>, e.g. $5^0 = 1$, $67^0 = 1$, $x^0 = 1$.

Four Easy Rules:

> *Warning: Rules 1 & 2 <u>don't work</u> for things like $2^3 \times 3^7$, only for <u>powers of the same number</u>.*

1) When <u>MULTIPLYING</u>, you <u>ADD THE POWERS</u>.   e.g. $3^4 \times 3^6 = 3^{4+6} = 3^{10}$

2) When <u>DIVIDING</u>, you <u>SUBTRACT THE POWERS</u>.   e.g. $c^4 \div c^2 = c^{4-2} = c^2$

3) When <u>RAISING one power to another</u>, you <u>MULTIPLY THE POWERS</u>.   e.g. $(3^2)^4 = 3^{2\times4} = 3^8$

4) <u>FRACTIONS</u> — Apply the power to <u>both TOP and BOTTOM</u>.   e.g. $\left(\frac{2}{3}\right)^3 = \frac{2^3}{3^3} = \frac{8}{27}$

> **EXAMPLE** $a = 5^9$ and $b = 5^4 \times 5^2$. **What is the value of $\frac{a}{b}$?**
>
> 1) Work out b — <u>add</u> the powers: $b = 5^4 \times 5^2 = 5^{4+2} = 5^6$
> 2) <u>Divide</u> a by b — <u>subtract</u> the powers: $\frac{a}{b} = 5^9 \div 5^6 = 5^{9-6} = 5^3 = 125$

One Trickier Rule

To find a <u>negative power</u> — turn it <u>upside-down</u>.

People have real difficulty remembering this — whenever you see a <u>negative power</u> you need to immediately think: "Aha, that means turn it the other way up and make the power positive".

E.g. $7^{-2} = \frac{1}{7^2} = \frac{1}{49}$, $\left(\frac{3}{5}\right)^{-2} = \left(\frac{5}{3}\right)^2 = \frac{5^2}{3^2} = \frac{25}{9}$

Practise these power rules — you never know when you'll need them

If you can add, subtract and multiply, there's nothing on this page you can't do — just learn the rules.

Q1 a) Find $3^3 + 4^2$ without a calculator.
   b) Use your calculator to find 6.2^3.
   c) Write ten thousand as a power of 10.
   [4 marks]

Q2 Simplify: a) $4^2 \times 4^3$ b) $\frac{7^6}{7^3}$ c) $(q^2)^4$ **[3 marks]**

Q3 Without using a calculator, find
   a) $\frac{6^3 \times 6^5}{6^6}$ b) 2^{-4} **[4 marks]**

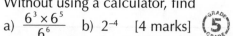

Roots

Take a deep breath, and get ready to tackle this page.

Square Roots

'Squared' means 'multiplied by itself': $8^2 = 8 \times 8 = 64$
SQUARE ROOT $\sqrt{}$ is the reverse process: $\sqrt{64} = 8$

> **'Square Root' means
> 'What Number <u>Times by Itself</u> gives...'**

EXAMPLES

1. What is $\sqrt{49}$?

49 is a <u>square number</u> — make sure you know all the <u>square numbers</u> on p.1 so you can answer questions like this <u>without a calculator</u>.

7 times by itself gives 49: $49 = 7 \times 7$
So $\sqrt{49} = 7$

2. What is $\sqrt{29.16}$?

Use your calculator. Press: $\boxed{29.16}$ $\boxed{=}$ 5.4

3. Find <u>both</u> square roots of 36.

$6 \times 6 = 36$, so positive square root = 6
$-6 \times -6 = 36$, so negative square root = -6

> **All numbers also have a
> <u>NEGATIVE SQUARE ROOT</u>
> — it's just the '−' version of
> the normal positive one.**

This little rule for multiplying roots might come in <u>handy</u> in your exam:

$$\sqrt{a} \times \sqrt{a} = a$$

<u>Be careful</u> — this is <u>only true</u> if you're multiplying together two roots which are the <u>same</u>.

Cube Roots

'Cubed' means '<u>multiplied by itself and then by itself again</u>': $2^3 = 2 \times 2 \times 2 = 8$
CUBE ROOT $\sqrt[3]{}$ is the <u>reverse process</u>: $\sqrt[3]{8} = 2$

> **'Cube Root' means 'What Number <u>Times by Itself and then by Itself Again</u> gives...'**

You need to be able to write down the <u>cube roots</u> of the <u>cube numbers</u> given on p.1 <u>without a calculator</u>.
To find the cube root of any other number you can use your calculator — press .

EXAMPLES

1. What is $\sqrt[3]{27}$?

27 is a <u>cube number</u>.

3 times by itself and then by itself again gives 27: $27 = 3 \times 3 \times 3$
So $\sqrt[3]{27} = 3$

2. What is $\sqrt[3]{4913}$?

Press: $\boxed{4913}$ $\boxed{=}$ 17

You can use your calculator to find <u>any root</u> of a number, using the buttons.

Make sure you know how to use your calculator to find higher order roots — the buttons might be slightly different to these ones.

Learn the difference between square roots and square numbers

A square root is a number that, when multiplied by itself, gives the number under the root symbol.

Q1 Find a) $\sqrt{196}$ without using a calculator.   b) $\sqrt[3]{9261}$ c) $\sqrt[7]{2187}$ [3 marks]

Q2 The volume of a cube is 1.728 cm³. Find the length of one of its sides, in cm.   [2 marks]

Q3 Work out $\sqrt[3]{19.34} + (1.3 + 2.5)^2$. Write down the full calculator display.   [1 mark]

Standard Form

*Standard form is useful for writing **VERY BIG** or **VERY SMALL** numbers in a more convenient way.*

E.g.   56 000 000 000 would be 5.6 × 10^10 in standard form.

   0.000 000 003 45 would be 3.45 × 10^-9 in standard form.

*But **ANY NUMBER** can be written in standard form and you need to know how to do it:*

What it **Actually** is:

A number written in standard form must <u>always</u> be in <u>exactly</u> this form:

This <u>number</u> must <u>always</u> be <u>between 1 and 10</u>.

(The fancy way of saying this is 1 ≤ A < 10)

$$A \times 10^n$$

This number is just the <u>number of places</u> the <u>decimal point</u> moves.

> **Learn the <u>THREE RULES</u>:**
> 1) The <u>front number</u> must always be <u>between 1 and 10</u>.
> 2) The power of 10, n, is <u>how far the decimal point moves</u>.
> 3) n is <u>positive for BIG numbers</u>, n is <u>negative for SMALL numbers</u>.
>   (This is much better than rules based on which way the decimal point moves.)

Four **Important** Examples:

1 **Express 35 600 in standard form.**

   1) <u>Move the decimal point</u> until 35 600 becomes 3.56 (1 ≤ A < 10)
   2) The decimal point has moved <u>4 places</u> so n = 4, giving: 10^4
   3) 35 600 is a <u>big number</u> so n is +4, not −4

   3 5 6 0 0.0

   $= 3.56 \times 10^4$

2 **Express 0.0000623 in standard form.**

   1) The decimal point must move <u>5 places</u> to give 6.23 (1 ≤ A < 10). So the power of 10 is 5.
   2) Since 0.0000623 is a <u>small number</u> it must be 10^{-5} not 10^{+5}

   0.0 0 0 0 6 2 3

   $= 6.23 \times 10^{-5}$

3 **Express 4.95 × 10^-3 as an ordinary number.**

   1) The power of 10 is <u>negative</u>, so it's a <u>small number</u> — the answer will be less than 1.
   2) The power is −3, so the decimal point moves <u>3 places</u>.

    0 0 0 4.9 5 × 10^-3

   $= 0.00495$

4 **Which is the largest number in the following list?** 9.5×10^8 2.7×10^5 3.6×10^8 5.6×10^6

   1) Compare the <u>powers</u> first.

   9.5×10^8 and 3.6×10^8 have the biggest powers so one of them is the largest.

   2) Then, compare the <u>front numbers</u>.

   9.5 is greater than 3.6 So 9.5×10^8 is the largest number.

Standard Form

*You might be asked to add, subtract, multiply or divide using numbers in standard form **without** using a calculator.*

Multiplying and Dividing

1) Rearrange to put the <u>front numbers</u> and the <u>powers of 10 together</u>.
2) Multiply or divide the front numbers, and use the <u>power rules</u> (see p.28) to multiply or divide the powers of 10.
3) Make sure your answer is still in <u>standard form</u>.

EXAMPLES

1. Find $(2 \times 10^3) \times (6 \times 10^5)$ without using a calculator. Give your answer in standard form.

Multiply front numbers and powers separately

$(2 \times 10^3) \times (6 \times 10^5)$
$= (2 \times 6) \times (10^3 \times 10^5)$
$= 12 \times 10^{3+5}$ — Add the powers (see p.28)

Not in standard form so convert it — divide the number by 10...

$= 12 \times 10^8$
$= 1.2 \times 10^9$ — ... and multiply the power by 10.

2. Calculate $(2 \times 10^5) \div (4 \times 10^{10})$ without using a calculator. Give your answer in standard form.

$(2 \times 10^5) \div (4 \times 10^{10})$

Divide front numbers and powers separately

$= \dfrac{2 \times 10^5}{4 \times 10^{10}} = \dfrac{2}{4} \times \dfrac{10^5}{10^{10}}$
$= 0.5 \times 10^{5-10}$ — Subtract the powers (see p.28)

Not in standard form so convert it — multiply the number by 10...

$= 0.5 \times 10^{-5}$
$= 5 \times 10^{-6}$ — ... and divide the power by 10.

Adding and Subtracting

1) Make sure the <u>powers of 10</u> are <u>the same</u>.
2) Add or subtract the <u>front numbers</u>.
3) Convert the answer to <u>standard form</u> if necessary.

To put standard form numbers into your calculator, use the [EXP] or the [×10ˣ] button.

E.g. enter 2.67×10^{15} by pressing

[2.67] [EXP] [15] [=] or [2.67] [×10ˣ] [15] [=] .

EXAMPLE **Calculate $(2.8 \times 10^4) + (6.6 \times 10^4)$ without using a calculator. Give your answer in standard form.**

1) <u>Check</u> that both powers of 10 are equal. $(2.8 \times 10^4) + (6.6 \times 10^4)$
2) Then add the <u>front numbers</u>. $= (2.8 + 6.6) \times 10^4$
3) This is in standard form, so you <u>don't</u> need to convert it. $= 9.4 \times 10^4$

Remember, n tells you how far the decimal point moves

Make sure you understand all the examples on these pages. Then answer these Exam Practice Questions:

Q1 Write a) 4.32×10^8 as an ordinary number.   [1 mark]
         b) 0.000387 in standard form.   [1 mark]

Q2 Which of these numbers is the smallest? 2.6×10^{-3} 1.9×10^{-3} 3.4×10^{-2} [1 mark]

Q3 Work out the following. Give your answers in standard form.
         a) $(9 \times 10^7) \div (3 \times 10^4)$ [3 marks]   b) $(6.7 \times 10^{10}) - (4.8 \times 10^{10})$ [2 marks]

Warm-up and Worked Exam Questions

I know that you'll be champing at the bit to get into the exam questions, but these warm-up questions are invaluable for getting the basic facts straight first.

Warm-up Questions

1) a) Use your calculator to find 0.8^4.
   b) Without a calculator, work out $3^4 - 2^5$.
   c) What is 1 000 000 as a power of 10?

2) Simplify: a) $4^1 \times 4^5$ b) $(5^3)^2$ c) $\dfrac{x^8}{x^2}$

3) Without using a calculator, find: a) $\dfrac{7^{12}}{7^3 \times 7^7}$ b) 3^{-3}

4) Find a) $\sqrt{225}$ b) $\sqrt[3]{6859}$ c) $\sqrt[5]{7776}$

5) The volume of a football is $\dfrac{4000\pi}{3}$ cm³.
   Given that the volume of a sphere $= \dfrac{4}{3}\pi r^3$, find the radius, r, of the ball in cm.

6) Work out $0.3^2(4.2 + 1.7)^3 + \sqrt{75.69}$ on your calculator. Write down your answer exactly.

7) Write a) 2 890 000 in standard form.
          b) 7.11×10^{-5} as an ordinary number.

8) Which of these numbers is the largest? 1.8×10^4 2.1×10^4 6.3×10^3

9) Work out the following. Give your answers in standard form.
   a) $(2 \times 10^{-4}) \times (6 \times 10^5)$ b) $(5.4 \times 10^{-7}) + (8.9 \times 10^{-7})$

Worked Exam Question

With the answers written in, it's very easy to just skim over this worked exam question.
But that's not really going to help you, so take the time to make sure you've really understood it.

1   The table on the right shows the masses of four different particles. (5)

   a)   Which particle is the heaviest?

         Look at the power first.
         −6 moves the decimal point fewer
         places to the left than the others.

         ....C...........
         [1 mark]

Particle	Mass (g)
Particle A	2.1×10^{-7}
Particle B	8.6×10^{-8}
Particle C	1.4×10^{-6}
Particle D	3.2×10^{-7}

   b)   What is the mass of particle C?
         Give your answer as an ordinary number.

   $1.4 \times 10^{-6} = 0.0000014$ g

   Move the decimal
   point 6 places.

                        ....0.0000014........... g
                        [1 mark]

   c)   How much more does particle D weigh than particle A?
         Give your answer in standard form.

                                                              The power of 10 is the same
                                                              for particles D and A, so it's
                                                              just a simple subtraction.
   $(3.2 \times 10^{-7}) - (2.1 \times 10^{-7}) = (3.2 - 2.1) \times 10^{-7}$

                        $= 1.1 \times 10^{-7}$ g

                                          ....1.1×10^{-7}........... g
                                          [2 marks]

Exam Questions

2   A square has an area of 6.25 cm². Find the length of one side of the square.   (3)

.... cm

[1 mark]

3   $A = 4.834 \times 10^9$, $B = 2.4 \times 10^5$, $C = 5.21 \times 10^3$ (4)

a)   Write A as an ordinary number.

....

[1 mark]

b)   Put A, B and C in order from smallest to largest.

.........., ..., ...

[1 mark]

4   Simplify the expression $\dfrac{3^4 \times 3^7}{3^6}$. Leave your answer in index form.   (5)

....

[2 marks]

5   Work out the value of:

a) $6^5 \div 6^3$ (4)

....

[1 mark]

b) $(2^4 \times 2^7) \div (2^3 \times 2^2)^2$ (5)

....

[2 marks]

6   Light travels at approximately 2×10^5 miles per second.
The distance from the Earth to the Sun is approximately 9×10^7 miles.   (5)

How long will it take light to travel this distance?

Use the formula:
time (s) = distance (miles) ÷ speed (miles/s)

.... seconds

[2 marks]

Revision Questions for Section One

That wraps up <u>Section One</u> — time to find out <u>what you know</u>.
- <u>Tick off each question</u> when you've <u>got it right</u>.
- When you're <u>completely happy</u> with a topic, tick that off too.

For even more practice, try the Sudden Fail Quiz for Section One — just scan this QR code!

Section One Quiz

Calculators are <u>only allowed</u> in questions 2, 7, 9, 10, 15 and 22. Sorry.

Arithmetic (p1-6) ☐

1) What are square numbers? Write down the first ten of them. ☑

2) Using the numbers 2, 4 and 5, and +, −, × and ÷, what is the smallest possible positive number you can make? You can use each number/operation a maximum of once. You may also use brackets. ☑

3) Tickets for a show cost £12 each. A senior's ticket is half price. A child's ticket is a third of the full price. How much does it cost for a family of 2 adults, 2 children and 1 senior to watch the show? ☑

4) Find: a) £1.20 × 100 b) £150 ÷ 300 ☑

5) Work out: a) 51 × 27 b) 338 ÷ 13 c) 3.3 × 19 d) 4.2 ÷ 12 ☑

6) Find: a) −10 − 6 b) −35 ÷ −5 c) −4 + −5 + 22 − −7 ☑

Prime Numbers, Factors and Multiples (p9-12) ☐

7) Find all the prime numbers between 40 and 60 (there are 5 of them). ☑

8) What are multiples? Find the first six multiples of: a) 10 b) 4 ☑

9) Express each of these as a product of prime factors: a) 210 b) 1050 ☑

10) Find: a) the HCF of 42 and 28 b) the LCM of 8 and 10 ☑

Fractions and Decimals (p15-19) ☐

11) Work out without a calculator: a) $\frac{25}{6} \div \frac{8}{3}$ b) $\frac{2}{3} \times 4\frac{2}{5}$ c) $\frac{5}{8} + \frac{9}{4}$ d) $\frac{2}{3} - \frac{1}{7}$ ☑

12) Calculate a) $\frac{4}{7}$ of 560 b) $\frac{2}{5}$ of £150 ☑

13) Amy, Brad and Cameron are all playing a video game. Amy has completed $\frac{5}{8}$ of the game, Brad has completed $\frac{7}{11}$ of the game and Cameron has completed $\frac{15}{22}$ of the game. Who has the largest fraction of the game left to complete? ☑

14) Write: a) 0.04 as: (i) a fraction (ii) a percentage b) 65% as: (i) a fraction (ii) a decimal ☑

15) a) What is a recurring decimal? b) Write $\frac{2}{9}$ as a recurring decimal. ☑

Rounding and Estimating (p22-25) ☐

16) Round: a) 17.65 to 1 d.p. b) 6743 to 2 s.f. c) 3 643 510 to the nearest million. ☑

17) Estimate the value of a) $\frac{17.8 \times 32.3}{6.4}$ b) $\frac{96.2 \times 7.3}{0.463}$ ☑

18) Give the error interval for x if $x = 200$ when rounded to 1 s.f. ☑

Powers and Roots (p28-29) ☐

19) If $f = 7^6 \times 7^4$ and $g = 7^5$, what is $f \div g$? ☑

20) What is the value of 5^{-2}? Give your answer as a fraction. ☑

21) Find without using a calculator: a) $\sqrt{121}$ b) $\sqrt[3]{64}$ c) $8^2 - 2^3$ d) 100 000 as a power of ten. ☑

22) Use a calculator to find: a) 7.5^3 b) $\sqrt{23.04}$ c) $\sqrt[3]{512}$ d) $\sqrt[5]{161051}$ ☑

Standard Form (p30-31) ☐

23) What are the three rules for writing numbers in standard form? ☑

24) Write: a) 3 560 000 000 in standard form b) 2.75×10^{-6} as an ordinary number. ☑

25) Calculate: a) $(3.2 \times 10^6) \div (1.6 \times 10^3)$ b) $(5 \times 10^{11}) + (7 \times 10^{11})$
Give your answers in standard form. ☑

Algebra — Simplifying

Algebra really terrifies so many people. But honestly, it's not that bad.
*Make sure you **understand and learn** these **basics** for dealing with algebraic expressions.*

Terms

Before you can do anything else with algebra, you must understand what a <u>term</u> is:

> **A <u>TERM</u> is a collection of numbers, letters and brackets, all multiplied/divided together**

Terms are separated by <u>+ and − signs</u>. Every term has a + or − attached to the <u>front of it</u>.

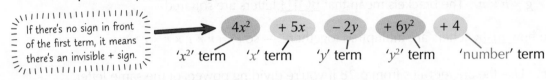

If there's no sign in front of the first term, it means there's an invisible + sign.

$4x^2$ $+ 5x$ $- 2y$ $+ 6y^2$ $+ 4$

'x^2' term   'x' term   'y' term   'y^2' term   'number' term

Simplifying or 'Collecting Like Terms'

To <u>simplify</u> an algebraic expression made up of all the <u>same terms</u>, just <u>add</u> or <u>subtract</u> them.

EXAMPLES

1. Simplify $q + q + q + q + q$

'q' just means '$1q$'.

Just <u>add up</u> all the q's:

$q + q + q + q + q = 5q$

2. Simplify $4t + 5t - 2t$

Again, just <u>combine the terms</u> —
don't forget there's a '−' before the $2t$:

$4t + 5t - 2t = 7t$

If you have a mixture of <u>different terms</u>, it's a bit more tricky. To <u>simplify</u> an algebraic expression like this, you combine '<u>like terms</u>' (e.g. all the x terms, all the y terms, all the number terms etc.).

EXAMPLE   **Simplify $2x - 4 + 5x + 6$**

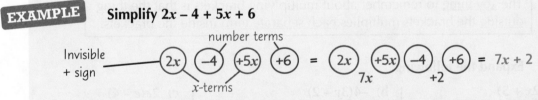

number terms

Invisible + sign $2x$ -4 $+5x$ $+6$ $=$ $2x$ $+5x$ -4 $+6$ $=$ $7x + 2$

x-terms $7x$ $+2$

1) Put <u>bubbles</u> round each term — be sure you capture the <u>+/− sign</u> in front of each.
2) Then you can move the bubbles into the <u>best order</u> so that <u>like terms</u> are together.
3) <u>Combine like terms</u>.

EXAMPLE   **Simplify $4 + \sqrt{3} - 1 + 3\sqrt{3}$**

Just treat $\sqrt{3}$-terms like x-terms — don't combine them with the number terms.

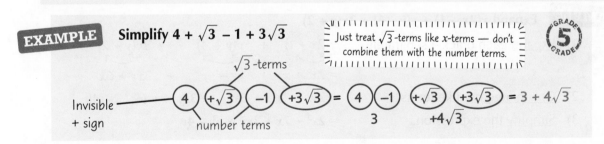

$\sqrt{3}$-terms

Invisible + sign 4 $+\sqrt{3}$ -1 $+3\sqrt{3}$ $=$ 4 -1 $+\sqrt{3}$ $+3\sqrt{3}$ $=$ $3 + 4\sqrt{3}$

number terms 3 $+4\sqrt{3}$

You need to know what terms are — and how to collect like ones

Terms are collections of numbers and letters separated by + and − signs. When you collect like terms together, you combine x terms, or y terms, or xy terms, or x^2 terms, or y^2 terms, or number terms, or...

Q1   Simplify: a) $2a + 7a + 4a$ [1 mark]   b) $6b + 8b - 3b - b$ [1 mark]

Q2   Simplify: a) $5x + y - 2x + 7y$ [1 mark]   b) $6 + 5\sqrt{5} + 3 - 2\sqrt{5}$ [2 marks]

Algebra — Multiplying and Dividing

*Multiplying algebra is a lot like multiplying numbers — here are a **few rules** to get you started.*

Multiplying and Dividing Letters

Watch out for these combinations of letters in algebra that regularly catch people out:

1) abc means $a \times b \times c$ and $3a$ means $3 \times a$. The ×'s are often left out to make it clearer.

2) gn^2 means $g \times n \times n$. Note that only the n is squared, not the g as well.

3) $(gn)^2$ means $g \times g \times n \times n$. The brackets mean that <u>BOTH</u> letters are squared.

4) <u>Powers</u> tell you <u>how many</u> letters are multiplied together — so $r^6 = r \times r \times r \times r \times r \times r$.

5) $\frac{a}{b}$ means $a \div b$. Use the <u>power rules</u> from p.28 if you're dividing powers of the same letter.

EXAMPLES

1. Simplify $k \times k \times k \times k$

Careful — k times itself 4 times is k^4, not 4k (4k means $k + k + k + k$ or $4 \times k$).

You have 4 k's <u>multiplied together</u>:

$k \times k \times k \times k = k^4$

2. Simplify $2p \times 3q \times 5$

Multiply the <u>numbers</u> together, then the <u>letters</u> together:

$2p \times 3q \times 5 = 2 \times 3 \times 5 \times p \times q = 30pq$

3. Simplify $6m^2 \div 8m$

Write as a <u>fraction</u> then simplify: $6m^2 \div 8m = \dfrac{6m^2}{8m} = \dfrac{3}{4}m$

$m^2 \div m = m$

Leave the number in front of the letter as a fraction not a decimal.

Multiplying Brackets

The <u>key thing</u> to remember about multiplying brackets is that the thing <u>outside</u> the brackets multiplies <u>each separate term</u> inside the brackets.

EXAMPLE **Expand the following:**

a) $3(2x + 5)$

$= (3 \times 2x) + (3 \times 5)$

$= 6x + 15$

b) $-4(3y - 2)$

$= (-4 \times 3y) + (-4 \times -2)$

$= -12y + 8$

c) $2e(e - 4)$

$= (2e \times e) + (2e \times -4)$

$= 2e^2 - 8e$

EXAMPLE **Expand $x(2x + 1) + y(y - 4) + 3x(y + 2)$**

1) <u>Expand</u> each bracket separately.

$x(2x + 1) \quad + \quad y(y - 4) \quad + \quad 3x(y + 2)$

$= 2x^2 + x \quad + \quad y^2 - 4y \quad + \quad 3xy + 6x$

2) <u>Group together</u> like terms.

$= 2x^2 \quad + x + 6x \quad + 3xy \quad + y^2 \quad - 4y$

3) <u>Simplify</u> the expression.

$= 2x^2 + 7x + 3xy + y^2 - 4y$

Watch out when multiplying letters together

In the cases where multiplying and dividing letters gets a bit tricky, just remember the five points above. Remember the power rules — when multiplying, add powers, and when dividing, subtract powers.

Q1 Simplify the following expressions:

a) $5r \times -2s \times 6$ [1 mark] b) $7(3m - 2)$ [1 mark] c) $4p(p + 2q)$ [1 mark]

Q2 Show that $5(x + 8) + 2(x - 12) = 7x + 16$. [2 marks]

Q2 Video Solution

Multiplying Double Brackets

Double brackets are a bit more tricky than single brackets — this time, you have to multiply everything in the first bracket by everything in the second bracket.

Use the FOIL Method to Multiply Out Double Brackets

There's a handy way to multiply double brackets — it's called the <u>FOIL method</u> and works like this:

> <u>F</u>irst — multiply the first term in each bracket together
>
> <u>O</u>utside — multiply the outside terms (i.e. the first term in the first bracket by the second term in the second bracket)
>
> <u>I</u>nside — multiply the inside terms (i.e. the second term in the first bracket by the first term in the second bracket)
>
> <u>L</u>ast — multiply the second term in each bracket together

When multiplying double brackets, you get <u>4 terms</u> — and 2 of them usually combine to leave <u>3 terms</u>.

EXAMPLES

1. **Expand and simplify $(x + 3)(x + 8)$**

$$\begin{array}{cccc} & F & O & I & L \\ (x + 3)(x + 8) = & (x \times x) + (x \times 8) + (3 \times x) + (3 \times 8) \\ = & x^2 & + 8x & + 3x & + 24 \\ = & x^2 + 11x + 24 \end{array}$$

The two x-terms <u>combine together</u>.

2. **Expand and simplify $(n - 2)(2n + 7)$**

$$\begin{array}{cccc} & F & O & I & L \\ (n - 2)(2n + 7) = & (n \times 2n) + (n \times 7) + (-2 \times 2n) + (-2 \times 7) \\ = & 2n^2 & + 7n & - 4n & - 14 \\ = & 2n^2 + 3n - 14 \end{array}$$

Write Out Squared Brackets as Double Brackets

Always write out <u>squared</u> brackets as <u>two brackets</u> (to avoid mistakes) — then multiply them out using the <u>FOIL</u> method above.

EXAMPLE **Expand and simplify $(3x + 2)^2$**

$$\begin{aligned} (3x + 2)^2 &= (3x + 2)(3x + 2) \\ &= 9x^2 + 6x + 6x + 4 \\ &= 9x^2 + 12x + 4 \end{aligned}$$

— Write out the expression as <u>two brackets</u>, then use the <u>FOIL</u> method.

> **DON'T** make the mistake of thinking that $(3x + 2)^2 = 9x^2 + 4$ (this is <u>wrong wrong wrong</u>).

Use the FOIL method to make sure you don't miss out any terms

When multiplying out double brackets, don't rush — you'll make mistakes and throw away easy marks. Remember to keep an eye out for minus signs too, and combine like terms. Now, have a go at these...

Q1   Expand and simplify: a) $(x + 6)(x - 5)$ [2 marks]   b) $(2y - 1)(y + 9)$ [2 marks]

Q2   Expand and simplify: a) $(x - 3)^2$ [2 marks]   b) $(4y + 5)^2$ [2 marks]

Factorising

*Right, now you know how to expand brackets, it's time to put them back in. This is known as **factorising**.*

Factorising — Putting Brackets In

This is the <u>exact reverse</u> of multiplying out brackets. You have to look for <u>common factors</u> — numbers or letters that go into <u>every term</u>. Here's the method to follow:

> 1) Take out the <u>biggest number</u> that goes into all the terms.
> 2) <u>For each letter in turn</u>, take out the <u>highest power</u> (e.g. x, x^2, etc.) that will go into EVERY term.
> 3) Open the bracket and fill in all the bits needed to <u>reproduce each term</u>.
> 4) <u>Check</u> your answer by <u>multiplying out</u> the bracket and making sure it matches the original expression.

EXAMPLES

1. Factorise $8y + 4$

Biggest number that goes into 8 and 4

Decide what you need to multiply 4 by to get $8y$ and 4.

$$4(2y + 1)$$

Check: $4(2y + 1) = 8y + 4$ ✓

2. Factorise $3x^2 + 6x$

Biggest number that goes into 3 and 6

Highest power of x that will go into both terms

$$3x(x + 2)$$

Check: $3x(x + 2) = 3x^2 + 6x$ ✓

> <u>REMEMBER</u>: The bits <u>taken out</u> and put at the front are the <u>common factors</u>. The bits <u>inside the bracket</u> are what's needed to get back to the <u>original terms</u> if you multiply the bracket out again.

D.O.T.S. — The **D**ifference **O**f **T**wo **S**quares

The 'difference of two squares' (D.O.T.S. for short) is where you have 'one thing squared' <u>take away</u> 'another thing squared'. There's a quick and easy way to factorise it — just use the rule below:

$$a^2 - b^2 = (a + b)(a - b)$$

EXAMPLE

Factorise:
a) $t^2 - 1$ $t^2 - 1 = (t + 1)(t - 1)$
Don't forget that 1 is a square number.

b) $s^2 - 64$ $s^2 - 64 = (s + 8)(s - 8)$
$64 = 8^2$, so in the formula above, $b = 8$.

c) $25m^2 - 1$ $25m^2 - 1 = (5m + 1)(5m - 1)$
Here you have to remember that it's 5m, not just m.

d) $9p^2 - 16q^2$ $9p^2 - 16q^2 = (3p + 4q)(3p - 4q)$
This time you had to spot that 9 and 16 are square numbers.

Factorising is the opposite of multiplying out brackets

You can check your answer by multiplying the brackets out again, so there's no excuse for mistakes...

Q1   Factorise $12x + 30$ [1 mark]

Q2   Factorise $6y + 15y^2$ [2 marks]

Q3   Factorise $x^2 - 25$ [2 marks]

Q4   Factorise $36x^2 - 49y^2$ [2 marks]

Q4 Video Solution

Warm-up and Worked Exam Questions

It's time to test your basic algebra skills — have a go at these warm-up questions to see what you know. If you get any wrong, go back over this section, then try again.

Warm-up Questions

1) Simplify the following expressions:
   a) $4a - 2a - 5a + a$
   b) $6p - 3q + p - 7q$
   c) $2\sqrt{7} + 8 - 2 + 5\sqrt{7}$

2) Simplify the following expressions:
   a) $-3m \times 2n \times 4$
   b) $-3(2r - 11)$
   c) $5x(x - 7y)$

3) Show that $3(x + 4) - 6(3 - 2x) = 15x - 6$.

4) Expand and simplify:
   a) $(x + 3)(x - 6)$
   b) $(5a + 2)(a - 4)$
   c) $(x + 8)^2$
   d) $(2y - 3)^2$

5) Factorise the following expressions:
   a) $3x - 9$
   b) $4y + 20y^2$
   c) $x^2 - 16$
   d) $16x^2 - 25y^2$

Worked Exam Questions

I've gone through these questions and written in answers, just like you'll do in the exam.
They should really help with the questions which follow, so don't say I never do anything for you.

1   Circle the simplified version of $4s - 3s + 9s$. **(2)** They're all s-terms so just add/subtract the numbers: $4 - 3 + 9 = 10$.

   $16s$ $12s$ $(10s)$ $-8s$ $11s$

   [1 mark]

2   Expand and simplify where possible. **(3)** Multiply out the brackets first, then collect like terms.

   a) $3(x - 1) + 5(x + 2)$

   $(3 \times x) + (3 \times -1) + (5 \times x) + (5 \times 2) = 3x - 3 + 5x + 10$
   $= 8x + 7$

   $8x + 7$
   [2 marks]

   b) $3a(a - 5b)$

   $(3a \times a) + (3a \times -5b) = 3a^2 - 15ab$

   $3a^2 - 15ab$
   [1 mark]

   c) $9 - 3(x + 2)$

   $9 + (-3 \times x) + (-3 \times 2) = 9 - 3x - 6$
   $= 3 - 3x$

   Careful with the minus signs here.

   $3 - 3x$
   [2 marks]

Exam Questions

3   Simplify the following.

a) $p + p + p + p$

....
[1 mark]

b) $m + 3m - 2m$

....
[1 mark]

c) $7r - 2p - 4r + 6p$

....
[2 marks]

4   Factorise the expression below.

$6x + 3$

....
[1 mark]

5   Expand and simplify the following:

a) $(x + 2)(x + 4)$ ④

....
[2 marks]

b) $(y + 3)(y - 3)$ ④

....
[2 marks]

c) $(2z - 1)(z - 5)$ ⑤

....
[2 marks]

6   Factorise the following expressions. ⑤

   a) $x^2 - 49$

Use the special rule for factorising
the difference of two squares.

....
[2 marks]

b) $9x^2 - 100$

....
[2 marks]

c) $y^2 - m^2$

....
[2 marks]

Solving Equations

*'**Solving equations**' basically means 'find the **value of x** (or whatever letter is used) that makes the equation **true**'. To do this, you usually have to **rearrange** the equation to get x **on its own**.*

The '**Common Sense**' Approach

The trick here is to realise that the <u>unknown quantity</u> 'x' is just a <u>number</u> and the '<u>equation</u>' is a <u>cryptic clue</u> to help you find it.

EXAMPLE **Solve the equation $3x + 4 = 46$.**

> This just means 'find the value of x'.

This is what you should say to yourself:

'Something + 4 = 46', hmmm, so that 'something' must be 42.

So that means $3x = 42$, which means '3 × something = 42'.

So it must be 42 ÷ 3 = 14, so $x = 14$.

> If you were writing this down in an exam question, just write down the bits in blue.

In other words don't think of it as algebra, but as '<u>find the mystery number</u>'.

The '**Proper**' Way

The 'proper' way to solve equations is to keep <u>rearranging</u> them until you end up with '<u>x = </u>' on one side. There are a few <u>important points</u> to remember when rearranging.

Golden Rules

1) Always do the <u>SAME thing</u> to <u>both sides of the equation</u>.
2) To get rid of something, do the <u>opposite</u>.
   The opposite of + is − and the opposite of − is +.
   The opposite of × is ÷ and the opposite of ÷ is ×.
3) Keep going until you have a letter <u>on its own</u>.

EXAMPLES

1.   Solve $x + 7 = 11$.

$$x + 7 = 11$$

The opposite of +7 is −7

$$(-7) \quad x + 7 - 7 = 11 - 7$$
$$x = 4$$

> This means 'take away 7 from both sides'.

2.   Solve $x − 3 = 7$.

The opposite of −3 is +3

$$x - 3 = 7$$
$$(+3) \quad x - 3 + 3 = 7 + 3$$
$$x = 10$$

3.   Solve $5x = 15$.

$$5x = 15$$

5x means 5 × x, so do the opposite — divide both sides by 5

$$(\div 5) \quad 5x \div 5 = 15 \div 5$$
$$x = 3$$

4.   Solve $\frac{x}{3} = 2$.

$$\frac{x}{3} = 2$$

$\frac{x}{3}$ means x ÷ 3, so do the opposite — multiply both sides by 3

$$(\times 3) \quad \frac{x}{3} \times 3 = 2 \times 3$$
$$x = 6$$

That's it — all the steps you need to solve any of these equations

It's always good to know the proper way to solve equations, just in case you get thrown a curveball in the exam and they give you a real nightmare of an equation to solve. Have a go at this Practice Question:

Q1   Solve these equations: a) $x + 2 = 8$ [1 mark]   b) $x − 6 = 8$ [1 mark]

c) $4x = 12$ [1 mark]   d) $\frac{x}{5} = 3$ [1 mark]

Solving Equations

You're not done with solving equations yet — not by a long shot.

Two-Step Equations

If you come across an equation like $4x + 3 = 19$ (where there's an <u>x-term</u> and a <u>number</u> on the <u>same side</u>), use the methods from the previous page to solve it — just do it in <u>two steps</u>:

1) <u>Add or subtract</u> the number first.   2) <u>Multiply or divide</u> to get '$x = $'.

EXAMPLE **Solve the equation $4x - 3 = 17$.**

$$4x - 3 = 17$$ — The opposite of -3 is $+3$, so add 3 to both sides.
$$(+3) \quad 4x - 3 + 3 = 17 + 3$$
$$4x = 20$$ — The opposite of $\times 4$ is $\div 4$, so divide both sides by 4.
$$(\div 4) \quad 4x \div 4 = 20 \div 4$$
$$x = 5$$

Equations with an 'x' on **Both Sides**

For equations like $2x + 3 = x + 7$ (where there's an x-term on <u>each side</u>), you have to:

1) Get all the x's on one side and all the <u>numbers</u> on the other.
2) <u>Multiply or divide</u> to get '$x = $'.

EXAMPLE **Solve the equation $3x + 5 = 5x + 7$.**

$$3x + 5 = 5x + 7$$ — To get the x's on only one side, subtract $3x$ from each side.
$$(-3x) \quad 3x + 5 - 3x = 5x + 7 - 3x$$
$$5 = 2x + 7$$ — Now subtract 7 to get the numbers on the other side.
$$(-7) \quad 5 - 7 = 2x + 7 - 7$$
$$-2 = 2x$$ — The opposite of $\times 2$ is $\div 2$, so divide both sides by 2.
$$(\div 2) \quad -2 \div 2 = 2x \div 2$$
$$-1 = x$$

Don't be put off by the fact that the x ends up on the right, not the left. $-1 = x$ is exactly the same as $x = -1$.

Equations with **Brackets**

If the equation has <u>brackets</u> in, you have to <u>multiply out</u> the brackets (see p.36) before solving it as above.

EXAMPLE **Solve the equation $5x + 3 = 4(x + 2)$.**

$$5x + 3 = 4(x + 2)$$ — Multiply out the brackets.
$$5x + 3 = 4x + 8$$ — To get the x's on only one side, subtract $4x$ from each side.
$$(-4x) \quad 5x + 3 - 4x = 4x + 8 - 4x$$
$$x + 3 = 8$$ — The opposite of $+3$ is -3, so subtract 3 from each side.
$$(-3) \quad x + 3 - 3 = 8 - 3$$
$$x = 5$$

You can use the same methods to solve all sorts of equations

If your equation has brackets, multiply them out before solving it as normal.
You can check your answer by putting it back into the original equation to see if it works.

Q1   Solve $6x - 5 = 3x + 10$ [2 marks]   Q2   Solve $4(y - 2) = 2y + 6$ [3 marks]

Expressions, Formulas and Functions

*Before we get started, there are a few **definitions** you need to know:*

1) EXPRESSION — a <u>collection</u> of <u>terms</u> (see p.35). Expressions <u>DON'T</u> have an = sign in them.

2) EQUATION — an expression with an = sign in it (so you can solve it)

3) FORMULA — a <u>rule</u> that helps you work something out (it will also have an = sign in it).

4) FUNCTION — an expression that takes an <u>input</u> value, <u>processes</u> it and produces an <u>output</u> value.

Putting **Numbers** into **Formulas**

You might be given a <u>formula</u> and asked to work out its <u>value</u> when you put in <u>certain numbers</u>.
All you have to do here is follow this <u>method</u>.

1) Write out the <u>formula</u>.

2) Write it <u>again</u>, directly underneath, but <u>substituting numbers for letters</u> on the <u>RHS</u> (right-hand side).

3) Work it out <u>in stages</u>. Use <u>BODMAS</u> (see p.1) to work things out in the <u>right order</u>.
Write down values for each bit as you go along.

4) <u>DO NOT</u> attempt to do it <u>all in one go</u> on your calculator — you're more likely to make <u>mistakes</u>.

> **EXAMPLE** The formula for converting from Celsius (C) to Fahrenheit (F) is F = $\frac{9}{5}$C + 32.
> Use this formula to convert –10 °C into Fahrenheit.
>
> $F = \frac{9}{5}C + 32$ ———— 1) Write out the <u>formula</u>.
> $F = \frac{9}{5} \times -10 + 32$ ———— 2) Write it <u>again</u>, <u>substituting numbers for letters</u> on the <u>RHS</u>.
> $F = -18 + 32$ ———— 3) Use <u>BODMAS</u> to work things out in the <u>right order</u>
> — do the <u>multiplication</u> first, then do the <u>addition</u>.
> $F = 14$ so –10 °C = 14 °F
>
> Be careful when substituting negative numbers into a formula — just do it step-by-step.

Functions Produce Outputs from Inputs

1) A <u>function</u> takes an <u>input</u>, <u>processes</u> it (e.g. multiplies it by 5 and adds 2) and <u>outputs</u> a value.

2) If you have to use a <u>function machine</u>, just put in the number, follow the steps and see what comes out.

3) If you're given the <u>output</u> and have to find the <u>input</u>, use the function machine <u>in reverse</u>.

> **EXAMPLE** The function machine below represents the function 'multiply by 5 and add 2'.
>
>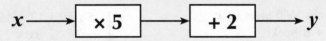
>
> If this was an equation, it'd be written as $y = 5x + 2$.
>
> **a) Find the value of y when $x = 5$.**
> Just put 5 into the machine: $5 \xrightarrow{\times 5} 25 \xrightarrow{+2} 27$. So $y = 27$.
>
> **b) Find the value of x when $y = 42$.**
> This time, put $y = 42$ into the machine and <u>work backwards</u>:
>
> 42   40   8. So $x = 8$.
>
> | Don't forget to reverse each step as well — so +2 becomes –2 and ×5 becomes ÷5. |

Function machines are just a series of operations

Given the input, it's easy to find the output of a function machine — just do the operations step-by-step.
Finding the input if you're given the output is trickier — work through backwards and reverse each step.

Q1 $v = u + at$. Find the value of v when $u = 5$, $a = 4$ and $t = 6$.   [2 marks]

Q2   Using the function machine above, find the value of x when $y = 57$.   [2 marks]

Formulas and Equations from Words

*Making **expressions** or **formulas** from **words** can be a bit confusing as you're given a lot of **information** in one go. You just have to go through it slowly and carefully and **extract the maths** from it.*

Make Expressions or Formulas from Given Information

Here are some of <u>examples</u> of how to use the information to write expressions and formulas.

 Tiana is x years old. Leah is 5 years younger than Tiana. Martin is 4 times as old as Tiana. Find a simplified expression for the sum of their ages in terms of x.

Tiana's age is x

Leah is 5 years younger, so subtract 5

Leah's age is $x - 5$

Martin's age is $4 \times x = 4x$ 4 times older

The sum of their ages is:

$x + (x - 5) + 4x = 6x - 5$

If you'd been <u>told</u> the sum of their ages, you'd have to set your expression equal to the sum and solve it to find x.

 In rugby union, tries score 5 points and conversions score 2 points. A team scores a total of P points, made up of t tries and c conversions. Write a formula for P in terms of t and c.

Tries score 5 points ——— t tries will score $5 \times t = 5t$ points

Conversions score ——— c conversions will score $2 \times c = 2c$ points

2 points   So total points scored are $P = 5t + 2c$

Because you're asked for a formula, you must include the '$P =$ ' bit to get full marks (i.e. don't just put $5t + 2c$).

Use Your Expression to Solve Equations

Sometimes, you might be asked to <u>use</u> an expression to <u>solve an equation</u>.

 A zoo has x zebras and four times as many lemurs. The difference between the number of zebras and the number of lemurs is 45. How many zebras does the zoo have?

The zoo has x zebras and $4 \times x = 4x$ lemurs.

The difference is $4x - x = 3x$, so $3x = 45$, which means $x = 15$.

So the zoo has 15 zebras.

Once you've formed the equation, you need to solve it to find the value of x.

EXAMPLE **Will, Naveed and Camille give some books to charity. Naveed gives 6 more books than Will, and Camille gives 7 more books than Naveed. Between them, they give away 46 books. How many books did they give each?**

Let the number of books Will gives be x.

Then Naveed gives $x + 6$ books

and Camille gives $(x + 6) + 7 = x + 13$ books

So in total they give $x + x + 6 + x + 13 = 3x + 19$ books

So $3x + 19 = 46$ ——— You're told this in the question.

$3x = 27$

$x = 9$

So Will gives 9 books,
Naveed gives $9 + 6 = 15$ books and
Camille gives $15 + 7 = 22$ books.

Writing expressions and formulas is easy once you get the idea

Exam questions might not tell you to write an equation or formula — sometimes you have to come up with one for yourself to be able to answer the question, so make sure you practise.

Q1   Ali, Ava and Ann sell 73 raffle tickets between them. Ava sells twice as many tickets as Ali, and Ann sells 8 more tickets than Ava. How many tickets does each person sell?   [3 marks]

Q2   Three positive whole numbers have a sum of 48. The second number is five times the first, and the third number is double the second. What are the three numbers?   [3 marks]

Formulas and Equations from Diagrams

*Formulas and equations can even sneak into **area** and **perimeter** questions*
— have a look at page 112 if you need to brush up on those topics.

Use **Shape Properties** to Find **Formulas** and **Equations**

In some questions, you'll need to use what you know about <u>shapes</u> (e.g. <u>side lengths</u> or <u>areas</u>)
to come up with a formula or an equation to solve.

EXAMPLE

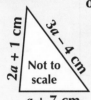

a) **Write a formula for *P*, the perimeter of the triangle below, in terms of *a*.**

Form an <u>expression</u> for the <u>perimeter</u>:
$P = (a + 7) + (2a + 1) + (3a − 4)$
$P = (6a + 4)$ cm

b) **If the triangle has a perimeter of 58 cm, find the value of *a*.**

$P = 58$, so set your formula equal to <u>58</u> and <u>solve</u> to find *a*:
$6a + 4 = 58$
$6a = 54$
$a = 9$

Compare **Dimensions** of **Two Shapes** to Find Equations

You might get a question that involves <u>two shapes</u> with related <u>areas</u> or <u>perimeters</u>
— you'll have to use this fact to find <u>side lengths</u> or <u>missing values</u>.

EXAMPLE

The perimeter of the rectangle is the same as the perimeter of the square. Find the value of *x*.

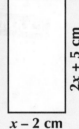

Perimeter of square = $2x + 2x + 2x + 2x = 8x$ cm
Perimeter of rectangle = $(2x + 5) + (x − 2) + (2x + 5) + (x − 2)$
$= 6x + 6$ cm

Set the perimeter of the rectangle equal to the perimeter of the square and solve:
$8x = 6x + 6$
$2x = 6$
$x = 3$

EXAMPLE

The area of the square is the same as the area of the triangle. Find the length of the base of the triangle.

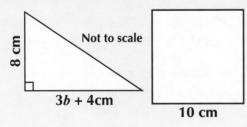

Area of triangle: $\frac{1}{2} × (3b + 4) × 8 = 12b + 16$ cm^2
Area of square: $10^2 = 100$ cm^2

Set the areas equal to each other and solve:
$12b + 16 = 100$
$12b = 84$
$b = 7$
So base length = $(3 × 7) + 4 = 25$ cm

Formulas and equations can crop up in lots of different topics

Don't be put off by the shapes — once you turn the information into an equation, it's just algebra.
As long as you can find the perimeter and area of simple shapes you won't have much trouble.

Q1   A regular pentagon has sides of length *x* cm. A square with sides of length *x* + 4 cm
        has the same perimeter as the pentagon. Find the value of *x*.   [3 marks]

Rearranging Formulas

*The **subject** of a formula is the letter **on its own** before the = (so x is the subject of x = 2y + 3z).*

Changing the Subject of a Formula

<u>Rearranging formulas</u> means making a different letter the <u>subject</u>, e.g. getting '*y* = ' from '*x* = 3*y* + 2'.
Fortunately, you can use the <u>same methods</u> that you used for <u>solving equations</u> (see p.41-42)
— here's a quick reminder:

Golden Rules

1) Always do the <u>SAME thing</u> to <u>both sides of the formula</u>.
2) To get rid of something, do the <u>opposite</u>.
   The opposite of + is – and the opposite of – is +.
   The opposite of × is ÷ and the opposite of ÷ is ×.
3) Keep going until you have the letter you want <u>on its own</u>.

EXAMPLE **Rearrange $a = 3b + 4$ to make b the subject of the formula.**

$$a = 3b + 4$$
The opposite of +4 is −4, so take away 4 from both sides.

(−4) $$a - 4 = 3b + 4 - 4$$

$$a - 4 = 3b$$
The opposite of ×3 is ÷3, so divide both sides by 3.

(÷3) $$(a - 4) \div 3 = 3b \div 3$$

$$\frac{a-4}{3} = b \text{ OR } b = \frac{a-4}{3}$$

Careful here — you divide the <u>whole side</u> by 3, not just one term.

EXAMPLE **Rearrange $p = 5(q + 2)$ to make q the subject of the formula.**

$$p = 5q + 10$$
Multiply out the brackets.

(−10) $$p - 10 = 5q + 10 - 10$$
The opposite of +10 is −10, so take away 10 from both sides.

$$p - 10 = 5q$$

(÷5) $$(p - 10) \div 5 = 5q \div 5$$
The opposite of ×5 is ÷5, so divide both sides by 5.

$$\frac{p-10}{5} = q \text{ OR } q = \frac{p-10}{5}$$

EXAMPLE **Rearrange $m = \frac{n}{4} - 7$ to make n the subject of the formula.**

$$m = \frac{n}{4} - 7$$
The opposite of −7 is +7, so add 7 to both sides.

(+7) $$m + 7 = \frac{n}{4} - 7 + 7$$

$$m + 7 = \frac{n}{4}$$
The opposite of ÷4 is ×4, so multiply both sides by 4.

(×4) $$(m + 7) \times 4 = \frac{n}{4} \times 4$$

$$4(m + 7) = n \text{ OR } n = 4m + 28$$

Just remember — the subject is the letter on its own

Rearranging formulas is really just like solving equations — so if you learn the method for one,
you know the method for the other. All you have to do is remember the golden rules and you'll be set.

Q1   Rearrange $u = \frac{v}{3} - 2$ to make v the subject of the formula.   [2 marks]

Q2   Rearrange $c = 6d - 12$ to make d the subject of the formula.   [2 marks]

Warm-up and Worked Exam Questions

I know it was a pretty tough section, but being able to rearrange and solve equations and formulas is likely to come in handy in the exam. See how you fare with these warm-up questions.

Warm-up Questions

1) Solve these equations:
   a) $x + 4 = 6$ b) $x - 3 = 8$ c) $3x = 18$ d) $\frac{x}{4} = 5$

2) a) Solve $4x - 5 = 7 + x$ b) Solve $5(y - 3) = 3y + 7$

3) $s = \frac{1}{2}(u + v)t$. Find the value of s when $u = 4$, $v = 8$ and $t = 2$.

4) Use the function machine on the right to find the value of: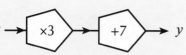
   a) y when $x = 6$ b) x when $y = 40$

5) A jar contains blue, red and green sweets. There are three times as many red sweets as blue, and ten more green sweets than red. Find an expression for the number of sweets in the jar.

6) Khaled, Rachel and Adam collect football stickers. They have 180 stickers in total. Rachel has twice as many stickers as Khaled and Adam has 3 times as many stickers as Rachel. How many stickers does Khaled have?

7) The triangle on the right has a perimeter of 33 cm. Find the value of x.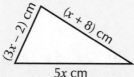

8) Rearrange $a = \frac{b}{5} + 4$ to make b the subject of the formula.

9) Rearrange $p = 3q - 8$ to make q the subject of the formula.

Worked Exam Question

I'd like an exam question, and the answers written in — and a surprise. Two out of three's not bad.

1   The perimeter of the isosceles triangle below is double the perimeter of the square. Find the length of the base of the triangle. **(5 GRADE)**

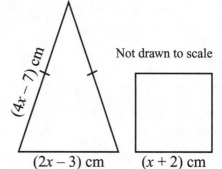

Not drawn to scale

Perimeter of triangle = $(4x - 7) + (4x - 7) + (2x - 3)$
= $10x - 17$ cm   *Work out the perimeter of both shapes.*

Perimeter of square = $4 \times (x + 2) = 4x + 8$ cm

Perimeter of triangle = 2 × perimeter of square
$$10x - 17 = 2 \times (4x + 8)$$
$$10x - 17 = 8x + 16$$
$$2x = 33$$
$$x = 16.5 \text{ cm}$$

Use the information from the question to make your equation.

Solve your equation to find x.

So base of triangle = $(2 \times 16.5) - 3 = 30$ cm

Don't forget to use the value of x to find the length of the base of the triangle.

.............30............ cm
[4 marks]

Exam Questions

2 $S = 4m^2 + 2.5n$ **(2)**

a) Calculate the value of S when $m = 2$ and $n = 10$.

....

[2 marks]

b) Calculate the value of S when $m = 6.5$ and $n = 4$.

....

[2 marks]

3 Solve the following equations. **(3)**

a) $40 - 3x = 17x$

$x =$ ....

[2 marks]

b) $2y - 5 = 3y - 12$

$y =$ ....

[2 marks]

4 Find the length of one side of this equilateral triangle. **(4)**

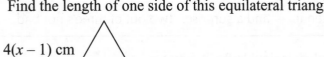

$4(x - 1)$ cm

$3x + 5$ cm

.... cm

[3 marks]

5 Rearrange the formula $\dfrac{a+2}{3} = b - 1$ to make a the subject. **(4)**

....

[2 marks]

6 At a football match between Redwood Rovers and Whitewater Wanderers,
there were three times as many Redwood fans as Whitewater fans.
The difference between the number of fans for each team was 7000. **(5)**
How many fans were there in total?

....

[3 marks]

Sequences

*Sequences are **lists** of numbers or shapes that follow a **rule**. You need to be able to spot what the rule is.*

Finding **the Rule** for **Number Sequences**

The trick to <u>finding the rule</u> for number sequences is to <u>write down</u> what you have to do to get from one number to the next in the <u>gaps</u> between the numbers. There are <u>2 main types</u> to look out for:

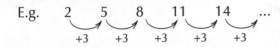 **1) Add or subtract the same number** These are known as <u>arithmetic</u> or <u>linear</u> sequences.

E.g. 2   5   8   11   14   ... | 30   24   18   12   ...
+3 +3 +3 +3 +3 | −6   −6   −6   −6

The RULE: 'Add 3 to the <u>previous term</u>' | 'Subtract 6 from the <u>previous term</u>'

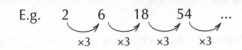 **2) Multiply or divide by the same number each time** These are known as <u>geometric</u> sequences.

E.g. 2   6   18   54   ... | 40 000   4000   400   40   ...
×3 ×3 ×3 ×3 | ÷10   ÷10   ÷10   ÷10

The RULE: 'Multiply the <u>previous term</u> by 3' | 'Divide the <u>previous term</u> by 10'

Sometimes you might get sequences that follow a <u>different</u> rule — e.g. you might have to add or subtract a <u>changing number</u> each time, or add together the <u>two previous terms</u> (see the examples below).

EXAMPLE **Find the next two terms in each of the following sequences.**

a) 1, 3, 6, 10, 15, ...

<u>'The number you add on increases by one each time'</u> (i.e. +2, +3, +4, ...) so the next two terms are:

15 + 6 = 21   This is the sequence of
21 + 7 = 28   triangular numbers.

b) 1, 1, 2, 3, 5, ...

The rule is <u>'add together the two previous terms'</u>, so the next two terms are:

3 + 5 = 8   This is known as the
5 + 8 = 13   Fibonacci sequence.

Finding **the Rule** for **Shape Sequences**

If you have a sequence of <u>shape</u> patterns, you need to be able to <u>continue</u> the sequence. You might also have to find the <u>rule</u> for the sequence to work out <u>how many</u> shapes there'll be in a later pattern.

EXAMPLE **On the right, there are some patterns made of circles.**
a) Draw the next pattern in the sequence.
b) Work out how many circles there will be in the 10th pattern.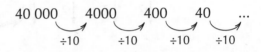

a) Just continue the sequence — the circles make a <u>square pattern</u>. ➡

b) Find the rule for the number of circles: there's $1^2 = 1$ circle in the first pattern, $2^2 = 4$ circles in the second pattern, $3^2 = 9$ circles in the third pattern etc. The rule is 'square the number of the pattern'. So in the 10th pattern, there'll be $10^2 = 100$ circles.

Always write the change in the gaps between the numbers

It's the most straightforward way to spot the pattern — you'll see straight away if the difference is the same, changing by a certain amount, or multiplying. Now, have a go at this Exam Practice Question:

Q1 A sequence starts 3, 6, 12, ... There are two possible rules for this sequence.
Write down both possible rules and find the next two terms of the sequence in each case.   [2 marks]

Sequences

*You might be asked to "find an **expression** for the **nth term** of a sequence" — this is a rule with n in, like 5n – 3. It gives **every term in a sequence** when you put in different values for n.*

Finding the **nth Term** of a **Sequence**

This method works for sequences with a <u>common difference</u> — where you <u>add</u> or <u>subtract</u> the <u>same number</u> each time.

EXAMPLE **Find an expression for the *n*th term of the sequence that starts 5, 8, 11, 14, ...**

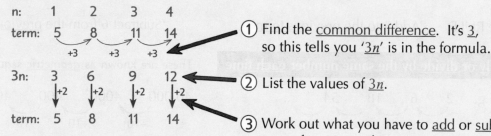

n: 1   2   3   4
term: 5   8   11   14
              +3   +3   +3

① Find the <u>common difference</u>. It's <u>3</u>, so this tells you '<u>3n</u>' is in the formula.

3n: 3   6   9   12
        +2   +2   +2   +2
term: 5   8   11   14

② List the values of <u>3n</u>.

③ Work out what you have to <u>add</u> or <u>subtract</u> to get from 3n to the term. So it's <u>+2</u>.

So the expression for the nth term is 3n + 2

④ Put '<u>3n</u>' and '<u>+2</u>' together.

<u>Check</u> your formula by putting the first few values of *n* back in:
n = 1 gives 3n + 2 = 3 + 2 = 5 ✓
n = 2 gives 3n + 2 = 6 + 2 = 8 ✓

Deciding if a Term is in a Sequence

You might be given the *n*th term and asked if a <u>certain value</u> is in the sequence. The trick here is to <u>set the expression equal to that value</u> and solve to find *n*. If *n* is a <u>whole number</u>, the value is <u>in</u> the sequence.

EXAMPLE   **A sequence is given by the rule 6*n* – 2.**

a) Find the 6th term in the sequence.	**b) Is 45 a term in this sequence?**

Have a look at p.41-42 for more on solving equations.

a) Just put n = 6 into the expression:
(6 × 6) – 2 = 36 – 2
= 34

b) Set it equal to 45...   6n – 2 = 45
                               6n = 47   ...and solve for n.
                               n = 47 ÷ 6 = 7.8333...
n is not a whole number, so 45 is <u>not</u> in the sequence 6n – 2.

It might be even <u>easier</u> to decide if a number is in a sequence or not — for example, if the sequence was all <u>odd numbers</u>, there's <u>no way</u> that an <u>even number</u> could be in the sequence. You just have to use your common sense — e.g. if all the terms in the sequence ended in <u>3</u> or <u>8</u>, 44 would <u>not</u> be in the sequence.

Follow the steps above to find the nth term of a sequence

Learn the steps above for finding the *n*th term. With it, you can easily find the 500th term, or the 500 000th — but without it, you'll need a dozen extra sheets of paper and a spare pen. Now, have a go at these:

Q1   A sequence starts 2, 9, 16, 23, ...
    a) Find an expression for the *n*th term of the sequence.   [2 marks]
    b) Use your expression to find the 8th term in the sequence.   [1 mark]
    c) Is 63 a term in the sequence? Explain your answer.   [2 marks]

Q1 Video Solution

Inequalities

*Inequalities are a bit tricky, but once you've learned the tricks involved, most of the **algebra** for them is **identical** to ordinary **equations** (have a look back at pages 41-42 if you need a reminder).*

The **Inequality Symbols**

> $>$ means 'Greater than' $\quad$ $\geq$ means 'Greater than or equal to'
> $<$ means 'Less than' $\quad$ $\leq$ means 'Less than or equal to'

<u>REMEMBER</u> — the one at the <u>BIG</u> end is <u>BIGGEST</u> so $x > 4$ and $4 < x$ both mean: '<u>x is greater than 4</u>'.

EXAMPLE **x is an integer such that $-4 < x \leq 3$. Write down all possible values of x.**

Work out what each bit of the inequality is telling you:

$-4 < x$ means 'x is greater than -4',

and $x \leq 3$ means 'x is less than or equal to 3'.

Remember, integers are just whole numbers (+ve and −ve, including O).

Now just write down all the values that x can take: $-3, -2, -1, O, 1, 2, 3$

-4 <u>isn't</u> included because of the $<$ but 3 <u>is</u> included because of the $\leq$.

You Can Show Inequalities on **Number Lines**

Drawing inequalities on a <u>number line</u> is dead easy — all you have to remember is that you use an <u>open circle</u> (O) for $>$ or $<$ and a <u>coloured-in circle</u> (●) for $\geq$ or $\leq$.

EXAMPLE **Show the inequality $-4 < x \leq 3$ on a number line.**

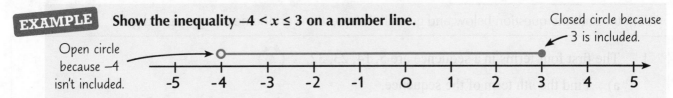

Open circle because −4 isn't included.

Closed circle because 3 is included.

Algebra with **Inequalities**

Solve inequalities <u>like regular equations</u> but <u>WITH ONE BIG EXCEPTION</u>:

> Whenever you <u>MULTIPLY</u> OR <u>DIVIDE</u> by a <u>NEGATIVE NUMBER</u>, you must <u>FLIP THE INEQUALITY SIGN</u>.

EXAMPLES

1. Solve $3x - 2 \leq 13$.

Just solve it like an equation — but leave the inequality sign in your answer:

$(+2)$ $\quad 3x - 2 + 2 \leq 13 + 2$
$\qquad\qquad 3x \leq 15$
$(\div 3)$ $\quad 3x \div 3 \leq 15 \div 3$
$\qquad\qquad x \leq 5$

2. Solve $2x + 7 > x + 11$.

Again, solve it like an equation:

(-7) $\quad 2x + 7 - 7 > x + 11 - 7$
$\qquad\qquad 2x > x + 4$
$(-x)$ $\quad 2x - x > x + 4 - x$
$\qquad\qquad x > 4$

3. Solve $9 - 2x > 15$.

Watch out for the sign change:

(-9) $\quad 9 - 2x - 9 > 15 - 9$
$\qquad\qquad -2x > 6$
$(\div -2)$ $\quad -2x \div -2 < 6 \div -2$
$\qquad\qquad x < -3$

The $>$ has turned into a $<$, because we divided by a <u>negative number</u>.

Treat inequalities like equations

Learn the golden rules for solving equations and you'll be able to solve inequalities too. Just remember the extra rule about flipping the inequality sign if you multiply or divide by a negative number.

Q1 $\quad n$ is an integer such that $-1 \leq n < 5$. Write down all the possible values of n. [2 marks]

Q2 $\quad$ Solve the following inequalities: a) $4x + 3 < 27$ [2 marks] $\qquad$ b) $4x \geq 18 - 2x$ [2 marks]

Warm-up and Worked Exam Questions

Sequences and inequalities — love them or hate them, you have to do them — it's just a case of learning the method and practising lots of questions. So let's start with some warm-up questions...

Warm-up Questions

1) Write down the next two terms in each of these sequences:
   a) 2, 6, 10, 14   b) 1, 3, 9, 27   c) 2, 3, 5, 8, 12

2) A sequence starts 1, 4, 9, 16, 25...
   a) What is the rule for this sequence?
   b) Find the next two terms of the sequence.
   c) Is 100 a term in this sequence? Explain your answer.

3) For each of the sequences, say whether it is an arithmetic or geometric sequence and explain why.   a) 5, 9, 13, 17...   b) 4, 12, 36, 108...

4) A sequence starts 27, 23, 19, 15...
   a) Find an expression for the nth term of the sequence.
   b) What is the 20th term in the sequence?

5) n is an integer such that $-3 < n \le 4$. Write down all the possible values of n.

6) Solve these inequalities: a) $6x - 2 < 28$ b) $5x \ge 49 - 2x$

Worked Exam Question

Work through the question below and give all the questions on the next page a good go.

1 The first four terms in a sequence are 5, 14, 23, 32, ...

a) Find the nth term of the sequence.

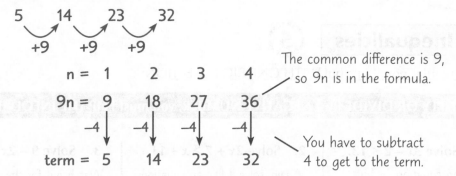

The common difference is 9, so 9n is in the formula.

You have to subtract 4 to get to the term.

So the expression for the nth term is 9n − 4

$$9n - 4$$
[2 marks]

b) What is the 20th term of the sequence?

20th term = (9 × 20) − 4 = 176

176
[1 mark]

c) Is 87 a term in this sequence? Explain your answer.

If 87 is a term in the sequence, then 9n − 4 = 87, 9n = 91 so n = 10.111...

n is not a whole number, so 87 is not a term in the sequence.

[2 marks]

Exam Questions

2   n is an integer. List all the possible values of n that satisfy the inequality $-3 \leq n < 2$. (**3**)

....

[2 marks]

3   The patterns in the sequence below represent the first three triangle numbers. (**3**)

a)   Draw the next pattern in the sequence.

[1 mark]

b)   How many circles are in the tenth pattern in the sequence? Give a reason for your answer.

....

....

[2 marks]

4   To find the next term in the sequence below, you add together the two previous terms. (**4**)
    Fill in the gaps to complete the sequence.

| 3 | .... | 7 | .... | .... | 29 |

[2 marks]

5   A quadratic sequence starts 2, 6, 12, 20, ...   (**4**)
    Find the next term in the sequence.

    Find the pattern in the differences
    between each pair of terms and
    use this to find the next term.

....

[2 marks]

6   p and q are integers. $p \leq 45$ and $q > 25$. (**4**)
    What is the largest possible value of $p - q$?

....

[2 marks]

Quadratic Equations

*A **quadratic** equation is one where the highest power is x^2.*
The standard format for a quadratic equation is $x^2 + bx + c = 0$.

You can **Factorise Quadratic Equations**

1) You can <u>solve</u> quadratic equations by <u>factorising</u>.
2) '<u>Factorising a quadratic</u>' means '<u>putting it into 2 brackets</u>'.

> **Factorising Quadratics**
>
> 1) <u>ALWAYS</u> rearrange into the <u>STANDARD FORMAT</u>: $x^2 + bx + c = 0$.
> 2) Write down the <u>TWO BRACKETS</u> with the x's in: $(x \quad)(x \quad) = 0$.
> 3) Then <u>find 2 numbers</u> that <u>MULTIPLY to give 'c'</u> (the number term) but also <u>ADD/SUBTRACT to give 'b'</u> (the number in front of the x term).
> 4) Fill in the +/− signs and make sure they work out properly.
> 5) As an <u>ESSENTIAL CHECK</u>, <u>EXPAND</u> the brackets to make sure they give the original equation.

Ignore any minus signs at this stage.

3) As well as factorising a quadratic, you might be asked to <u>solve</u> the equation. This just means finding the values of x that make each bracket <u>0</u> (see example below).

EXAMPLE **Solve $x^2 - x = 12$.**

1) $x^2 - x - 12 = 0$
   $(b = -1, c = -12)$

2) $(x \quad)(x \quad) = 0$

3)
   1 × 12 Add/subtract to give: 13 or 11
   2 × 6   Add/subtract to give: 8 or 4
   3 × 4   Add/subtract to give: 7 or ①

   $(x \quad 3)(x \quad 4) = 0$ This is what we want.

4) $(x + 3)(x - 4) = 0$

5) Check:
   $(x + 3)(x - 4) = x^2 - 4x + 3x - 12$
   $= x^2 - x - 12$ ✓

6) $(x + 3) = 0 \Rightarrow x = -3$
   $(x - 4) = 0 \Rightarrow x = 4$

1) <u>Rearrange</u> into the standard format.

2) Write down <u>two brackets</u> with x's in.

3) Find the right <u>pair of numbers</u> that <u>multiply to give c</u> (= 12), and <u>add or subtract to give b</u> (= 1) (remember, we're ignoring the +/− signs for now).

4) <u>Now fill in the +/− signs</u> so that 3 and 4 add/subtract to give −1 (= b).

5) <u>ESSENTIAL check</u> — <u>EXPAND the brackets</u> to make sure they give the original expression.

But we're not finished yet — we've only factorised it, we still need to...

6) <u>SOLVE THE EQUATION</u> by setting each bracket <u>equal to 0</u>.

To help you work out which <u>signs</u> you need, <u>look at c</u>.

- If c is <u>positive</u>, the signs will be <u>the same</u> — both positive or both negative.
- If c is <u>negative</u> the signs will be <u>different</u> — one positive and one negative.

Factorising quadratics is not easy — but it is important

Make sure you learn the method, then it's a case of practise, practise, practise. People often get the signs the wrong way round, so make sure you always check your answer by expanding the brackets.

Q1 Factorise $x^2 + 2x - 15$ [2 marks]   Q2 Solve $x^2 - 9x + 20 = 0$ [3 marks]

Q2 Video Solution

Simultaneous Equations

Simultaneous equations might sound a bit scary, but they're just a **pair** of equations that you have to solve **at the same time**. You have to find values of x and y that work in **both** equations.

Six Steps for **Simultaneous Equations**

EXAMPLE   Solve the simultaneous equations $2x + 4y = 6$
$4x + 3y = -3$

Your equations should be in the form $ax + by = c$, where a, b and c are numbers, so rearrange them if you need to.

1 Label your equations ① and ②.

$2x + 4y = 6$ — ①
$4x + 3y = -3$ — ②

2 Match up the numbers in front of either the x's or y's in both equations.
You may need to multiply one or both equations by a suitable number.
Relabel the equations ③ and ④ if you need to change them.

① × 2: $4x + 8y = 12$ — ③
$4x + 3y = -3$ — ②

You don't need to change equation 2 for this example.

3 Add or subtract the two equations to eliminate the terms with the same number in front.

③ − ②: $4x + 8y = 12$
$-\ 4x + 3y = -3$
$\overline{0x + 5y = 15}$

If the numbers have the same sign (both +ve or both −ve) then subtract. If the numbers have opposite signs (one +ve and one −ve) then add.

4 Solve the resulting equation.

$5y = 15 \Rightarrow \underline{y = 3}$

5 Substitute the value you've found back into equation ① and solve it.

Sub $y = 3$ into ①: $2x + (4 \times 3) = 6 \Rightarrow 2x + 12 = 6 \Rightarrow 2x = -6 \Rightarrow \underline{x = -3}$

6 Substitute both these values into equation ② to make sure it works.
If it doesn't then you've done something wrong and you'll have to do it all again.

Sub x and y into ②: $(4 \times -3) + (3 \times 3) = -12 + 9 = -3$, which is right, so it's worked.
So the solutions are: $x = -3$, $y = 3$

It doesn't matter if you eliminate the x's or y's... do whatever's easiest

It might just be me, but I think simultaneous equations are quite fun... well, maybe not fun... but quite satisfying. Anyway, it doesn't matter whether you like them or not — you have to learn how to do them.

Q1   Solve the simultaneous equations $x + y = 3$
$4x + 3y = 10$ [3 marks]

Q2   Solve the simultaneous equations $2x + 4y = 2$
$5x - 3y = 18$ [3 marks]

Q2 Video Solution

Proof

*I'm not going to lie — **proof questions** can look a bit terrifying.*
But there are a couple of tricks you can use that make them a bit less scary.

Prove Statements are True or False

1) The most straightforward proofs are ones where you're given a <u>statement</u> and asked if it's <u>true</u> or <u>false</u>.

2) To show that it's <u>false</u>, all you have to do is find <u>one example</u> that doesn't <u>work</u>.

3) Showing that something is <u>true</u> is a bit trickier — you might have to do a bit of <u>rearranging</u> to show that two things are <u>equal</u>, or show that one thing is a <u>multiple</u> of a certain number.

 EXAMPLE **Find an example to show that the statement below is not correct.**
"The difference between two prime numbers is always even."

2 and 5 are both prime, so try them:
5 − 2 = 3, which is odd —
so the statement is not correct.

> It was easy to find an example for this one
> — but sometimes you might have to try a few
> different numbers to find a pair that doesn't work.

 EXAMPLE **Prove that $(n + 3)^2 - (n - 2)^2 \equiv 5(2n + 1)$.**

Take one side of the equation and play about
with it until you get the other side:

LHS: $(n + 3)^2 - (n - 2)^2 \equiv n^2 + 6n + 9 - (n^2 - 4n + 4)$
$\equiv n^2 + 6n + 9 - n^2 + 4n - 4$
$\equiv 10n + 5$
$\equiv 5(2n + 1) = $ RHS ✓

> See p.38 for a reminder on factorising.

> $\equiv$ is the <u>identity symbol</u>,
> and means that two things
> are <u>identically equal</u> to each
> other. So $a + b \equiv b + a$ is
> true for <u>all values</u> of a and b
> (unlike an equation, which is
> only true for certain values).

Show that One Thing is a Multiple of Another

1) To show that something is a <u>multiple</u> of a particular number (let's say <u>5</u>), you need to <u>rearrange</u> the thing you're given to get it into the form <u>5 × a whole number</u>, which means it's a multiple of 5.

2) If it <u>can't</u> be written as 5 × a whole number, then it's <u>not</u> a multiple of 5.

EXAMPLE $a = 3(b + 9) + 5(b − 2) + 3$.
Show that a is a multiple of 4 for any whole number value of b.

$a = 3(b + 9) + 5(b − 2) + 3$
$= 3b + 27 + 5b − 10 + 3$ —— Expand the brackets...
$= 8b + 20$ ————————— ... simplify...
$= 4(2b + 5)$ ———————— ... and factorise.

> $2b + 5$ is a whole
> number because b
> is a whole number.

a can be written as 4 × something (where the something is $2b + 5$)
so it is a multiple of 4.

3) It's always a good idea to keep in mind what you're <u>aiming for</u> — here, you're trying to write the expression for a as '<u>4 × a whole number</u>', so you'll need to take out a <u>factor of 4</u> at some point.

Proof questions aren't as bad as they look

If you're asked to prove that two things are equal, rearranging should do the trick. If you're asked to prove something is wrong, just find an example of it not working. <u>Always</u> keep in mind what you're aiming for.

Q1   For each of the following statements, find an example to prove that they are false.
   a) All square numbers end in 1, 4, 6 or 9.   [1 mark]
   b) The product of two prime numbers is always odd.   [1 mark]

Warm-up and Worked Exam Questions

A mixed bag of tricky topics to end the algebra section — the only way you're going to get your head around them is to do some practice questions. Start by warming up with these questions.

Warm-up Questions

1) Factorise the following expressions:
   a) $x^2 - 6x + 8$　　　　b) $x^2 - 2x - 3$　　　　c) $x^2 + 7x + 12$

2) Solve the following equations:
   a) $x^2 + 7x + 10 = 0$　　　b) $x^2 + 5x - 14 = 0$　　　c) $x^2 - 5x + 3 = -3$

3) Solve the simultaneous equations: $x + y = 5$ and $2y - 3x = 5$.

4) Solve the simultaneous equations: $3x + 5y = 12$ and $4x - 3y = -13$.

5) Give an example to prove that each of the following statements is false.
   a) The product of two square numbers is never square.
   b) The sum of two prime numbers is always prime.

6) Prove that $(x + 2)^2 + (x - 2)^2 = 2(x^2 + 4)$ for all values of x.

Worked Exam Questions

That's enough warming up, it's time for the real thing. Take a look at these worked examples first and then turn over and have a go at some practice questions yourself.

1　The equation $x^2 + x - 20 = 0$ is an example of a quadratic equation.

　　a)　Fully factorise the expression $x^2 + x - 20$.

Number pairs that multiply to give 20 are:　　　5 and −4 add to give 1
1 × 20,　2 × 10,　4 × 5

$$x^2 + x - 20 = (x + 5)(x - 4)$$

$(x + 5)(x - 4)$
....
[2 marks]

　　b)　Use your answer to part a) to solve the equation $x^2 + x - 20 = 0$.

$(x + 5)(x - 4) = 0$
So, $x + 5 = 0$ or $x - 4 = 0$
$x = -5$ or $x = 4$

$x =$ ....−5........... or　$x =$ ....4..........
[1 mark]

2　Solve this pair of simultaneous equations.

$4x + 3y = 16$ ①　　①−②:　$4x + 3y = 16$　　　Eliminate the x term by
$4x + 2y = 12$ ②　　　　　　$- \underline{4x + 2y = 12}$　　subtracting the equations
　　　　　　　　　　　　　　　　　$y = 4$

Substitute $y = 4$
into equation ①.　$4x + (3 \times 4) = 16$
　　　　　　　　　　　$4x = 4$ so $x = 1$

Check your answer by putting
$x = 1$ and $y = 4$ into ② ——— $(4 \times 1) + (2 \times 4) = 12$ ✓

$x =$ ....1........... $y =$ ....4..........
[2 marks]

Exam Questions

3   For each statement below, write down an example to show that the statement is incorrect. (**4**)

   a)   There are no factors of 48 between 15 and 20.

   ....
                                                                [1 mark]

   b)   The sum of two square numbers is always odd.

   ....
                                                                 [1 mark]

   c)   All numbers that end in an 8 are multiples of either 4, 6 or 8.

   ....
                                                                 [1 mark]

4   Solve this pair of simultaneous equations. (**5**)

$$x + 3y = 11$$
$$3x + y = 9$$

                                                 $x =$ .... $y =$ ....
                                                                     [3 marks]

5   Solve the equation $x^2 + 4x - 12 = 0$. (**5**)

                                              $x =$ ....   or $x =$ ....
                                                                       [3 marks]

6   q is a whole number. Show that $2(18 + 3q) + 3(3 + q)$ is a multiple of 9. (**5**)

                                                                                              [3 marks]

Revision Questions for Section Two

Now, let's see how much of that <u>tricky algebra</u> you've learned.
- Try these questions and <u>tick off each one</u> when you <u>get it right</u>.
- When you're done <u>completely happy</u> with it, tick off the topic.

For even more practice, try the Sudden Fail Quiz for Section Two — just scan this QR code!

Section Two Quiz

Algebra (p35-38) ☐

1) Simplify: a) $e + e + e$ b) $6f + 7f - f$

2) Simplify: a) $2x + 3y + 5x - 4y$ b) $11a + 2 - 8a + 7$

3) Simplify: a) $m \times m \times m$ b) $p \times q \times 7$ c) $2x \times 9y$

4) Expand: a) $6(x + 3)$ b) $-3(3x - 4)$ c) $x(5 - x)$

5) Expand and simplify $4(3 + 5x) - 2(7x + 6)$

6) Expand and simplify: a) $(x + 2)(2x - 5)$ b) $(5y + 2)^2$

7) What is factorising?

8) Factorise: a) $8x + 24$ b) $18x^2 + 27x$ c) $36x^2 - 81y^2$

Solving Equations (p41-42) ☑

9) Solve: a) $x + 9 = 16$ b) $x - 4 = 12$ c) $6x = 18$

10) Solve: a) $4x + 3 = 19$ b) $3x + 6 = x + 10$ c) $3(x + 2) = 5x$

Expressions, Formulas and Functions (p43-46) ☑

11) $Q = 5r + 6s$. Work out the value of Q when $r = -2$ and $s = 3$.

12) A function takes a number, doubles it and subtracts 8.
What is the result when 11 is put in the machine?

13) Tony and Robbie have the same number of marbles. Nadia has 26 marbles.
Between them, they have 100 marbles. How many marbles does Tony have?

14) A rectangle measures $2x$ cm by $7x$ cm. An equilateral triangle has the same perimeter
as the rectangle. Find the length of one side of the triangle in terms of x.

15) Rearrange the formula $W = 4v + 5$ to make v the subject.

Sequences and Inequalities (p49-51) ☑

16) For each of the following sequences, find the next term and write down the rule you used.
a) 3, 10, 17, 24, ...   b) 1, 4, 16, 64, ...   c) 2, 5, 7, 12, ...

17) Find an expression for the nth term of the sequence that starts 4, 10, 16, 22, ...

18) Is 34 a term in the sequence given by the expression $7n - 1$?

19) Write the following inequalities out in words: a) $x > -7$ b) $x \le 6$

20) $0 < k \le 7$. Find all the possible integer values of k.

21) Solve the following inequalities: a) $x + 4 < 14$ b) $3x + 5 \le 26$.

Quadratic Equations (p54) ☑

22) Factorise the following quadratic expressions: a) $x^2 + 10x + 16$ b) $x^2 - 6x - 7$

23) Solve the quadratic equation $x^2 + 3x - 18 = 0$.

Simultaneous Equations and Proof (p55-56) ☑

24) Solve the following pair of simultaneous equations: $4x + 5y = 33$ and $-x + 3y = 13$

25) Find an example to show that the statement
"if a number ends in a 9, it must divide by 3" is not true.

26) Show that x is never a multiple of 5 if $x = 3(y + 2) + 2(y + 6)$ for any whole number y.

Coordinates and Midpoints

*What could be more fun than points in one quadrant? Points in **four quadrants**, that's what...*

The Four **Quadrants**

A graph has <u>four different quadrants</u> (regions).

The top-right region is the easiest because
<u>ALL THE COORDINATES IN IT ARE POSITIVE</u>.

You have to be careful in the <u>other regions</u> though,
because the *x*- and *y*- coordinates could be <u>negative</u>,
and that makes life much more difficult.

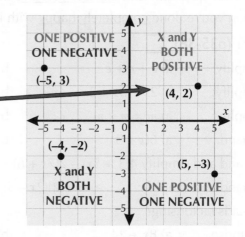

THREE IMPORTANT POINTS ABOUT COORDINATES:

1) The coordinates are always in <u>ALPHABETICAL ORDER, *x* then *y*</u>.   **(x , y)**

2) *x* is always the flat axis going <u>ACROSS</u> the page. In other words '*x* is a...cross'.

3) Remember it's always <u>IN THE HOUSE</u> (→) and then <u>UP THE STAIRS</u> (↑)
    so it's <u>ALONG first</u> and <u>then UP</u>, i.e. *x*-coordinate first, and then *y*-coordinate

The **Midpoint** of a Line

The '<u>MIDPOINT OF A LINE SEGMENT</u>' is the <u>POINT THAT'S BANG IN THE MIDDLE</u> of it.

Finding the coordinates of a midpoint is pretty easy.
<u>LEARN THESE THREE STEPS</u>...

> 1) Find the <u>average</u> of the <u>*x*-coordinates</u>.
> 2) Find the <u>average</u> of the <u>*y*-coordinates</u>.
> 3) **Plonk them in <u>brackets</u>.**

EXAMPLE   P and Q have coordinates (1, 2) and (6, 6).
Find the midpoint of the line PQ.

Average of *x*-coordinates = $\dfrac{1+6}{2}$ = 3.5

Average of *y*-coordinates = $\dfrac{2+6}{2}$ = 4

Coordinates of midpoint = (3.5, 4)

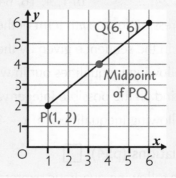

Coordinates should always be written as (x, y)

Learn the three points for getting *x* and *y* the right way round and the three easy steps for finding the
midpoint of a line segment. Then, put your skills to the test with these Exam Practice Questions.

Q1   a) Plot point A(–3, 2) and point B(3, 5) on a grid.   [2 marks]

       b) Find the coordinates of the midpoint of AB.   [2 marks]

Q1 Video
Solution

Straight-Line Graphs

*Here are the basic straight-line graphs — you need to be able to **draw them** and give their **equations**.*

Vertical and Horizontal lines: 'x = a' and 'y = a'

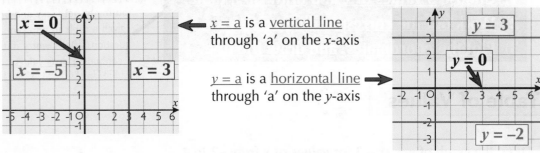

$x = a$ is a <u>vertical line</u> through 'a' on the *x*-axis

$y = a$ is a <u>horizontal line</u> through 'a' on the *y*-axis

The Main Diagonals: 'y = x' and 'y = -x'

'$y = x$' is the <u>main diagonal</u> that goes <u>UPHILL</u> from left to right.

'$y = -x$' is the <u>main diagonal</u> that goes <u>DOWNHILL</u> from left to right.

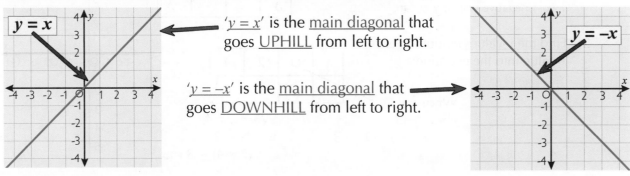

Other Lines Through the Origin: 'y = ax' and 'y = -ax'

$y = ax$ and $y = -ax$ are the equations for
A SLOPING LINE THROUGH THE ORIGIN.

The value of '<u>a</u>' (known as the <u>gradient</u>) tells you the steepness of the line. The bigger 'a' is, the steeper the slope. A <u>MINUS SIGN</u> tells you it slopes <u>DOWNHILL</u>.

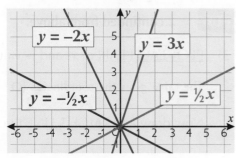

Learn to Spot Straight Lines from their Equations

All straight-line equations just contain '<u>something *x*</u>, <u>something *y*</u> and <u>a number</u>'.

Straight lines:		NOT straight lines:	
$x - y = 0$	$y = 2 + 3x$	$y = x^3 + 3$	$\dfrac{1}{y} + \dfrac{1}{x} = 2$
$2y - 4x = 7$	$4x - 3 = 5y$	$x^2 = 4 - y$	$xy + 3 = 0$

There's more on x^2 graphs on page 68.

Get it straight — which lines are straight (and which aren't)

It's definitely worth learning all the graphs above. Once you've done that, test yourself with this question.

Q1   On a grid with *x*-axis from −5 to 5 and *y*-axis from −5 to 5, draw these lines:

     a) $y = -1$ b) $y = -x$ c) $x = 2$ [3 marks]

Drawing Straight-Line Graphs

You might be asked to **DRAW THE GRAPH** of an equation in the exam.
This **EASY METHOD** will net you the marks every time:

> 1) **Choose 3 values of x and draw up a table.**
> 2) **Work out the corresponding y-values.**
> 3) **Plot the coordinates, and draw the line.**

You might get lucky and be <u>given</u> a table in an exam question. Don't worry if it contains <u>5 or 6 values</u>.

Doing the 'Table of Values'

EXAMPLE **Draw the graph of $y = 2x - 3$ for values of x from –2 to 4.**

1) <u>Choose 3 easy x-values for your table:</u>

   Use x-values from the grid you're given.
   Avoid negative ones if you can.

x	O	2	4
y			

2) <u>Find the y-values</u> by putting each x-value into the equation:

x	O	2	4
y	–3	1	5

   When $x = $ O,
   $y = 2x - 3$
   $= (2 \times O) - 3 = -3$

   When $x = 4$,
   $y = 2x - 3$
   $= (2 \times 4) - 3 = 5$

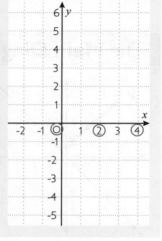

Plotting the Points and Drawing the Graph

EXAMPLE **...continued from above.**

3) <u>PLOT EACH PAIR</u> of x- and y- values from your table.

   The table gives the coordinates (O, –3), (2, 1) and (4, 5).

   Now draw a <u>STRAIGHT LINE</u> through your points.

   If one point looks a bit wacky, check 2 things:
   – the <u>y-values</u> you worked out in the table
   – that you've <u>plotted</u> the points properly.

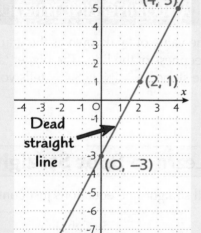

Dead straight line

(4, 5)
(2, 1)
(O, –3)

Spot and plot a straight line — then check it looks right

In the exam you might get an equation like $3x + y = 5$ to plot, making finding the y-values a bit trickier.
Just substitute in the x-value and find the y-value that makes the equation true.
E.g. when $x = 1$, $3x + y = 5 \rightarrow (3 \times 1) + y = 5 \rightarrow 3 + y = 5 \rightarrow y = 2$.

Q1 Draw the graph of $y = x + 4$ for values of x from –6 to 2. [3 marks]

Q2 Draw the graph of $y + 3x = 2$ for values of x from –2 to 2. [3 marks]

Q2 Video Solution

Straight-Line Graphs — Gradients

Time to hit the slopes. Well, find them anyway...

Finding the **Gradient**

The <u>gradient</u> of a line is a measure of its <u>slope</u>. The <u>bigger</u> the number, the <u>steeper</u> the line.

EXAMPLE **Find the gradient of the straight line shown.**

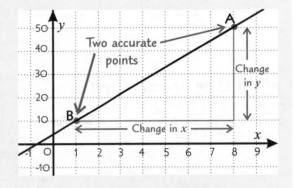

1 Find <u>two accurate points</u> and complete the triangle.

Choose easy points with positive coordinates.

Two points that can be read accurately are:

Point A: (8, 50)   Point B: (1, 10)

2 Find the <u>change in y</u> and the <u>change in x</u>.

Change in y = 50 − 10 = <u>40</u>

Change in x = 8 − 1 = <u>7</u>

Make sure you subtract the x-coordinates the <u>SAME WAY ROUND</u> as you do the y-coordinates.
E.g. y-coord. of pt A − y-coord. of pt B and x-coord. of pt A − x-coord. of pt B

3 <u>LEARN</u> this formula, and use it:

$$\text{GRADIENT} = \frac{\text{CHANGE IN Y}}{\text{CHANGE IN X}}$$

Gradient = $\frac{40}{7}$ = <u>5.71</u> (to 2 d.p.)

Make sure you get the formula the right way up.
Remember it's <u>VER</u>y <u>HO</u>t — <u>VER</u>tical over <u>HO</u>rizontal.

4 Check the <u>sign's</u> right.   If it slopes <u>uphill</u> left → right (⟋) then it's <u>positive</u>.
If it slopes <u>downhill</u> left → right (⟍) then it's <u>negative</u>.

As the graph goes uphill, the gradient is <u>positive</u>. So the gradient is <u>5.71</u> (not -5.71).

1) In real life, <u>gradients</u> are often given as a <u>ratio</u> or a <u>percentage</u>.
2) You'll often see them on <u>road signs</u> to describe the <u>steepness</u> of hills and slopes.
3) E.g. if the <u>gradient</u> = $\frac{1}{4}$, it has a ratio of <u>1 : 4</u>, a percentage of <u>25%</u> and you say it's "<u>1 in 4</u>" (for every 4 units you move horizontally, you move 1 unit vertically).

Gradient = change in y over change in x

Learn the four steps for finding a gradient then have a shot at this Exam Practice Question. Take care — you might not be able to pick two points with nice, positive coordinates.

Q1   Find the gradient of the line shown.   [2 marks]

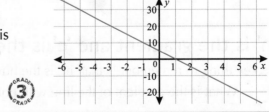

Straight-Line Graphs — y = mx + c

This sounds a bit scary, but give it a go and you might like it.

y = mx + c is the Equation of a **Straight Line**

$y = mx + c$ is the general equation for a
straight-line graph, and you need to remember:

> 'm' is equal to the **GRADIENT** of the graph,
> 'c' is the value **WHERE IT CROSSES THE Y-AXIS** and is called the **Y-INTERCEPT**.

'm' and 'c' are always just <u>numbers</u>
— so $y = 3x - 1$ and $y = -x + 2$
are in $y = mx + c$ form.

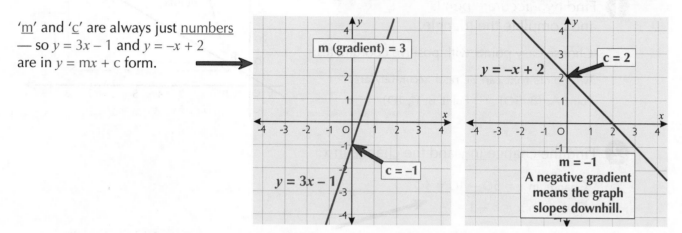

You might have to <u>rearrange</u> a straight-line equation to get it into this form:

<u>Straight line:</u>		<u>Rearranged into '$y = mx + c$'</u>	
$y = 2 + 3x$	$\rightarrow$	$y = 3x + 2$	(m = 3, c = 2)
$x - y = 4$	$\rightarrow$	$y = x - 4$	(m = 1, c = −4)
$4 - 3x = y$	$\rightarrow$	$y = -3x + 4$	(m = −3, c = 4)

<u>WATCH OUT</u>: people mix up 'm' and 'c' when they get something like $y = 5 + 2x$.
Remember, 'm' is the number <u>in front of the 'x'</u> and 'c' is the number <u>on its own</u>.

Finding the **Equation** of a Straight-Line **Graph**

EXAMPLE   **Find the equation of the line on the graph in the form y = mx + c.**

1 Find '<u>m</u>' (gradient) $m = \dfrac{\text{change in } y}{\text{change in } x} = \dfrac{15}{30} = \dfrac{1}{2}$
     It's an uphill graph,
     so the gradient is positive.

2 Read off '<u>c</u>' (y-intercept)   c = 15

3 Use these to write the equation
     in the form $y = mx + c$. $y = \dfrac{1}{2}x + 15$

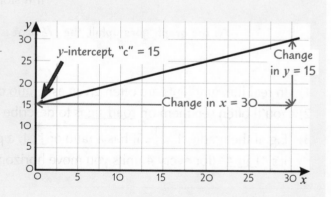

'm' is the gradient and 'c' is the y-intercept

The key thing to remember is that 'm' is the number in front of the x, and 'c' is the number on its own.

Q1   What is the gradient of the line with equation $y = 4 - 2x$?   [1 mark]

Using y = mx + c

This page covers some of the awkward questions you might get asked about straight lines.

Parallel Lines Have the Same Gradient

GRADE 5

Parallel lines all have the <u>same gradient</u>, which means their $y = mx + c$ equations all have the same value of <u>m</u>.
So the lines: $y = 2x + 3$, $y = 2x$ and $y = 2x - 4$ are all parallel.

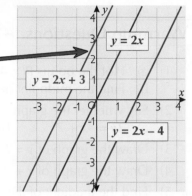

EXAMPLE **Line J has a gradient of –3. Find the equation of Line K, which is parallel to Line J and passes through point (2, 3).**

Lines J and K are <u>parallel</u> so their <u>gradients</u> are the same $\Rightarrow$ m = –3

$y = -3x + c$

When x = 2, y = 3:
$3 = (-3 \times 2) + c \Rightarrow 3 = -6 + c$
c = 9

$y = -3x + 9$

1) First find the <u>'m' value</u> for Line K.
2) Substitute the value for 'm' into <u>y = mx + c</u> to give you the 'equation so far'.
3) Substitute the <u>x and y values</u> for the given point on Line K and solve for '<u>c</u>'.
4) Write out the <u>full equation</u>.

Finding the Equation of a Line Through Two Points

GRADE 5

If you're given <u>two points</u> on a line you can find the <u>gradient</u>, then you can <u>use</u> the gradient and one of the points to find the <u>equation</u> of the line. It's a bit <u>tricky</u>, but try to follow the <u>method</u> used in this example.

EXAMPLE **Find the equation of the straight line that passes through (–2, 9) and (3, –1). Give your answer in the form $y = mx + c$.**

1) Use the <u>two</u> points to find '<u>m</u>' (gradient).

$m = \dfrac{\text{change in } y}{\text{change in } x} = \dfrac{-1 - 9}{3 - (-2)} = \dfrac{-10}{5} = -2$

So $y = -2x + c$

2) <u>Substitute</u> one of the points into the equation you've just found.

Substitute (–2, 9) into eqn: $9 = (-2 \times -2) + c$
$9 = 4 + c$

3) <u>Rearrange</u> the equation to find '<u>c</u>'.

$c = 9 - 4$
$c = 5$

4) Write out the <u>full equation</u>.

$y = -2x + 5$

Sometimes you'll be asked to give your equation in other forms, such as $ax + by + c = 0$.
Just <u>rearrange</u> your $y = mx + c$ equation to get it in this form.

Parallel lines have the same gradient

To check that lines are parallel, rearrange each equation into the form $y = mx + c$ and then compare their values of m — if they're the same then the lines are parallel, if they're different then they aren't parallel.

Q1 a) Line Q goes through (0, 5) and (4, 7).
Find the equation of Line Q in the form $y = mx + c$. [3 marks]
b) Line R is parallel to line Q. It intersects the y-axis at (0, 10).
Write down the equation of line R in the form $y = mx + c$. [1 mark]

Q1 Video Solution

Warm-up and Worked Exam Questions

In the exam, you'll have to know straight-line graphs like the back of your hand. If you struggle with any of the warm-up questions, go back over the section again before you go any further.

Warm-up Questions

1) a) Plot the points P(1, 4) and point M(−1, 1) on a coordinate grid.
   b) Find the midpoint of the line segment PM.

2) Say whether the graph of each of the following equations will be a straight line.
   a) $2y = -x + 7$
   b) $y = 4x^2 - 1$
   c) $x = 3y$
   d) $x + 2y = 2 - 3x$

3) Draw the graph of $y = 2x + 1$ for values of x from −4 to 4.

4) Draw the graph of $x + y = 5$ for values of x from −5 to 3.

5) Find the gradient of the line shown on the right.

6) What is the gradient of the line with equation $y = 3(1 + x)$?

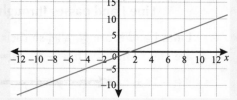

7) a) The points (1, −5) and (−3, 3) both lie on line A.
      Find the equation of line A in the form $y = mx + c$.
   b) Line B is parallel to line A, and passes through the point (2, 5).
      What is the equation of line B in the form $y = mx + c$?

Worked Exam Question

You know the routine by now — work carefully through this question and make sure you understand it. Then it's on to the real test of doing some exam questions for yourself.

1   Use the grid for the questions below. **(3)**

a)   Draw and label the following lines.

   $y = 3$ A horizontal line through
             3 on the y-axis.

   $x = -2$ A vertical line through
             −2 on the x-axis.

   $y = x$ The diagonal with gradient 1,
             going through the origin.

   [3 marks]

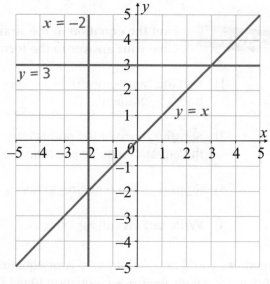

b)   What are the coordinates of the point where the lines $y = 3$ and $y = x$ meet?

(......3......, ...3......)

[1 mark]

Exam Questions

2   Points **A** and **B** have been plotted on the grid below.

a)   Write down the coordinates of the midpoint of the line segment **AB**.

(..............., ...)
[2 marks]

b)   Point **C** has the coordinates $(0, -1)$. Given that line **AB** and line **CD** have the same midpoint, find the coordinates of point **D**.

(..............., ...)
[2 marks]

3   Look at the graph on the right.

Find the equation of the straight line.
Give your answer in the form $y = mx + c$.

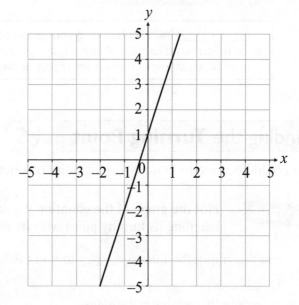

....
[3 marks]

4   $y = 4x - 3$ is the equation of a straight line.

Find the equation of the line parallel to $y = 4x - 3$ that passes through the point $(-1, 0)$.

....
[3 marks]

Quadratic Graphs

Enough of straight lines. You now get to move on to lovely, smooth curves. Quadratic ones to be precise.

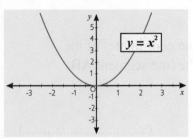

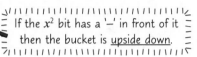

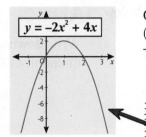

Quadratic graphs are of the form <u>y = anything with x^2</u> (but not higher powers of x).

They all have the same <u>symmetrical</u> bucket shape.

If the x^2 bit has a '−' in front of it then the bucket is <u>upside down</u>.

Plotting **Quadratics** **GRADE 5**

EXAMPLE **Complete the table of values for the equation $y = x^2 + 2x - 3$ and then plot the graph.**

x	−4	−3	−2	−1	0	1	2
y	5	O	−3	−4	−3	0	5

1) Substitute each <u>x-value</u> into the equation to get each <u>y-value</u>.

   E.g. $y = (-4)^2 + (2 \times -4) - 3 = 5$

2) Plot the points and join them with a <u>completely smooth curve</u>.

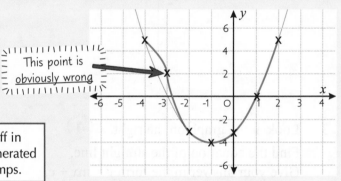

This point is <u>obviously wrong</u>

> <u>NEVER EVER</u> let one point drag your graph off in some ridiculous direction. When a graph is generated from an equation, you never get spikes or lumps.

Finding the **Turning Point** **GRADE 5**

You could be asked to find the turning point of a quadratic, so here's a nifty method to do just that.

EXAMPLE **Plot the graph of the equation $y = -x^2 - x + 2$, labelling its turning point with its coordinates.**

x	−3	−2	−1	0	1	2
y	−4	0	2	2	0	−4

Plot the graph, then use <u>symmetry</u> to find the turning point of the curve:

1) Choose <u>two points</u> on the curve where the y-value is the <u>same</u>.

   At $x = -1$ and $x = 0$, $y = 2$

2) The <u>x-coordinate</u> of the turning point is <u>halfway</u> between these two values.

   x-coordinate of the turning point = −0.5

3) Put the x-coordinate <u>back</u> into the equation to find the <u>y-coordinate</u>.

   $y = -(-0.5)^2 - (-0.5) + 2$
   $= 2.25$

   The turning point is (−0.5, 2.25).

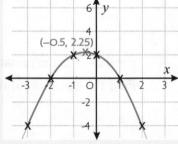

(−0.5, 2.25)

Quadratic graphs have an x² term, but no higher powers of x

Learn how to draw quadratic graphs and practise drawing some smooth curves. Then try these:

Q1   a) Draw the graph of $y = x^2 + 3x - 7$ for values of x between −3 and 3.   [4 marks] **GRADE 5**

      b) Find the turning point of the graph $y = x^2 + 3x - 7$.   [2 marks]

Q1 Video Solution

Harder Graphs

Graphs come in all sorts of shapes, sizes and wiggles — here are just a couple:

x^3 (Cubic) Graphs

1) <u>Cubic graphs</u> have the form <u>$y = $ anything with x^3</u> (but no higher powers of x).

2) All x^3 graphs have a <u>wiggle</u> in the middle.

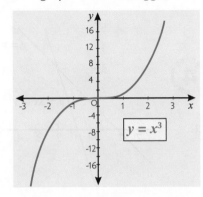

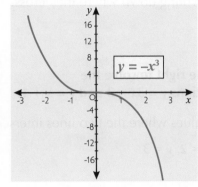

$y = -x^3$

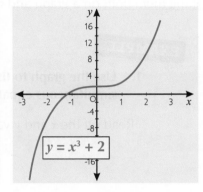

$y = x^3$

$y = x^3 + 2$

EXAMPLE

Draw the graph of $y = -x^3 - 10$ for values of x between -3 and $+2$.

Start by making a <u>table of values</u>.

x	-3	-2	-1	0	1	2
$y = -x^3 - 10$	17	-2	-9	-10	-11	-18

E.g. $y = -(-2)^3 - 10 = -2$

Plot the points and join them with a lovely <u>smooth curve</u>.
<u>Don't</u> use your ruler — that would be a trifle daft.

1/x (Reciprocal) Graphs

These appear as <u>two</u> symmetrical curves — one in the top right, one in the bottom left. They never touch the axes.

They're <u>symmetrical</u> about the lines <u>$y = x$</u> and <u>$y = -x$</u>.

The <u>general form</u> of a reciprocal graph is $\frac{A}{x}$, where A is <u>just a number</u>.

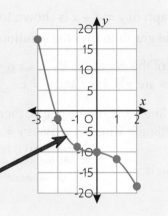

$y = \frac{1}{x}$

$y = x$

$y = -x$

> If you're not sure what a graph is supposed to look like in the exam, remember you can always use a <u>table of values</u> — even if it's just to refresh your memory.

Learn these two different types of graph

Cubic graphs and reciprocals can look pretty confusing, but all you really need to do is recognise the shape and be able to sketch them. Remember — cubics have a wiggle and reciprocal is two symmetrical curves.

Q1   Draw the graph of $y = x^3 + 8$ from $x = -2$ to $x = 2$.   [4 marks]

Solving Equations Using Graphs

*You can plot graphs to find **solutions** (or **approximate** solutions) to simultaneous equations and other equations. Plot the equations you want to solve and the solution lies where the lines **intersect**.*

Solving **Simultaneous Equations**

 See p.55 for more on simultaneous equations.

If you want to <u>solve</u> a pair of simultaneous equations with a graph, it's just a matter of <u>plotting them both</u> on a graph and writing down where they cross.

EXAMPLES

1. **Use the graph to the right to solve the simultaneous equations $y = 3x - 3$ and $y = x + 1$.**

   Read off the x and y values where the two lines intersect.

   $x = 2, y = 3$

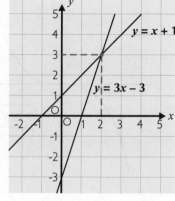

2. **The graph of $y = 4 - x$ is shown to the right. Use the graph to find the solution to $4 - x = x$.**

   Each side of the equation $4 - x = x$ <u>represents a line</u>. These lines are $y = 4 - x$ and $y = x$.

   Draw the line $y = x$ on the graph, then read off the <u>x-coordinate</u> where it crosses $y = 4 - x$.

   The solution is $x = 2$.

    At the point where the lines cross, both sides of the equation are equal, so this is the <u>solution</u>.

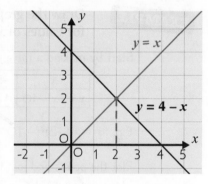

Solving **Quadratic Equations**

EXAMPLE

Use the graph of $y = 2x^2 - 3x$ (on the right) to find both solutions of the equation $2x^2 - 3x = 0$.

The left-hand side of the equation $2x^2 - 3x = 0$ represents the curve $y = 2x^2 - 3x$, and the right-hand side represents the line $y = 0$ (the <u>x-axis</u>).

Read off the <u>x-values</u> where the curve <u>crosses</u> the x-axis — these are the <u>solutions</u>.

The solutions are $x = 0$ and $x = 1.5$. 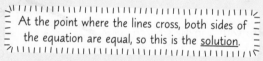 Quadratic equations usually have <u>2 solutions</u> (see p.54).

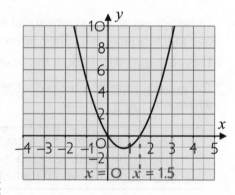

The solutions lie where the graphs intersect

The x and y values at these points are the solutions to your equations. Try these questions:

Q1 By plotting the graph, find the solutions to the equations $y = 2x - 4$ and $y = x + 2$. [4 marks]

Q2 Using the quadratic graph above, estimate the solutions to $2x^2 - 3x = 6$. [2 marks]

Q2 Video Solution

Distance-Time Graphs

Here is another type of graph for you to learn about... You can easily identify a distance-time graph by the axis labels — distance on the y-axis and time on the x-axis. Surprising isn't it?

Distance-Time Graphs

Distance-time graphs can look a bit awkward at first, but they're not too bad once you get your head around them.

Just remember these <u>4 important points</u>:

1) At any point, <u>GRADIENT = SPEED</u>.
2) The <u>STEEPER</u> the graph, the <u>FASTER</u> it's going.
3) <u>FLAT SECTIONS</u> are where it is <u>STOPPED</u>.
4) If the gradient's negative, it's <u>COMING BACK</u>.

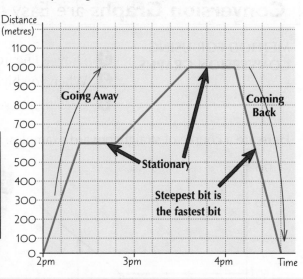

EXAMPLE **Henry went out for a ride on his bike. After a while he got a puncture and stopped to fix it. This graph shows the first part of Henry's journey.**

a) **What time did Henry leave home?**

He left home at the point where the line starts. **At 8:15**

b) **How far did Henry cycle before getting a puncture?**

The horizontal part of the graph is where Henry stopped. **12 km**

c) **What was Henry's speed before getting a puncture?**

Using the speed formula (p.98) is the same as finding the gradient.

$$\text{speed} = \frac{\text{distance}}{\text{time}} = \frac{12\text{ km}}{0.5\text{ hours}}$$
$$= 24\text{ km/h}$$

d) **At 9:30 Henry turns around and cycles home at 24 km/h. Complete the graph to show this.**

You have to work out how long it will take Henry to cycle the 18 km home:

$$\text{time} = \frac{\text{distance}}{\text{speed}} = \frac{18\text{ km}}{24\text{ km/h}} = \underline{0.75\text{ hours}}$$

Convert the decimal time to <u>minutes</u>.

$$0.75 \times 60\text{ mins} = \underline{45\text{ mins}}$$

45 minutes after 9:30 is 10:15, so that's the time Henry gets home. Now you can complete the graph.

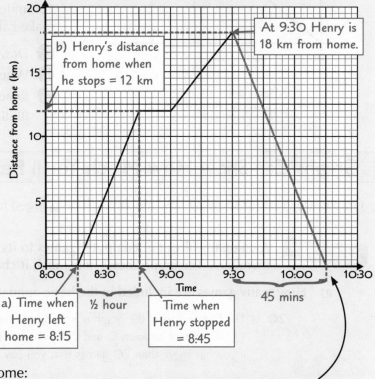

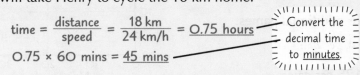

The gradient of a distance-time graph equals the speed

Learn the four important details about distance-time graphs, then test your skills on these questions.

Q1 a) Using the graph above, how long did Henry stop for? [1 mark]

b) What was Henry's speed after he had repaired the puncture, before he turned back home? [2 marks]

Q1 Video Solution

Real-Life Graphs

*In the exam you might get a graph which converts something like **£ to dollars** or **mph to km/h**.*

Conversion Graphs are Easy to Use

METHOD FOR USING CONVERSION GRAPHS:

1 Draw a line from a value on one axis.

2 When you hit the LINE, change direction and go straight to the other axis.

3 Read off the value from this axis. The two values are equivalent.

Here are a couple of straightforward examples: This graph converts between miles and kilometres

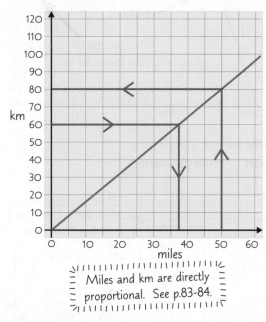

Miles and km are directly proportional. See p.83-84.

EXAMPLE   **How many miles is 60 km?**

1 Draw a line across from '60' on the 'km' axis.

2 When it hits the line, go down to the 'miles' axis.

3 Read off the answer: 37.5 miles

EXAMPLE   **How many km is 150 miles?**

150 miles is way off the graph, so find a point which will make calculating easy. Use 50 miles, then multiply by 3.

1 Draw a line up from '50' on the 'miles' axis.

2 When it hits the line, go across to the 'km' axis.

3 Read off the answer and multiply by 3 to find 150 miles.   80 × 3 = 240 km

Graphs Can Show How Much You'll Pay

Graphs are great for showing how much you'll be charged for using a service or buying multiple items.

EXAMPLE   **A company hires out computer games to its members. The graph shows how much it charges.**

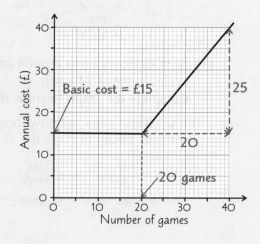

a)   **How many games are included in the basic annual cost?**

20   The first section of the graph is horizontal. You pay £15 if you rent between 0 and 20 games. It's only if you hire more than 20 games that you pay more.

b)   **Estimate the cost per game for additional games.**

Gradient of sloped section = cost per game

$\frac{\text{vertical change}}{\text{horizontal change}} = \frac{25}{20}$ = £1.25 per game

---

Learn how to convert graph questions into marks

Draw your conversion lines on the graph in the exam. If all else fails, that might be enough for a mark.

Q1   The distance between Tokyo and London is 6000 miles.
Use the graph at the top of the page to estimate this distance in km.   [2 marks]

Real-Life Graphs

Graphs can tell you just about anything. I can't show you all the possibilities due to health and safety concerns about back injuries resulting from the weight of the book. But here are some useful examples.

Gradients Show the **Rate of Change**

Basically, gradients always show you the '<u>change in something per something else</u>'.

The gradient is always | **(*y*-axis UNITS) PER (*x*-axis UNITS)** |

The graph below shows the distance travelled by a remote control car.

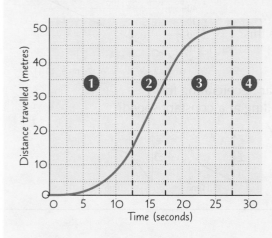

The <u>gradient</u> of the <u>graph</u> tells you the <u>speed</u> of the remote control car in <u>metres per second</u> (see p.71).

1 In this section of the graph the gradient is <u>increasing</u> (i.e. the graph is getting steeper) so the speed of the car is increasing — it's <u>accelerating</u>.

2 Here, the gradient doesn't change so the car is travelling at a <u>constant speed</u>.

3 The gradient is <u>decreasing</u> (i.e. the graph is getting flatter) so the speed of the car is decreasing — it's <u>decelerating</u>.

4 The gradient is zero so the car has <u>stopped</u>.

Graphs Can Show **Changes with Time**

 EXAMPLE

Four different-shaped glasses are shown on the right. Juice is poured into each glass at a constant rate.

Each graph below shows how the height of juice in one glass changes. Match each graph to the correct glass.

> A <u>steeper</u> slope means that the juice height is changing <u>faster</u>.

Glass C

Glass C has <u>straight vertical sides</u>, so the juice height increases steadily.

Glass B

Glass B is <u>widest at the bottom</u>, so the juice height increases <u>slowly at first</u>.

Glass D

Glass D is <u>narrowest in the middle</u>, so the height will increase <u>fastest</u> in the <u>middle part</u> of the graph.

Glass A

Glass A is <u>narrowest at the bottom</u>, so the height will increase <u>fastest</u> at the start of the graph.

The gradient tells you the number of y-axis units per x-axis unit

If the question talks about 'rate' or 'something per something else', it's a big clue that the gradient's involved.

Q1 A bath is being filled using only the hot tap. After 3 minutes the cold tap is also turned on. Which graph, A or B, shows how the depth of water in the bath changes over time?

[1 mark]

Warm-up and Worked Exam Questions

There were a few tough pages in that section — unfortunately the exam questions can be quite tough too.
These warm-up questions will get you in shape to tackle the practice exam questions on the next page.

Warm-up Questions

1) a) Draw the graph of $y = x^2 - 5x + 8$ for values of x between 0 and 6.
   b) Find the turning point of the graph $y = x^2 - 5x + 8$.

2) Draw the graph of $y = 1 - x^3$ from $x = -2$ to $x = 2$.

3) By plotting the graph, find the solutions to the equations
   $y = x - 2$ and $y + 2x = 7$.

4) Use the graph opposite to answer the questions below.
   a) A water tank holds 8 gallons. How many litres is this?
   b) Approximately how many gallons of water would
      fit into a 20 litre container?

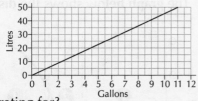

5) a) Using the graph on page 73, how long was the car decelerating for?
   b) What was the speed of the car, when it was travelling at a constant speed?

6) The container shown on the right is
   filled with water at a constant rate.
   Which graph, A or B, shows how the height
   of water in the container changes over time?

Worked Exam Question

Wow, an exam question with the answer written in. Make the most of it... you know what's coming.

1   A table of values for $y = x^2 - 5$ is shown below. **(5)** GRADE

x	-3	-2	-1	0	1	2
y	4	-1	-4	-5	-4	-1

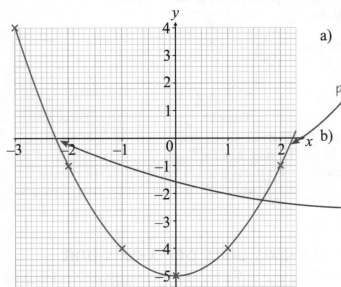

a) Draw the graph of $y = x^2 - 5$ on the grid.

Make sure you join the
points with a smooth curve.

[2 marks]

b) Use your graph to estimate the negative
   solution to the equation $x^2 - 5 = 0$.
   Give your answer to 1 decimal place.

Find the x-coordinate where
the graph crosses the x-axis.

$x = $ ....-2.2..........
[1 mark]

Exam Questions

2   The table to the right shows how much petrol a car used on 3 journeys.

Distance (miles)	16	40	72
Petrol used (litres)	2	5	9

a)   Using the table above, draw a conversion
      graph on the grid to the left.

[2 marks]

b)   Find the gradient of the line.

....
[2 marks]

c)   What does the gradient of the line represent?

....
[1 mark]

3   The graph of $y = x^2 + 2x + c$ is shown below.

a)   Circle the correct value of c.

        −2   1   0   −1   −4

[1 mark]

b)   Circle both solutions of $x^2 + 2x = 0$.

        −1   −2   3   0   1

[1 mark]

c)   Write down the coordinates of the
      turning point of the curve.

(............, ...)
[1 mark]

Exam Questions

4 Sketch the following graphs on the axes below. Label the points where they intersect the axes.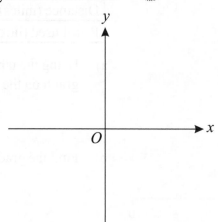

a) $y = -x^2$

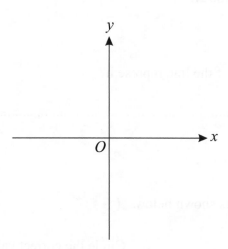

When you're sketching a curve just draw the general shape, but make sure the important bits are in the right place.

[2 marks]

b) $y = x^3$

[2 marks]

5 The diagram below shows the lines $y = x + 1$ and $y = 4 - 2x$.

a) Use the diagram to solve $x + 1 = 4 - 2x$

$x = $ ....
[1 mark]

b) By drawing another straight line, solve these simultaneous equations:

$y = x + 1$
$3y = x + 9$

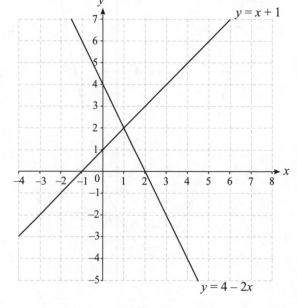

$x = $ .... $y = $ ....
[3 marks]

Revision Questions for Section Three

Well, that wraps up <u>Section Three</u> — let's see what you <u>remember</u>.
- Try these questions and <u>tick off each one</u> when you <u>get it right</u>.
- When you're <u>completely happy</u> with a topic, tick that off too.

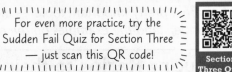

For even more practice, try the Sudden Fail Quiz for Section Three — just scan this QR code!

Section Three Quiz

Coordinates and Midpoints (p60) ☐

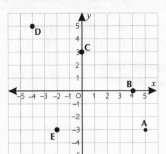

1) Give the coordinates of points A to E in the diagram on the right.

2) Find the midpoint of a line segment with endpoints B and C.

Straight-Line Graphs (p61-65) ☑

3) Draw these lines on a grid: a) $y = -x$, b) $y = -4$, c) $x = 2$

4) By making a table of values, draw the graph of $y = -4x - 2$.

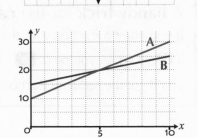

5) a) Find the gradient of line A on the right.
   b) Find the equation of line B on the right, giving your answer in the form $y = mx + c$.

6) Find the equation of the line passing through (4, 2) which is parallel to $y = 2x - 1$.

7) Find the equation of the line passing through (3, –6) and (6, –3).

Quadratic and Harder Graphs (p68-70) ☐

8) Describe the shapes of the graphs $y = x^2 - 8$ and $y = -x^2 + 2$.

9) a) Create and complete a table of values for values of x between –3 and 1 for the equation $y = x^2 + 3x$.
   b) Plot the graph of $y = x^2 + 3x$, labelling the turning point of the curve with its coordinates.

10) Describe in words and with a sketch the forms of these graphs:
    a) $y = ax^3$ b) $y = 1/x$

11) Plot the graph $y = 2x - 1$ and use it to find the solution to $5 = 2x - 1$.

Distance-Time Graphs (p71) ☑

12) What does a horizontal line mean on a distance-time graph?

13) The graph on the right shows Ben's car journey to the supermarket and home again.
    a) Did he drive faster on his way to the supermarket or on his way home?
    b) How long did he spend at the supermarket?

Real-Life Graphs (p72-73) ☑

14) On a straight-line graph, how would you find the rate of change?

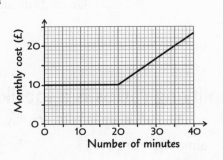

15) This graph shows the monthly cost of a mobile phone contract.
    a) How many minutes does the basic monthly fee include?
    b) Mary uses her phone for 35 minutes one month. What will her bill be?
    c) Stuart is charged £14 one month. Estimate how long he used his phone for.
    d) Estimate the cost per minute for additional minutes. Give your answer to the nearest 1p.

Ratios

Ratios are a pretty important topic — they can crop up in all sorts of questions, so you need to be prepared. If you understand the **examples** on the next three pages, you'll have a fighting chance in the exams.

Reducing **Ratios** to their **Simplest Form**

To reduce a ratio to a <u>simpler form</u>, divide <u>all the numbers</u> in the ratio by the <u>same thing</u> (a bit like simplifying a fraction — see p.15). It's in its <u>simplest form</u> when there's nothing left you can divide by.

> **EXAMPLE**   **Write the ratio 15:18 in its simplest form.**
>
> For the ratio 15:18, both numbers have a <u>factor</u> of 3, so <u>divide them by 3</u>.
>
> We can't reduce this any further. So the simplest form of 15:18 is **5:6**.
>
> $$\div 3 \left(\begin{matrix} 15:18 \\ = 5:6 \end{matrix} \right) \div 3$$

A handy trick for the calculator papers — use the fraction button

If you enter a fraction with the ▭ or ▣ button, the calculator automatically cancels it down when you press ▬. So for the ratio 8:12, just enter $\frac{8}{12}$ as a fraction, and you'll get the reduced fraction $\frac{2}{3}$. Now you just change it back to ratio form, i.e. <u>2 : 3</u>.

The More **Awkward Cases**:

1) If the ratio contains <u>decimals</u> or <u>fractions</u> — <u>multiply</u>

> *For fractions, multiply by a number that gets rid of both <u>denominators</u>.*

> **EXAMPLE**   **Simplify the ratio 2.4:3.6 as far as possible.**
>
> 1) <u>Multiply both sides by 10</u> to get rid of the decimal parts.
> 2) Now <u>divide</u> to reduce the ratio to its simplest form.
>
> $$\times 10 \left(\begin{matrix} 2.4:3.6 \\ = 24:36 \end{matrix} \right) \times 10$$
> $$\div 12 \left(\begin{matrix} \\ = 2:3 \end{matrix} \right) \div 12$$

2) If the ratio has <u>mixed units</u> — convert to the <u>smaller unit</u>

> **EXAMPLE**   **Reduce the ratio 24 mm:7.2 cm to its simplest form.**
>
> 1) <u>Convert</u> 7.2 cm to millimetres.
> 2) <u>Simplify</u> the resulting ratio. Once the units on both sides are the same, <u>get rid of them</u> for the final answer.
>
> $$\begin{matrix} 24 \text{ mm}:7.2 \text{ cm} \\ = 24 \text{ mm}:72 \text{ mm} \\ \div 24 \searrow 1:3 \swarrow \div 24 \end{matrix}$$

3) To get to the form <u>1 : n</u> or <u>n : 1</u> — just <u>divide</u>

> **EXAMPLE**   **Reduce 5:54 to the form 1:n.**
>
> Divide both sides by 5:
>
> $$\div 5 \left(\begin{matrix} 5:54 \\ = 1:\frac{54}{5} \end{matrix} \right) \div 5 \quad \text{or} \quad 1:10.8$$

Simplifying ratios is a lot like simplifying fractions

Whole number ratios are easy to simplify, but you need to make sure you can do the awkward cases too.

Q1   Simplify: a) 25:35   b) $\frac{9}{4}:\frac{15}{2}$ c) 8:18 to the form 1:n   [4 marks]

Ratios

*Another page on **ratios** coming up — it's more **interesting** than the first but not as exciting as the next one...*

Scaling Up Ratios

If you know the <u>ratio between parts</u> and the actual size of <u>one part</u>,
you can <u>scale the ratio up</u> to find the other parts.

> **EXAMPLE** **Mortar is made from mixing sand and cement in the ratio 7 : 2. How many buckets of mortar will be made if 21 buckets of sand are used in the mixture?**
>
> You need to <u>multiply by 3</u> to go from 7 to 21 on the left-hand side (LHS) — so do that to <u>both sides</u>:
>
> So <u>21 buckets of sand</u> and <u>6 buckets of cement</u> are used.
>
> sand : cement
>
> ×3 (7 : 2) ×3
> = 21 : 6
>
> Amount of mortar made = 21 + 6 = 27 buckets

The two parts of a ratio are always in <u>direct proportion</u> (see p.83-84). So in the example above, sand and cement are in direct proportion, e.g. if the amount of sand <u>doubles</u>, the amount of cement <u>doubles</u>.

Writing Ratios as Fractions

1) To write one part as a <u>fraction of another part</u> — put <u>one number over the other</u>

E.g. if apples and oranges are in the ratio 2 : 9 then we say there are
$\frac{2}{9}$ as many apples as oranges or $\frac{9}{2}$ times as many oranges as apples.

2) To write one part as a <u>fraction of the total</u> — <u>add up the parts</u> to find the <u>total</u>, then put the part you want <u>over the total</u>.

E.g. a pie dough is made by mixing flour, butter and water in the ratio 3 : 2 : 1.
The total number of parts is 3 + 2 + 1 = <u>6</u>.
So $\frac{3}{6} = \frac{1}{2}$ of the dough is flour, $\frac{2}{6} = \frac{1}{3}$ is butter and $\frac{1}{6}$ is water.

Part : Whole Ratios

You might come across a ratio where the LHS is <u>included</u> in the RHS — these are called <u>part : whole ratios</u>.

> **EXAMPLE** **Mrs Miggins owns tabby cats and ginger cats. The ratio of tabby cats to the total number of cats is 3 : 5.**
>
> **a) What fraction of Mrs Miggins' cats are tabby cats?**
> The ratio tells you that for every <u>5 cats</u>, <u>3</u> are <u>tabby cats</u>.
> $\frac{part}{whole} = \frac{3}{5}$
>
> **b) What is the ratio of tabby cats to ginger cats?**
> <u>3 in every 5</u> cats are tabby, so <u>2 in every 5</u> are ginger.
> 5 − 3 = 2
> For every <u>3 tabby</u> cats there are <u>2 ginger</u> cats.
> tabby : ginger = 3 : 2
>
> **c) Mrs Miggins has 12 tabby cats. How many ginger cats does she have?**
> <u>Scale up</u> the ratio from part b) to find the number of ginger cats.
> tabby : ginger
> ×4 (3 : 2) ×4
> = 12 : 8
> There are 8 ginger cats

Ratios

*If you were worried I was running out of **great stuff** to say about ratios then worry no more...*

Proportional **Division**

In a <u>proportional division</u> question a <u>TOTAL AMOUNT</u> is split into parts <u>in a certain ratio</u>.
The key word here is <u>PARTS</u> — concentrate on 'parts' and it all becomes quite painless:

EXAMPLE   **Jess, Mo and Suria share £9100 in the ratio 2 : 4 : 7. How much does Mo get?**

1) <u>ADD UP THE PARTS</u>:
   The ratio 2 : 4 : 7 means there will be a total of 13 <u>parts</u>:   2 + 4 + 7 = 13 parts

2) <u>DIVIDE TO FIND ONE "PART"</u>:
   Just divide the <u>total amount</u> by the number of <u>parts</u>:   £9100 ÷ 13 = £700   (= 1 part)

3) <u>MULTIPLY TO FIND THE AMOUNTS</u>:
   We want to know <u>Mo's share</u>, which is <u>4 parts</u>:   4 parts = 4 × £700 = £2800

Watch out for pesky proportional division questions that <u>don't</u> give you the <u>total amount</u>.
You can't just follow the method above, you'll have to be a bit more <u>crafty</u>.

EXAMPLE   **A baguette is cut into 3 pieces. The second piece is twice as long
as the first and the third piece is five times as long as the first.**

**a)   Find the ratio of the lengths of the 3 pieces.
      Give your answer in its simplest form.**

> If the first piece is 1 part,
> then the second piece is 1 × 2 = 2 parts
> and the third piece is 1 × 5 = 5 parts.
>
> So the ratio of the lengths = 1 : 2 : 5.

**b)   The first piece is 28 cm smaller than the third piece.
      How long is the second piece?**

1)   Work out <u>how many parts</u> 28 cm makes up.   28 cm = 3rd piece − 1st piece
                                                           = 5 parts − 1 part = 4 parts

2)   <u>Divide</u> to find <u>one part</u>.   28 cm ÷ 4 = 7 cm

3)   <u>Multiply</u> to find the length of the <u>2nd piece</u>.   2nd piece = 2 parts = 2 × 7 cm = 14 cm

---

You need to know how to answer all kinds of ratio questions

A good place to start is often to find one part and then go from there. Try that out in some of these questions.

Q1   Orange squash is made of water and concentrate in the ratio 11 : 2.
        a) What fraction of the squash is made up from concentrate?   [1 mark]
        b) How many litres of water are needed if 6 litres of concentrate are used?   [1 mark]

Q2   The ages of Ben, Graham and Pam are in the ratio 5 : 3 : 1.
        Their combined age is 108. How old is Graham?   [2 marks]

Q3   Square A has an area of 36 cm². The areas of square A and square B are
        in the ratio 4 : 9. What is the side length of square B?   [2 marks]

Q4   In an office, the ratio of people who drink tea to people who drink coffee is 8 : 5.
        18 more people drink tea than coffee. How many people drink coffee?   [3 marks]

Warm-up and Worked Exam Questions

You'll have to know ratios inside out for your exam — try these quick warm-up questions first and then you'll be ready to tackle those tricky exam practice questions on the next page.

Warm-up Questions

1) Write these ratios in their simplest forms:
   a) 4:8   b) 12:27   c) 1.2:5.4   d) $\frac{8}{3}:\frac{7}{6}$ e) 0.5 litres:400 ml

2) Reduce 5:22 to the form 1:n.

3) A recipe uses flour and sugar in the ratio 3:2.
   How much flour do you need if you're using 300 g of sugar?

4) A nursery group has 12 girls and 6 boys.
   a) Write the ratio of girls to boys.   b) What fraction of the class are girls?

5) Anja collects mugs. The ratio of red mugs to the total number of mugs is 6:15.
   Given that Anja has 50 mugs, how many of them are red?

6) Divide £2400 in the ratio 5:7.

7) Divide 180 in the ratio 3:4:5.

Worked Exam Question

I'm sure you're raring to get stuck into those exam practice questions — before you do, here's one I answered earlier. Read through it carefully and follow the working.

1 Pearl is making a fruit punch. She mixes apple juice, pineapple juice and cherryade in the ratio 4:3:7.

   a) What fraction of the fruit punch is pineapple juice?

   4 + 3 + 7 = 14 parts in total

   3 of the 14 parts are pineapple juice ——— $\frac{3}{14}$
   ....
   [1 mark]

   b) She makes 700 ml of fruit punch. What volume of each drink does she use?

   1 part = 700 ÷ (4 + 3 + 7)   First find how many ml
        = 700 ÷ 14 = 50 ml ——— 1 part is equal to.

   Multiply to find the amounts of each juice — apple juice is 4 parts, pineapple juice is 3 parts and cherryade is 7 parts.

   Apple juice: 50 ml × 4 = 200 ml
   Pineapple juice: 50 ml × 3 = 150 ml
   Cherryade: 50 ml × 7 = 350 ml

   Apple juice: ......200........ ml

   Pineapple juice: ......150........ ml

   Cherryade: ......350........ ml
   [3 marks]

Exam Questions

2   The grid on the right shows two shapes, A and B.   (3)

Give the following ratios in their simplest form.

a)   Shortest side of shape A : shortest side of shape B

....
[2 marks]

b)   Area of shape A : area of shape B

....
[3 marks]

3   Last month a museum received £21 000 in donations. After taking off the cost (3) of monthly bills, the museum spent the remaining money on new exhibitions.

The ratio of bills to donations was 5 : 14. How much did they spend on new exhibitions?

£ ....
[3 marks]

4   Mr Appleseed's Supercompost is made by mixing soil, compost and grit in the ratio 4 : 3 : 1.
Soil costs £8 per 40 kg, compost costs £15 per 25 kg and grit costs £12 per 15 kg. (5)
What is the total cost of materials for 16 kg of Mr Appleseed's Supercompost?

Start by working out how much of each material is needed for 16 kg of Supercompost.

£ ....
[5 marks]

Direct Proportion Problems

*Direct proportion problems all involve amounts that **increase** or **decrease** together.*

Learn the **Golden Rule** for **Proportion** Questions

There are lots of exam questions which at first sight seem completely different, but in fact they can all be done using the GOLDEN RULE...

Divide for ONE, then Times for ALL

EXAMPLE   **5 pints of milk cost £1.30. How much will 3 pints cost?**

The GOLDEN RULE tells you to:
Divide the price by 5 to find how much FOR ONE PINT,   1 pint: £1.30 ÷ 5 = 0.26 = 26p
then multiply by 3 to find how much FOR 3 PINTS.   3 pints: 26p × 3 = 78p

EXAMPLE   **Emma is handing out some leaflets. She gets paid per leaflet she hands out.**
If she hands out 300 leaflets she gets £12.
How many leaflets will she have to hand out to earn £42.50?

Divide by £12 to find how many leaflets
she has to hand out to earn £1.

To earn £1: 300 ÷ £12 = 25 leaflets

Multiply by £42.50 to find how many
leaflets she has to hand out to earn £42.50.

To earn £42.50: 25 × £42.50 = 1062.5

So she'll need to hand out **1063 leaflets**.

You need to round your answer up because 1062 wouldn't be enough.

Scaling **Recipes** Up or Down

EXAMPLE   **Judy is making orange and pineapple punch**
using the recipe shown on the right.
She wants to make enough to serve 20 people.
How much of each ingredient will Judy need?

> **Fruit Punch (serves 8)**
> **800 ml orange juice**
> **140 g fresh pineapple**

The GOLDEN RULE tells you to divide each amount by 8 to find how much
FOR ONE PERSON, then multiply by 20 to find how much FOR 20 PEOPLE.

So for 1 person you need:

800 ml ÷ 8 = 100 ml orange juice   ⇒

140 g ÷ 8 = 17.5 g pineapple   ⇒

And for 20 people you need:

20 × 100 ml = 2000 ml orange juice

20 × 17.5 g = 350 g pineapple

Divide for one, then times for all... divide for one, then times for all... divide for one...

Memorise this golden rule — it'll help make direct proportion questions a lot easier. Examiners love recipe
questions so learn how to use this golden rule to scale the ingredients up and down. Then try these questions.

Q1   Seven pencils cost £1.40.
   a) How much will four pencils cost?   [2 marks]
   b) What is the maximum number of pencils you could buy for £6.50?   [2 marks]

Q2   It costs £43.20 for 8 people to go on a rollercoaster 6 times.
   How much will it cost for 15 people to go on a rollercoaster 5 times?   [4 marks]

Q2 Video Solution

Direct Proportion Problems

There are many types of direct proportion question — here are another couple for you to learn.

Best Buy Questions

A slightly different type of direct proportion question is comparing the 'value for money' of 2 or 3 similar items. For these, follow the second <u>GOLDEN RULE</u>...

> ### Divide by the <u>PRICE in pence</u> (to get the amount <u>per penny</u>)

EXAMPLE
The local 'Supplies 'n' Vittals' stocks two sizes of Jamaican Gooseberry Jam, as shown on the right. Which of these represents better value for money?

Follow the <u>GOLDEN RULE</u> —
<u>divide</u> by the price in pence to get the <u>amount per penny</u>.

In the 350 g jar you get   350 g ÷ 80p = 4.38 g per penny
In the 100 g jar you get   100 g ÷ 42p = 2.38 g per penny

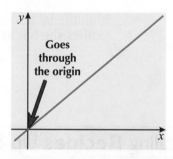
350 g at 80p   100 g at 42p

The 350 g jar is better value for money, because you get more jam per penny.

In some cases it might be easier to <u>divide by the weight</u> to get the <u>cost per gram</u>.
If you're feeling confident then you can do it this way — if not, the golden rule <u>always works</u>.

Graphing Direct Proportion

> **Two things are in direct proportion if, when you plot them on a graph, you get a straight line through the origin.**

Remember, the <u>general equation</u> for a straight line through the origin is $y = Ax$ (see p.61) where A is a number.
All direct proportions can be written as an equation in this form.

Goes through the origin

EXAMPLE
The amount of petrol, p litres, a car uses is directly proportional to the distance, d km, that the car travels. The car used 12 litres of petrol on a 160 km journey.

a) Write an equation in the form $p = Ad$ to represent this direct proportion.

1) Put the values of <u>$p = 12$</u> and <u>$d = 160$</u> into the equation to find the <u>value of A</u>.

$12 = A \times 160$

$A = \dfrac{12}{160}$

$A = 0.075$

2) Put the value of A <u>back into</u> the equation.

$p = 0.075d$

b) Sketch the graph of this direct proportion, marking two points on the line.

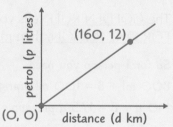

Direct proportion graphs are always straight lines through the origin

Graphing direct proportions is an important skill so put your knowledge to the test with these questions.

Q1   Tomato ketchup comes in bottles of three sizes: 250 g for 50p, 770 g for £1.40 and 1600 g for £3.20. Which bottle represents the best value for money?   [3 marks]

Q2   Brass is made by mixing copper and zinc in the ratio 3:2 by weight.
    a) Sketch a graph showing the weight of copper against the weight of zinc in a sample of brass. Mark two points on the graph.   [3 marks]
    b) What aspects of the graph show that copper and zinc are in direct proportion?   [1 mark]

Inverse Proportion Problems

Here's a trickier type of proportion — but once you've learnt this page you'll be an expert.

Graphing Inverse Proportion

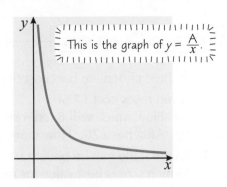

This is the graph of $y = \frac{A}{x}$.

**When two things are in inverse proportion,
one increases as the other decreases.**

On the graph you can see that as the value of <u>x increases</u>,
the value of <u>y decreases</u>. E.g. if x is <u>doubled</u>, y is <u>halved</u>,
or if x is <u>multiplied by 5</u>, y is <u>divided by 5</u>.

The general equation for inverse proportion is $y = \frac{A}{x}$.

EXAMPLE Circle each of the equations below that show that *s* is inversely proportional to *t*.

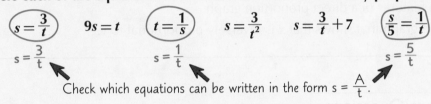

$$\left(s = \frac{3}{t}\right) \qquad 9s = t \qquad \left(t = \frac{1}{s}\right) \qquad s = \frac{3}{t^2} \qquad s = \frac{3}{t} + 7 \qquad \left(\frac{s}{5} = \frac{1}{t}\right)$$

$$s = \frac{3}{t} \qquad\qquad s = \frac{1}{t} \qquad\qquad\qquad\qquad\qquad s = \frac{5}{t}$$

Check which equations can be written in the form $s = \frac{A}{t}$.

Solving Inverse Proportion Questions

On page 83 you saw the 'divide and times'
method for direct proportions. Well, inverse
proportions are the opposite so you have to:

TIMES for ONE, then DIVIDE for ALL

EXAMPLES **1. It takes 3 farmers 10 hours to plough a field. How long would it take 6 farmers?**

<u>Multiply by 3</u> to find how long it would take <u>1 farmer</u>.   10 × 3 = 30 hours for 1 farmer

<u>Divide by 6</u> to find how long it would take <u>6 farmers</u>.   30 ÷ 6 = 5 hours for 6 farmers

Another way of looking at this question is that there are <u>twice</u> as
many farmers, so it will take <u>half</u> as long (10 ÷ 2 = 5 hours).

**2. 4 bakers can decorate 100 cakes in 5 hours.
If 5 bakers work at the same rate, how much quicker would they decorate 100 cakes?**

<u>Multiply by 4</u> to find how long it would take <u>1 baker</u>.   5 hours × 4 = 20 hours for 1 baker

<u>Divide by 5</u> to find how long it would take <u>5 bakers</u>.   20 ÷ 5 = 4 hours for 5 bakers

So 5 bakers are 5 − 4 = 1 hour quicker than 4.

Think of inverse proportions as the opposite of direct proportions

You should be able to identify, draw the graph of and solve inverse proportions. Have a go at solving these:

Q1   It takes 2 carpenters 6 hours to make a bookcase.
How long would it take 8 carpenters to make a bookcase?   [2 marks]

Q2   *m* is inversely proportional to *n*.
When *m* = 20, *n* = 5. What is the value of *m* when *n* is 32?   [2 marks]

Q2 Video Solution

Warm-up and Worked Exam Questions

Question pages take up a large proportion of this section, but that's just because we think they'll be really useful. Give these warm-up questions a shot when you're ready.

Warm-up Questions

1) If three chocolate bars cost 96p, how much will four of the bars cost?

2) 5 red roses cost £7.50.
   a) How much will 8 red roses cost?
   b) Afua has £20. How many red roses can she buy?

3) Marmalade can be bought in 3 different sizes: 250 g (£1.25), 350 g (£2.10) or 525 g (£2.50). Which size is best value for money?

4) It costs £240 to feed 2 elephants for 4 days.
   How much will it cost to feed 1 elephant for 7 days?

5) Give two features of a direct proportion graph.

6) Sketch the graph that shows that x is inversely proportional to y.

Worked Exam Questions

I've worked through one direct proportion and one inverse proportion question for you.
Go through both questions carefully and you'll be ready to tackle the next page.

1   Rani gets paid the same hourly rate whenever she works.
     In the first week of July, Rani worked for 28 hours and got paid £231.
     In each of the next 3 weeks of July, she worked for 25 hours.

     How much will Rani get paid in total for the 4 weeks she worked in July?

     Each hour Rani gets paid: £231 ÷ 28 = £8.25

     In the next three weeks she works 25 × 3 = 75 hours

     So in total she gets paid £231 + (75 × £8.25) = £849.75

     £ ....849.75........
     [2 marks]

2   Circle the **two** equations below that show that f is inversely proportional to g.

     $$f = g^2 \qquad f = g + 5 \qquad \boxed{fg = 7} \qquad f = \frac{g}{5} \qquad \boxed{g = \frac{3}{f}}$$

     Look for equations which can be rearranged
     to have the form $f = \frac{A}{g}$, where A is a number.

     [2 marks]

Exam Questions

3   Fresh orange juice can be bought in three different sizes.
    The price of each is shown on the right.
    Which size of bottle is the best value for money?

250 ml £2.00   330 ml £2.75   525 ml £3.75

.... ml
[3 marks]

4   A football coach buys a bottle of water for each child in a football club.
    All the bottles of water are the same price. There are 42 boys in the club.
    He spends £52.50 on water for the boys. He spends £35 on water for the girls.

    How many girls are there in the football club?

....
[2 marks]

5   A ship has enough food to cater for 250 people for 6 days.

    a)   For how many days can it cater for 300 people?

.... days
[2 marks]

    b)   How many more people can it cater for on a 2-day cruise than on a 6-day cruise?

.... people
[3 marks]

6   Bryn and Richard have just finished playing a game.
    The ratio of Bryn's points to Richard's was 5 : 2.

    a) On a set of axes, draw a graph that could be used to work out Bryn's points
       if you know Richard's points.

[2 marks]

    b) Richard scored 22 points. How many points did Bryn score?

.... points
[1 mark]

Percentages

You're going to see **6 different types** of percentage question on the next three pages.
The first few shouldn't give you too much trouble. Especially if you remember:

> 1) 'Per cent' means 'out of 100', so 20% means '20 out of 100' = $\frac{20}{100}$.
>
> 2) To work out the percentage <u>OF</u> something, replace the word <u>OF</u> with a <u>multiplication</u> (×).

Six **Different** Question Types

Type 1 — "Find x% of y"

If you have a <u>calculator</u>, turn the percentage into a <u>decimal</u>, then <u>multiply</u>.

> **EXAMPLE**   **Find 18% of £4.**
>
> Change 18% to a <u>decimal</u> and <u>multiply</u>.
>
> 18% of £4 → Replace '<u>of</u>' with '<u>x</u>'.
> = 18% × £4
> = 0.18 × £4 = £0.72

If you <u>don't have a calculator</u>, you can use this clever method instead:

> **EXAMPLE**   **Find 135% of 600 kg.**
>
> You can also find 1% by dividing by 100.
>
> 100% = 600 kg
> 1) Find <u>10%</u> by <u>dividing by 10</u>:   10% = 600 ÷ 10 = 60 kg
> 2) Find <u>5%</u> by <u>dividing 10% by 2</u>:   5% = 60 ÷ 2 = 30 kg
> 3) Use these values to <u>make 135%</u>:   135% = 100% + (3 × 10%) + 5%
>   = 600 + (3 × 60) + 30 = 810 kg

Type 2 — "Express x as a percentage of y"

<u>Divide</u> x by y, then multiply by <u>100</u>.

If you don't have a calculator you'll have to simplify the fraction (see p.15).

> **EXAMPLES**   **1. Give 36p as a percentage of 80p.**
>
> <u>Divide</u> 36p by 80p, <u>then multiply</u> by 100: $\frac{36}{80}$ × 100 = 45%

> **2. Farmer Littlewood measured the width of his prized pumpkin at the start and end of the month. At the start of the month it was <u>84 cm</u> wide and at the end of the month it was <u>1.32 m</u> wide. Give the <u>width at the end</u> of the month <u>as a percentage</u> of the <u>width at the start</u>.**
>
> 1) Make sure both amounts are in the <u>same units</u>.   1.32 m = 132 cm
>
> 2) <u>Divide</u> 132 cm by 84 cm, <u>then multiply</u> by 100: $\frac{132}{84}$ × 100 = 157.14% (2 d.p.)

Percentages are one of the most useful things you'll ever learn

Whenever you open a newspaper, see an advert, watch TV or do a maths exam paper you will see percentages. It's really important you get confident with using them — so here is some practise for you.

Q1 a) Without using a calculator, find 36% of 300.   [3 marks]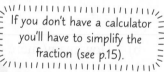
    b) Use a calculator to find 139% of 505.   [2 marks]

Q2 A full bottle of pearade holds 1.2 litres. After pouring a glass there is 744 ml left
    in the bottle. What percentage of the original amount is left in the bottle?   [2 marks]

Percentages

Type 3 — **New Amount** After a **% Increase or Decrease**

There are two different ways of finding the new amount after a percentage increase or decrease:

1) Find the % then Add or Subtract.

Find the % of the original amount. Add this on to (or subtract from) the original value.

EXAMPLE
**A dress has increased in price by 30%.
It originally cost £40. What is the new price of the dress?**

1) Find 30% of £40:   30% of £40 = 30% × £40
   = 0.3 × 40 = £12
2) It's an increase, so
   add on to the original: £40 + £12 = £52

2) The Multiplier Method

This time, you first need to find the multiplier — the decimal that represents the percentage change.

E.g. 5% increase is 1.05 (= 1 + 0.05)   26% decrease is 0.74 (= 1 − 0.26)

Then you just multiply the original value by the multiplier and voilà — you have the answer.

A % decrease has a multiplier less than 1,
a % increase has a multiplier greater than 1.

EXAMPLE
**A hat is reduced in price by 20% in the sales.
It originally cost £12. What is the new price of the hat?**

1) Find the multiplier: 20% decrease = 1 − 0.20 = 0.8
2) Multiply the original value by the multiplier: £12 × 0.8 = £9.60

Type 4 — **Simple Interest**

 Compound interest is covered on page 92.

Simple interest means a certain percentage of the original amount only is paid at regular intervals (usually once a year). So the amount of interest is the same every time it's paid.

EXAMPLE
**Regina invests £380 in an account which pays 3% simple interest each year.
How much interest will she earn in 4 years?**

1) Work out the amount of interest earned in one year: 3% = 3 ÷ 100 = 0.03
   3% of £380 = 0.03 × £380
   = £11.40
2) Multiply by 4 to get the total interest for 4 years: 4 × £11.40 = £45.60

Learn how to solve these simple question types

Another two types of percentages for you here — try the methods out on these practice questions.

Q1   A unicorn costing £4000 is reduced by 15% in a sale. What is its new price?   [2 marks]

Q2   Al puts £110 into a bank account that pays 6% simple interest each year. What will
his bank balance be after 3 years if he doesn't pay in or take out any money?   [3 marks]

Percentages

*Watch out for these **trickier types** of percentage question — they'll often include lots of real-life context.*

Type 5 — Finding the **Percentage Change**

1) This is the formula for giving a <u>change in value</u> as a <u>percentage</u> — <u>LEARN IT, AND USE IT</u>:

$$\text{Percentage 'Change'} = \frac{\text{'CHANGE'}}{\text{ORIGINAL}} \times 100$$

2) Typical questions will ask 'Find the percentage <u>increase</u>/<u>profit</u>/<u>error</u>' or 'Calculate the percentage <u>decrease</u>/<u>loss</u>/<u>discount</u>', etc.

> **EXAMPLE**
> **Tariq buys a plain plate for £2. He paints it, then sells it at a craft fair for £3.75. Find his profit as a percentage.**
>
> 1) Here the 'change' is <u>profit</u>, so the formula looks like this: $\text{percentage profit} = \frac{\text{profit}}{\text{original}} \times 100$
>
> 2) Work out the <u>profit</u> (amount made – original cost) $\text{profit} = £3.75 - £2 = £1.75$
>
> 3) Calculate the <u>percentage</u> profit: $\text{percentage profit} = \frac{£1.75}{£2} \times 100 = 87.5\%$

Type 6 — Finding the **Original Value**

This is the type that <u>most people get wrong</u> — but only because they <u>don't recognise</u> it as this type, and don't apply this <u>simple method</u>:

> 1) Write the amount in the question as a <u>percentage of the original value</u>.
> 2) <u>Divide</u> to find <u>1%</u> of the original value.
> 3) <u>Multiply by 100</u> to give the original value (= 100%).

> **EXAMPLE**
> **A house increases in value by 10% to £165 000. Find what it was worth before the rise.**
>
> Note: The <u>new</u>, not the original value is given.
>
> 1) An <u>increase</u> of 10% means £165 000 represents <u>110% of the original</u> value.
>
> 2) Divide by 110 to find <u>1%</u> of the original value.
>
> 3) Then multiply by 100.
>
>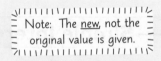
>
> ÷110 (£165 000 = 110%
>   £1500 = 1%
> ×100 (£150 000 = 100%
>
> If it was a <u>decrease</u> of 10%, then you'd put '£165 000 = <u>90%</u>' and divide by 90 instead of 110.
>
> So the original value was £150 000

Always set them out <u>exactly like this example</u>. The trickiest bit is deciding the top % figure on the right-hand side — the 2nd and 3rd rows are <u>always</u> 1% and 100%.

Learn the 6 different types of percentage question

The methods above are easy to follow but the questions can be a bit tricky. Have a go at these:

Q1   What is the percentage decrease when 1200 g is decreased to 900 g?   [3 marks]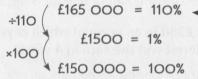

Q2   A junk shop is having a 20% off sale. A lobster statue is £4.88 in the sale. How much was the lobster statue before the sale?   [3 marks]

Q2 Video Solution

Trickier Percentage Problems

*This page is all about tackling tricky percentage questions. Once you know the **basic types** (pages 88-90), have a look at these **examples** and try to follow them step by step.*

Working with Percentages

1) Sometimes there <u>isn't</u> a set method you can follow to answer percentage questions.

2) You'll have to use what you've <u>learnt</u> on the last few pages and do a bit of <u>thinking</u> for yourself.

EXAMPLES

1. 80% of the members of a gym are male.
35% of the male members are aged 40 and over.
What percentage of gym members are males under 40 years old?

1) The percentage of <u>male members under 40</u> is: 100% − 35% = 65%

2) The percentage of <u>gym members</u>
that are <u>male</u> and <u>under 40</u> is:

65% of 80% = 0.65 × 80%
= 52%

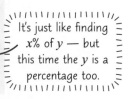

It's just like finding x% of y — but this time the y is a percentage too.

2. Yohan sells scarves. Each scarf costs £1.50 to make. One day he sold 500 scarves.
He sold 90% of them for £2 each and the rest at £1 each.
How much profit did Yohan make?

1) To make <u>500</u> scarves, it <u>costs him:</u>

500 × £1.50 = <u>£750</u>

2) Work out how many were sold <u>at each price</u>.

90% of 500 = 0.9 × 500
= 450 at £2 each

10% of 500 = 0.1 × 500
= 50 at £1 each

3) Work out the amount he made from <u>selling them</u>.

(450 × £2) + (50 × £1)
= £900 + £50 = <u>£950</u>

4) Calculate his <u>profit</u>.

£950 − £750 = £200

3. The number of visitors to a theme park in 2012 was 250 000. In 2013, the number of visitors was 12% lower than in 2012. In 2014, the number of visitors was 15% higher than in 2013. How many visitors were there in 2014?

1) First, work out the number of visitors in <u>2013</u>.

100% − 12% = 88%
88% of 250 000 = 0.88 × 250 000 = 220 000

2) Then work out the number of visitors in <u>2014</u>.
Make sure you use the value you've just found.

100% + 15% = 115%
115% of 220 000 = 1.15 × 220 000 = 253 000

Percentage questions can crop up in all shapes and sizes

The key thing is not to panic if you see an odd percentages question in your exam. It will always be a case of using one or more of the methods you've seen on the previous pages. Test your skills with these questions.

Q1   One day at a school, 70% of the students wore a polo shirt.
80% of the students wearing polo shirts were boys.
What percentage of students were boys who wore polo shirts?   [2 marks]

Q2   In May a bookshop sold 1600 books. 45% more books were sold in June than in May.
15% fewer books were sold in July than in June.
a) Find the number of books the bookshop sold in: i) June   ii) July   [2 marks]
b) What is the percentage increase in sales from May to July?   [3 marks]

Q2 Video Solution

Compound Growth and Decay

*One more sneaky % type for you... In **compound growth/decay** the amount added on/taken away **changes** each time — it's a percentage of the **new amount**, rather than the **original amount**.*

Compound Growth and Decay

Compound interest is a popular context for these questions — it means the interest is added on each time, and the next lot of interest is calculated using the new total rather than the original amount.

EXAMPLE **Daniel invests £10 000 in a savings account which pays 4% compound interest per annum. How much money will there be in his account after 3 years?**

1) Work out the multiplier:

   Multiplier = 4% increase = 1.04

2) Find the amount in the savings account each year until you get to 3 years.

   After 1 year: £10 000 × 1.04 = £10 400
   After 2 years: £10 400 × 1.04 = £10 816
   After 3 years: £10 816 × 1.04 = £11 248.64

   'Per annum' just means 'each year'.

Compound decay (depreciation) questions are about things that decrease in value or number over time.

EXAMPLE **Susan has just bought a car for £6500. The car depreciates by 8% each year. How many years will it be before the car is worth less than £5000?**

1) Work out the multiplier:

   8% decrease = 1 − 0.08 = 0.92

2) Calculate the value of the car each year — stop when the value drops below £5000.

   After 1 year: £6500 × 0.92 = £5980
   After 2 years: £5980 × 0.92 = £5501.60
   After 3 years: £5501.60 × 0.92 = £5061.472
   After 4 years: £5061.472 × 0.92 = £4656.55424

   So it will be 4 years before the car is worth less than £5000.

The Formula

If you're feeling confident with compound growth and decay then learn this formula. It'll speed things up...

Amount after n days/hours/years

$$N = N_0 \times (\text{multiplier})^n$$

Number of days/hours/years

Initial amount

Percentage change multiplier

EXAMPLE **The number of bacteria in a sample increases at a rate of 40% each day. Initially, there were 1000 bacteria. How many bacteria will there be after 10 days? Give your answer to the nearest 1000.**

1) Work out the multiplier:

   Multiplier = 40% increase = 1.4

2) Put an initial value of 1000, a time of 10 days and the multiplier into the formula.

   $1000 \times 1.4^{10} = 28\,925.465...$

   So after 10 days there will be 29 000 bacteria (to the nearest 1000).

Compound growth and decay — percentages applied again and again

This method gets the original value, increases it by the percentage, then increases that amount by the percentage, then takes that amount and increases it by the percentage, then... get it?

Q1 Pippa's bank account pays 2.5% compound interest per annum and her bank balance is £3200. After 3 years, how much will Pippa's bank balance be? [3 marks]

Q1 Video Solution

Warm-up and Worked Exam Questions

Have a go at these warm-up questions and see how you get on — the exam questions will be a bit more tricky, so it's important that you can do these first.

Warm-up Questions

1) Calculate 34% of £50.

2) What is 37 out of 50 as a percentage?

3) Find 15% of 60 (without using a calculator).

4) A suit costs £120 during a sale. Once the sale is over, the price of the suit rises by 15%. What is the new price of the suit?

5) You pay £200 into a bank account that pays 2.5% simple interest per year. How much money will be in the account after one year?

6) Matala buys a vintage watch for £800. After one year, the watch is worth £1300. By what percentage has the value of Matala's watch increased?

7) At a supermarket, a block of cheese is 40% off. With the offer, the cheese costs £1.80. What was the original price of the block of cheese?

8) £3000 is invested at 3% compound interest (per year). Work out how much money is in the account at the end of 4 years, to the nearest penny.

Worked Exam Question

Study this worked exam question well — then have a go at some for yourself on the next page.

1 Olivia and Benula each have a bank account that pays 8% simple interest per annum. They each deposit an amount of money and don't pay in or take out any other money.

a) Olivia deposits £2000 in the account. How much will be in the account after 3 years? **(3)**

$$8\% = 0.08$$

Each year she gets £2000 × 0.08 = £160 interest

After 3 years she'll have £2000 + (3 × £160) = £2480

£ ....2480............

[2 marks]

b) After the first year, Benula had £702 in her account. How much money did she originally put in the account?

$$\div 108 \; \left(\begin{array}{c} £702 = 108\% \\ £6.50 = 1\% \\ £650 = 100\% \end{array}\right) \div 108$$
$$\times 100 \qquad \qquad \times 100$$

£ ....650........

[3 marks]

Exam Questions

2   Jane owns a fashion shop.

Jane sells a pair of jeans for £33.25 plus VAT at 20%.

How much does she sell the pair of jeans for?   (3)

£ ....

[2 marks]

3   Franz always spends £2.40 a week on packs of football stickers.
The stickers normally cost 40p per pack but this week they are 40% cheaper.   (4)

How many more packs of stickers can he get this week than in a normal week?

....

[4 marks]

4   A pet rescue shelter houses cats and dogs. The ratio of cats : dogs is 3 : 7.
40% of the cats are black and 50% of the dogs are black.   (5)
What percentage of the animals at the shelter are black?

.... %

[4 marks]

5   Mrs Burdock borrows £750 to buy a sofa.   (5)
She is charged 6% compound interest per annum.

If Mrs Burdock doesn't pay back any of the money for 3 years, how much will she owe?
Give your answer to the nearest penny.

£ ....

[3 marks]

Unit Conversions

*A nice easy page for a change — just some **facts** to learn.*

Metric and Imperial Units

COMMON METRIC CONVERSIONS

1 cm = 10 mm	1 tonne = 1000 kg
1 m = 100 cm	1 litre = 1000 ml
1 km = 1000 m	1 litre = 1000 cm^3
1 kg = 1000 g	1 cm^3 = 1 ml

COMMON IMPERIAL CONVERSIONS

1 Yard = 3 Feet   1 Foot = 12 Inches
1 Gallon = 8 Pints
1 Stone = 14 Pounds
1 Pound = 16 Ounces

You only need to <u>remember</u> the <u>metric</u> conversions, but you should be able to <u>use</u> them <u>all</u>.

COMMON METRIC-IMPERIAL CONVERSIONS

1 kg ≈ 2.2 pounds   1 foot ≈ 30 cm   1 gallon ≈ 4.5 litres   1 mile ≈ 1.6 km

≈ means approximately equal to

3 Step Method for Converting Units

1. Find the <u>conversion factor</u> (always easy).
2. <u>Multiply AND divide by it</u>.
3. Choose the <u>common sense answer</u>.

Make sure you cross out the incorrect working or you could lose marks.

1 **Convert 7 litres into ml.**

1) Find the <u>conversion factor</u>.

2) <u>Multiply</u> and <u>divide</u> by it.

3) Choose the <u>sensible</u> answer — there should be <u>more millilitres than litres</u>.

1 litre = 1000 ml, so conversion factor = 1000

7 × 1000 = 7000   ~~7 ÷ 1000 = 0.007~~

7 litres = 7000 ml

2 **Neil's jet ski can hold 116 pints of fuel. How many gallons is this? (1 gallon = 8 pints)**

1) Find the <u>conversion factor</u>.

2) <u>Multiply</u> and <u>divide</u> by it.

3) Choose the <u>sensible</u> answer — there should be <u>fewer gallons than pints</u>.

1 gallon = 8 pints, so conversion factor = 8

~~116 × 8 = 928~~   116 ÷ 8 = 14.5

116 pints = 14.5 gallons

3 **Izumi unicycles 8 miles to work. How far is this in km? (1 mile ≈ 1.6 km)**

1) Find the <u>conversion factor</u>.

2) <u>Multiply</u> and <u>divide</u> by it.

3) Choose the <u>sensible</u> answer — there should be <u>more km than miles</u>.

1 mile ≈ 1.6 km, so conversion factor = 1.6

8 × 1.6 = 12.8   ~~8 ÷ 1.6 = 5~~

8 miles ≈ 12.8 km

Make sure you've learned all of the metric conversions

Any conversion involving imperial units will be given in the exam. Another thing to remember is the three step method for conversion — and don't forget to cross out any incorrect working.

Q1   A squash court is 9.75 m long. 1 foot ≈ 30 cm and 1 foot = 12 inches.
      How long is the court in: a) cm?   [1 mark]   b) feet and inches?   [2 marks]

Q1 Video Solution

Area and Volume Conversions

*Time for some **trickier conversions** to sink your teeth into. There are a **couple of methods** for you to remember so that when it comes to the exam you can feel confident converting areas and volumes.*

Converting **Areas**

You need to be really <u>careful</u> when converting areas — just because 1 m = 100 cm <u>DOES NOT</u> mean 1 m² = 100 cm².

Follow this <u>method</u> to avoid slipping up:

$1 \text{ m}^2 = 100 \text{ cm} \times 100 \text{ cm} = 10\,000 \text{ cm}^2$
$1 \text{ cm}^2 = 10 \text{ mm} \times 10 \text{ mm} = 100 \text{ mm}^2$

1) Find the <u>conversion factor</u> — it'll be the same as for converting units (see p.95).
2) <u>Multiply AND divide</u> by the conversion factor <u>TWO TIMES</u>.
3) Choose the <u>common sense answer</u>, and don't forget that the units come with a <u>2</u>, e.g. mm², cm²

EXAMPLE   **The area of the top of a table is 0.6 m². Find its area in cm².**

1) Find the <u>conversion factor</u>:

   $1 \text{ m} = 100 \text{ cm} \longrightarrow$ Conversion factor = 100

2) It's an area — multiply and divide <u>twice</u> by the conversion factor:

   $0.6 \times 100 \times 100 = 6000$
   ~~$0.6 \div 100 \div 100 = 0.00006$~~

   1 m = 100 cm so expect <u>more</u> cm than m.

3) Choose the <u>sensible</u> answer:

   $0.6 \text{ m}^2 = 6000 \text{ cm}^2$

Converting **Volumes**

$1 \text{ m}^3 = 100 \text{ cm} \times 100 \text{ cm} \times 100 \text{ cm} = 1\,000\,000 \text{ cm}^3$
$1 \text{ cm}^3 = 10 \text{ mm} \times 10 \text{ mm} \times 10 \text{ mm} = 1000 \text{ mm}^3$

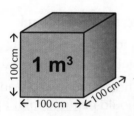

1) <u>Conversion factor</u> — it'll be the same as for converting units (see p.95).
2) <u>Multiply AND divide</u> by the conversion factor <u>THREE TIMES</u>.
3) Choose the <u>common sense answer</u>, and don't forget that the units come with a <u>3</u>, e.g. mm³, cm³.

EXAMPLE   **A glass has a volume of 72 000 mm³. What is its volume in cm³?**

1) Find the <u>conversion factor</u>:

   $1 \text{ cm} = 10 \text{ mm} \longrightarrow$ Conversion factor = 10

2) It's a volume — multiply and divide <u>3 times</u> by the conversion factor:

   ~~$72\,000 \times 10 \times 10 \times 10 = 72\,000\,000$~~
   $72\,000 \div 10 \div 10 \div 10 = 72$

   1 cm = 10 mm so expect <u>fewer</u> cm than mm.

3) Choose the <u>sensible</u> answer:

   $72\,000 \text{ mm}^3 = 72 \text{ cm}^3$

Remember — area comes with a 2 and volume comes with a 3

Learn the rules for converting between units for areas and volumes. Always check your answer to see if it is sensible or not. Common sense will get you a long way. Have a go at these questions to practise the rules.

Q1   The area of a forest is 6 km². What is its area in m²?   [2 marks]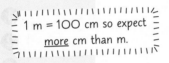

Q2   The volume of a golf ball is 40 cm³. What is its volume in mm³?   [2 marks]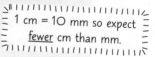

Time Intervals

*Make sure you can convert between **time units** — it's **simple** and might grab you a mark or two in the exam.*

Converting Time Units

1) You ought to know the standard <u>time unit conversions</u> by now.

2) Use these standard conversions to change the units of <u>other times</u>.

> 1 day = 24 hours
> 1 hour = 60 minutes
> 1 minute = 60 seconds

EXAMPLES

1. How many seconds are there in an hour?

1) First convert <u>hours</u> into <u>minutes</u>.   1 hour = 60 minutes

2) Then convert <u>minutes</u> into <u>seconds</u>.   60 minutes = 60 × 60 = 3600 seconds

Be <u>very careful</u> when using <u>calculators</u> — the decimal answers they give are confusing, e.g. <u>2.5 hours = 2 hours 30 mins</u>, <u>NOT 2 hours 50 mins</u>.

2. Write 186 minutes in hours and minutes.

1) Work out how many <u>complete hours</u> there are in 186 minutes.

   2 hours = 2 × 60 = 120 minutes
   <u>3 hours = 3 × 60 = 180 minutes</u> ✓
   4 hours = 4 × 60 = 240 minutes — too many

2) Find how many <u>minutes over 3 hours</u> it is.

   186 − 180 = <u>6 minutes</u>
   So 186 minutes = 3 hours 6 minutes

Break Time Calculations into Simple Stages

EXAMPLE   **Hiroko watched a film that started at 7.20 pm and finished at 10.05 pm. How long was the film in minutes?**

1) Split the time between 7.20 pm and 10.05 pm into <u>simple stages</u>.

   7.20 pm   →   9.20 pm   →   10.00 pm   →   10.05 pm
     + 2 hours   + 40 minutes   + 5 minutes

2) <u>Convert</u> the hours to minutes.   2 hours = 2 × 60 = 120 minutes

3) <u>Add</u> to get the total minutes.   120 + 40 + 5 = 165 minutes

Timetables

EXAMPLE   **Use the timetable to answer this question.**

Kofi wants to get a bus from the bus station to the train station in time for a train that leaves at 19:30. What is the latest bus he can catch?

Bus Timetable				
Bus Station	18 45	19 00	19 15	19 30
Market Street	18 52	19 07	19 22	19 37
Long Lane	19 01	19 16	19 31	19 46
Train Station	19 11	19 26	19 41	19 56

1) Read along the <u>train station</u> row.   19 11   (19 26)   19 41   19 56

   This is the latest time he could arrive before 19:30.

2) Move up this column to the <u>bus station</u> row and read off the entry.

   The bus that gets to the train station at 19:26 leaves the bus station at 19:00.

This page might look easy, but make sure you learn it all

It's easy to make mistakes doing time intervals on a calculator, so you best get plenty of practice...

Q1   a) How many minutes are there in 2 days?   [1 mark]

     b) Write 265 seconds in minutes and seconds.   [2 marks]

Q2   Zoe works 4 days a week at an owl sanctuary. She starts work at 6.20 am and finishes at 12.50 pm. She earns £7.20 per hour. How much does she earn in a week?   [3 marks]

Speed, Density and Pressure

*Let's see if you can speed through this page. You need to know the **formulas** and be able to substitute numbers into them — you should also be able to **convert** between different **units** (which is a bit tricky).*

Speed = Distance ÷ Time

Speed is the <u>distance travelled per unit time</u> — the number of <u>km per hour</u> or <u>metres per second</u>.

$$\text{SPEED} = \frac{\text{DISTANCE}}{\text{TIME}} \qquad \text{TIME} = \frac{\text{DISTANCE}}{\text{SPEED}} \qquad \text{DISTANCE} = \text{SPEED} \times \text{TIME}$$

A <u>formula triangle</u> is a mighty handy tool for remembering formulas. Here's the one for speed.
To <u>remember the order of the letters</u> ($S^D T$) we have the words <u>SaD Times</u>.
So if it's a question on speed, distance and time, just say <u>SAD TIMES</u>.

$$\triangle \frac{D}{S \times T}$$

How DO YOU USE Formula Triangles?
1) <u>COVER UP</u> the thing you want to find and <u>WRITE DOWN</u> what's left.
2) Now <u>PUT IN THE VALUES</u> for the other two things and <u>WORK IT OUT</u>.

E.g. to get the formula for <u>speed</u> from the triangle, cover up <u>S</u> and you're left with $\frac{D}{T}$.

EXAMPLES

1. Rob cycles 18 miles in 2 hours. What is his average speed?

1) You want speed so <u>covering S</u> gives: $S = \dfrac{D}{T}$

2) <u>Put in</u> the numbers — and don't forget the units. $S = 18 \div 2$ = 9 mph

CHECK YOUR UNITS MATCH
If the distance is in <u>miles</u> and the time is in <u>hours</u> then you'll get a speed in <u>mph</u>.

2. A cheetah runs at a constant speed of 27 m/s for 20 s. What distance does it cover?

1) You want distance so <u>covering D</u> gives: $D = S \times T$

2) <u>Put in</u> the numbers — and don't forget the units. $D = 27 \times 20$ = 540 m

UNITS CHECK: m/s and s go in so m comes out.

Density = Mass ÷ Volume

Density is the <u>mass per unit volume</u> of a substance. It's usually measured in <u>kg/m³</u> or <u>g/cm³</u>.

$$\text{DENSITY} = \frac{\text{MASS}}{\text{VOLUME}} \qquad \text{VOLUME} = \frac{\text{MASS}}{\text{DENSITY}} \qquad \text{MASS} = \text{DENSITY} \times \text{VOLUME}$$

Here's the formula triangle for <u>density</u>. To remember the order of the letters
in the formula triangle think $D^M V$ or <u>DiMoV</u> (the Russian agent).

EXAMPLE

A giant 'Wunda-Choc' bar has a density of 1.3 g/cm³. If the bar's volume is 1800 cm³, what is the mass of the bar in grams?

1) You want the mass, so <u>covering M</u> gives: $M = D \times V$

2) Put in the <u>numbers</u> — and remember the <u>units</u>. $M = 1.3 \text{ g/cm}^3 \times 1800 \text{ cm}^3$ = 2340 g

UNITS CHECK: g/cm³ and cm³ go in so g comes out.

Speed, Density and Pressure

Pressure = Force ÷ Area

'N' stands for 'Newtons'.

Pressure is the amount of <u>force acting per unit area</u>. It's usually measured in <u>N/m²</u>, or pascals (Pa).

PRESSURE = $\dfrac{\text{FORCE}}{\text{AREA}}$	AREA = $\dfrac{\text{FORCE}}{\text{PRESSURE}}$	FORCE = PRESSURE × AREA

Another formula triangle here — this one's for <u>pressure</u>. When you come across a pressure question, a handy trick to <u>remember the order</u> of the letters (P^{F}A) is to think about <u>Penguins Flapping Awkwardly</u>.

EXAMPLE
A cuboid box exerts a force of 200 N on the horizontal ground.
The side lengths of the face resting on the ground are 0.2 m and 0.8 m.
Calculate the pressure exerted by the box on the ground.

1) Work out the <u>area of the face</u> in contact with the ground: $0.2 \text{ m} \times 0.8 \text{ m} = 0.16 \text{ m}^2$

2) Use the <u>formula triangle</u> — you want pressure so <u>covering P</u> gives: $P = \dfrac{F}{A}$

3) Put in the <u>numbers</u>. $P = \dfrac{200\,\text{N}}{0.16\,\text{m}^2}$

4) <u>Check the units</u> — you put in <u>N</u> and <u>m²</u> so you'll get <u>N/m²</u>. $= 1250 \text{ N/m}^2$

Converting Speed, Density and Pressure

1) Units of speed, density and pressure are made up of <u>two measures</u> — a <u>distance</u> and a <u>time</u>, a <u>mass</u> and a <u>volume</u>, or a <u>force</u> and an <u>area</u>.

2) So to <u>convert units</u> of speed, density or pressure, you might need to do <u>two conversions</u> — one for each measure.

EXAMPLE **A rabbit's top speed is 54 km/h. How fast is this in m/s?**

1) First convert from km/h to m/h: 1 km = 1000 m, so conversion factor = 1000
   54 × 1000 = 54 000 ~~54 ÷ 1000 = 0.054~~
   54 km/h = 54 000 m/h

2) Now convert from m/h to m/s: 1 hour = 60 minutes = 60 × 60 = 3600 seconds
   So conversion factor = 3600
   ~~54 000 × 3600 = 194 400 000~~ 54 000 ÷ 3600 = 15
   54 km/h = 54 000 m/h = 15 m/s

Formula triangles are dead useful

Write down the formula triangles from the last two pages, then use them to make all nine formulas.

Q1 A cylinder rests with its 8 m² circular face on horizontal ground. The pressure it exerts on the ground is 350 N/m². What is the force of the cylinder on the ground? [2 marks]

Q2 A sprinter runs 400 m in 50 seconds. a) What was his average speed in m/s? [1 mark]
    b) What was his average speed in km/h? [3 marks]

Q3 A cube has a mass of 25 g and side length 2 cm.
    a) What is the density in g/cm³? [2 marks] b) What is the density in kg/m³? [3 marks]

Warm-up and Worked Exam Questions

Time to check all that lovely revision has sunk in. Try these first to make sure you've learnt the key stuff:

Warm-up Questions

1) a) How many mm is 6.5 cm?   b) How many kg is 250 g?
2) A machine was found to weigh 0.16 tonnes. What is this in kg?
3) A rod is 46 inches long. What is this in feet and inches?
4) a) Roughly how many km is 200 miles?   b) Roughly how many feet is 120 cm?
5) Convert these measurements: a) 23 m² to cm²   b) 34 500 cm² to m².
6) A train leaves at 9.37 am and arrives at 11.16 am. How long is the train journey in minutes?
7) A plane sets off at 10.15 am. The flight lasts 5 hrs 50 mins. What is the arrival time?
8) A cube rests on a horizontal surface. It exerts a pressure of 50 N/m² on the surface and it has a weight of 8 N. What is the area of one face of the cube?
9) A car travels 0.5 km in 25 seconds. What is the average speed of the car in m/s?
10) The mass of a candle is 300 g and its density is 0.8 g/cm³. What is the volume of this candle in cm³?

Worked Exam Question

Make sure you really take this stuff in — read the working thoroughly and then have a go yourself to check you've understood. You'll kick yourself if this comes up in the exam and you only gave it a quick glance.

1 Siobhan has been caught speeding by a pair of cameras measuring average speed.
The speed limit was 30 mph. The cameras are 2.5 km apart.
The time taken for her car to pass between them was 3 minutes.

a) What was Siobhan's average speed between the cameras?
Give your answer to the nearest mph. (1 mile ≈ 1.6 km) **(4)**

$$2.5 \text{ km} ≈ 2.5 ÷ 1.6 = 1.5625 \text{ miles}$$

$$\text{Speed} = \frac{\text{Distance}}{\text{Time}}$$

1 hour = 60 minutes, so 3 minutes = 3 ÷ 60 = 0.05 hours

Speed = 1.5625 miles ÷ 0.05 hours
= 31.25 mph = 31 mph (to nearest mph)

...........31........... mph

[3 marks]

b) If Siobhan had been travelling within the speed limit, what is the minimum time it should have taken her to pass between the cameras? **(5)**
Give your answer to the nearest second.

Time = 1.5625 miles ÷ 30 mph = 0.05208... hours $\text{Time} = \frac{\text{Distance}}{\text{Speed}}$

0.05208... hours × 60 × 60 = 187.5 seconds
= 188 seconds (to nearest second)

...........188........... s

[2 marks]

Exam Questions

2   Isaac and Ultan spent 13 days building a model robot.
    On the first 12 days they built from 4.30 pm till 7.15 pm and   (2)
    on the last day they built for a total of 7 hours 10 minutes.

    What is the total amount of time they spent building the robot?
    Give your answer in hours and minutes.

                                        .... hours .... minutes
                                                                    [4 marks]

3   1 gallon = 8 pints.   9 litres ≈ 2 gallons.   (3)
    Approximately how many litres are there in 64 pints?

                                                        .... litres
                                                                    [3 marks]

4   Nicole wants to post eight books to a friend in another country.   (3)
    Each book weighs 0.55 lb and postage is £0.50 per 100 g. (1 kg ≈ 2.2 lb)

    How much will it cost her to post all the books to her friend?

                                        £ ....
                                                                    [4 marks]

5   Look at the cuboid on the right. Three of its faces are   (4)
    labelled A, B and C. The cuboid has a weight of 40 N.

    Calculate the pressure, in N/m², that the cuboid exerts
    on horizontal ground when the cuboid is resting on face A.

    80 cm   C   B   4 m
             2 m   A

                                        .... N/m²
                                                                    [3 marks]

Revision Questions for Section Four

Lots to remember in <u>Section Four</u> — let's see what you've taken in...

- Try these questions and <u>tick off each one</u> when you <u>get it right</u>.
- When you're <u>completely happy</u> with a topic, tick that off too.

For even more practice, try the Sudden Fail Quiz for Section Four — just scan this QR code!

Section Four Quiz

Ratios (p78-80) ☑

1) Reduce: a) $18:22$ to its simplest form b) $49\,g:14\,g$ to the form $n:1$ ☑

2) Sarah is in charge of ordering stock for a clothes shop. The shop usually sells red scarves and blue scarves in the ratio $5:8$. Sarah orders 50 red scarves. How many blue scarves should she order? ☑

3) Pencils and rubbers are in the ratio $7:2$. How many times more pencils are there than rubbers? ☑

4) Ryan, Joel and Sam are sharing 800 lollipops. They split the lollipops in the ratio $5:8:12$.
a) What fraction of the lollipops does Ryan get? b) How many lollipops does Sam get? ☑

5) The recipe on the right shows CGP's secret pasta sauce recipe. The recipe serves 6 people. How much of each ingredient is needed to make enough for 17 servings? ☑

- 18 ml olive oil
- 360 g tomatoes
- 9 g garlic powder
- 72 g onions

Proportion Problems (p83-85) ☑

6) 3 gardeners can plant 360 flowers in a day. How many flowers could 8 gardeners plant in a day? ☑

7) 'y is directly proportional to x'. Sketch the graph of this proportion for $x \geq 0$. ☑

8) A DIY shop sells varnish in two different-sized tins. A 500 ml tin costs £8 and a 1800 ml tin costs £30. Which tin represents the better value for money? ☑

9) The amount of time it takes to wash a car is inversely proportional to the number of people washing it. 3 people take 12 minutes to wash a car. How many people are needed to wash a car in 2 minutes? ☑

Percentages (p88-92) ☑

10) If $x = 20$ and $y = 95$:   a) Find $x\%$ of y.   b) Find the new value after y is increased by $x\%$.
c) Express x as a percentage of y.   d) Express y as a percentage of x. ☑

11) What's the formula for finding a change in value as a percentage? ☑

12) An antique wardrobe decreased in value from £800 to £520. What was the percentage decrease? ☑

13) A tree's height has increased by 15% in the last year to 20.24 m. What was its height a year ago? ☑

14) 25% of the items sold by a bakery in one day were pies. 8% of the pies sold were chicken pies. What percentage of the items sold by the bakery were chicken pies? ☑

15) Collectable baseball cards increase in value by 10% each year. A particular card is worth £80.
a) How much will it be worth in 4 years? b) In how many years will it be worth over £140? ☑

Conversions and Time (p95-97) ☑

16) Convert: a) 5.6 litres to cm^3 b) 8 feet to cm   c) 2 weeks into hours
d) 12 m^3 to cm^3 e) 1280 mm^2 to cm^2 f) 2.75 cm^3 to mm^3 ☑

17) A musical production starts at 19:30. The musical is 118 minutes long plus a 20 minute interval. What time does the musical finish? Give your answer in 12-hour time. ☑

Speed, Density and Pressure (p98-99) ☑

18) Find the average speed, in km/h, of a car if it travels 63 miles in 1.5 hours. ☑

19) Find the volume, in cm^3, of a snowman if its density is 0.4 g/cm^3 and its mass is 5000 g. ☑

20) Find the area of an object in contact with horizontal ground, if the pressure it exerts on the ground is 120 N/m^2 and it pushes on the ground with a force of 1320 N. ☑

Properties of 2D Shapes

*Here's a nice easy page to get you started on **2D shapes**.*

Line Symmetry

This is where you draw one or more <u>MIRROR LINES</u> across a shape and both sides will <u>fold exactly</u> together.

| 2 LINES OF SYMMETRY | 1 LINE OF SYMMETRY | 1 LINE OF SYMMETRY | 3 LINES OF SYMMETRY | NO LINES OF SYMMETRY | 1 LINE OF SYMMETRY |

Rotational Symmetry

This is where you can <u>rotate</u> the shape into different positions that <u>look exactly the same</u>.

Order 1   Order 2   Order 2   Order 3   Order 4

The <u>ORDER OF ROTATIONAL SYMMETRY</u> is the posh way of saying: 'how many different positions look the same'. You should say the Z-shape above has '<u>rotational symmetry of order 2</u>'.

> When a shape has <u>only 1 position</u> you can <u>either</u> say that it has 'rotational symmetry of <u>order 1</u>' or that it has '<u>NO rotational symmetry</u>'.

Regular Polygons

All the <u>sides</u> and <u>angles</u> in a regular polygon are the <u>same</u>.
Learn the names of these <u>regular polygons</u> and how many <u>sides</u> they have.
(An <u>equilateral triangle</u> and a <u>square</u> are both regular polygons — see p.104 and p.105 for their properties.)

> In an <u>irregular</u> polygon, the sides and angles aren't all equal.

REGULAR PENTAGON
<u>5 sides</u>
<u>5 lines</u> of symmetry
Rotational symmetry of <u>order 5</u>

REGULAR HEXAGON
<u>6 sides</u>
<u>6 lines</u> of symmetry
Rotational symmetry of <u>order 6</u>

REGULAR HEPTAGON
<u>7 sides</u>
<u>7 lines</u> of symmetry
Rotational symmetry of <u>order 7</u>

REGULAR OCTAGON
<u>8 sides</u>
<u>8 lines</u> of symmetry
Rotational symmetry of <u>order 8</u>

REGULAR NONAGON
<u>9 sides</u>
<u>9 lines</u> of symmetry
Rotational symmetry of <u>order 9</u>

REGULAR DECAGON
<u>10 sides</u>
<u>10 lines</u> of symmetry
Rotational symmetry of <u>order 10</u>

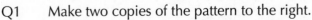

Make sure you learn the two types of symmetry

They'll get you some nice marks in the exam. Regular polygons have the same number of lines of symmetry and the same order of rotational symmetry as the number of sides.

Q1   Make two copies of the pattern to the right.
    a) Shade two squares to make a pattern with one line of symmetry.   [2 marks]
    b) Shade two squares to make a pattern with rotational symmetry of order 2.   [2 marks]

Properties of 2D Shapes

*These two pages have a load of details about **triangles** and **quadrilaterals** — these come in handy for all sorts of geometry problems, so you need to learn them all.*

Triangles

1) Equilateral Triangles

<u>3 equal sides</u> and
<u>3 equal angles</u> of <u>60°</u>.
<u>3 lines</u> of symmetry,
rotational symmetry <u>order 3</u>.

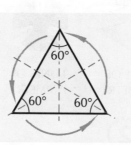

2) Right-angled Triangles

1 <u>right angle</u> (90°).
<u>No</u> lines of symmetry.
<u>No</u> rotational symmetry.

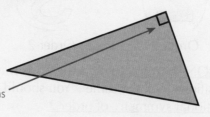

The little square means
it's a right angle.

3) Isosceles Triangles

<u>2 sides</u> the same.
<u>2 angles</u> the same.
<u>1 line</u> of symmetry.
<u>No</u> rotational symmetry.

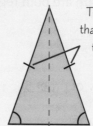

These dashes mean
that the two sides are
the same length.

4) Scalene Triangles

An <u>acute-angled triangle</u>
has 3 acute angles, and an
<u>obtuse-angled triangle</u> has
one obtuse angle (see p.126).

All three sides <u>different</u>.
All three angles <u>different</u>.
No symmetry (pretty obviously).

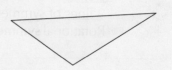

Triangles have three sides

Learn the names (and how to spell them) and the properties of all the triangles on this page.
These are easy marks in the exam — make sure you know them all.

Properties of 2D Shapes

Quadrilaterals

1) Square

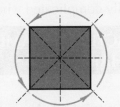

4 equal angles of 90° (right angles).
4 lines of symmetry,
rotational symmetry order 4.

2) Rectangle

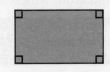 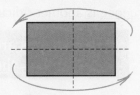

4 equal angles of 90° (right angles).
2 lines of symmetry, rotational symmetry order 2.

3) Rhombus

(A square pushed over)
Matching arrows show parallel sides.

A rhombus is the same as a diamond.

4 equal sides (opposite sides are parallel).
2 pairs of equal angles.
2 lines of symmetry, rotational symmetry order 2.

4) Parallelogram

(A rectangle pushed over)

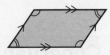

2 pairs of equal sides (each pair are parallel).
2 pairs of equal angles.
NO lines of symmetry,
rotational symmetry order 2.

5) Trapezium

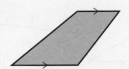

1 pair of parallel sides.   NO lines of symmetry*.
No rotational symmetry.

*In an isosceles trapezium, the sloping sides are
the same length. An isosceles trapezium has
1 line of symmetry.

6) Kite

2 pairs of equal sides.
1 pair of equal angles.
1 line of symmetry.
No rotational symmetry.

Quadrilaterals have four sides

There are six types of quadrilateral to learn on this page. Make sure you know their features — for example,
how many lines of symmetry they have and whether they have rotational symmetry. Now try this question:

Q1 A quadrilateral has all 4 sides the same length and two pairs of equal angles.
Identify the quadrilateral, and write down its order of rotational symmetry.   [2 marks]

Congruent Shapes

*Shapes can be **congruent**, which basically just means 'the same as each other'.*
Luckily for you, here's a full page on congruence.

Congruent — Same Shape, Same Size

<u>Congruence</u> is another ridiculous maths word which sounds really complicated when it's not:

> If two shapes are <u>**CONGRUENT**</u>, they are <u>**EXACTLY THE SAME**</u>
> — the <u>**SAME SIZE**</u> and the <u>**SAME SHAPE**</u>.

These shapes are all <u>congruent</u>:

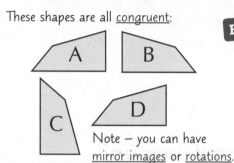

Note — you can have
<u>mirror images</u> or <u>rotations</u>.

EXAMPLE   **Two of the triangles below are congruent.**
Write down the letters of the congruent triangles.

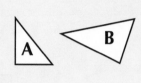

Just pick out the two triangles that are <u>exactly the same</u> —
remember that the shape might have been <u>rotated</u> or <u>reflected</u>.
By eye, you can see that the congruent triangles are **B and E**.

Conditions for Congruent Triangles

<u>Two triangles</u> are <u>congruent</u> if <u>one</u> of the four conditions below holds true:

<u>SSS</u>   <u>three sides</u> are the same
<u>AAS</u>   <u>two angles</u> and a <u>corresponding side</u> match up
<u>SAS</u>   <u>two sides</u> and the <u>angle between them</u> match up
<u>RHS</u>   a <u>right angle</u>, the <u>hypotenuse</u> and one other <u>side</u> all match up

The <u>hypotenuse</u> is the
<u>longest side</u> of a right-angled
triangle — the one <u>opposite</u>
the <u>right angle</u>.

SSS
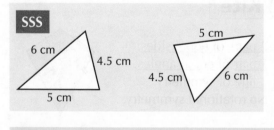
6 cm   4.5 cm   5 cm   5 cm   4.5 cm   6 cm

AAS
16 mm   81°   62°   62°   81°   16 mm

Make sure the sides
match up — here,
the side is opposite
the 81° angle.

SAS
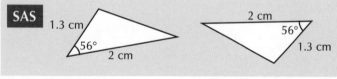
1.3 cm   56°   2 cm   2 cm   56°   1.3 cm

RHS
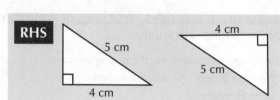
5 cm   4 cm   4 cm   5 cm

Congruent just means same size, same shape

You need to be able to recognise congruent shapes and learn all 4 conditions for
congruent triangles. Make sure you're using the right sides and angles in each shape.

Q1   The two triangles shown on the right are congruent.
Find the values of *x*, *y* and *z*.

[2 marks]

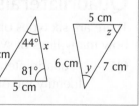
7 cm   44°   *x*   81°   5 cm   5 cm   *z*   6 cm   *y*   7 cm

Similar Shapes

Similar shapes are **exactly the same shape**, but can be **different sizes** (they can also be **rotated** or **reflected**).

SIMILAR — same shape, **different size**.

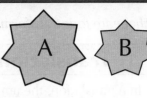

Similar Shapes Have the Same Angles

Generally, for two shapes to be <u>similar</u>, all the <u>angles</u> must match and the <u>sides</u> must be <u>proportional</u>. But for <u>triangles</u>, there are <u>three special conditions</u> — if any one of these is true, you know they're similar.

Two triangles are similar if:

1) All the <u>angles</u> match up.

2) All three <u>sides</u> are <u>proportional</u>.

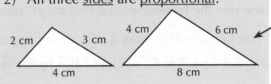

> Here, the sides of the bigger triangle are <u>twice</u> as long as the sides of the smaller triangle.

3) Any <u>two sides</u> are <u>proportional</u> and the <u>angle between them</u> is the <u>same</u>.

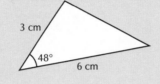

> Watch out — if one of the triangles has been rotated or flipped over, it might look as if they're not similar, but don't be fooled.

EXAMPLE Tony says, "Triangles ABC and DEF are similar." Is Tony correct? Explain your answer.

<u>Check</u> condition 3 holds — start by finding the <u>missing angle</u> in triangle DEF:

Angle DEF = 180° − 46° − 30° = 104° so angle ABC = angle DEF

Now check that <u>AB</u> and <u>BC</u> are <u>proportional</u> to <u>DE</u> and <u>EF</u>:

DE ÷ AB = 6 ÷ 2 = 3 and EF ÷ BC = 9 ÷ 3 = 3 so DE and EF are 3 times as long as AB and BC.

Tony is correct — two sides are proportional and the angle between them is the same so the triangles are similar.

Use Similarity to Find Missing Lengths

You might have to use the <u>properties</u> of similar shapes to find missing distances, lengths etc. — you'll need to use <u>scale factors</u> (see p.109) to find the lengths of missing sides.

EXAMPLE ABC and ADE are similar right-angled triangles. AC = 20 cm, AE = 50 cm and BC = 8 cm. Find the length of DE.

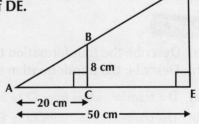

The triangles are <u>similar</u>, so work out the <u>scale factor</u>:

scale factor $= \dfrac{50}{20} = \underline{2.5}$

Now <u>use</u> the scale factor to work out the length of DE:

DE = 8 × 2.5 = 20 cm

Similar means the same shape but a different size

To help remember the difference between similarity and congruence, think '<u>similar siblings</u>, <u>congruent clones</u>' — siblings are alike but not the same, clones are identical.

Q1   Find the length of DB.   [3 marks]

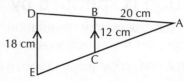

The Four Transformations

*There are four **transformations** you need to know — **translation, rotation, reflection** and **enlargement**.*

1) Translations

In a <u>translation</u>, the <u>amount</u> the shape moves by is given as a <u>vector</u> (see p.147-148) written $\begin{pmatrix} x \\ y \end{pmatrix}$ — where x is the <u>horizontal movement</u> (i.e. to the <u>right</u>) and y is the <u>vertical movement</u> (i.e. <u>up</u>). If the shape moves <u>left and down</u>, x and y will be <u>negative</u>.

EXAMPLE a) **Describe the transformation that maps triangle P onto Q.**
b) **Describe the transformation that maps triangle P onto R.**

a) To get from P to Q, you need to move <u>8 units left</u> and <u>6 units up</u>, so...

The transformation from P to Q is a translation by the vector $\begin{pmatrix} -8 \\ 6 \end{pmatrix}$.

b) The transformation from P to R is a translation by the vector $\begin{pmatrix} 0 \\ 7 \end{pmatrix}$.

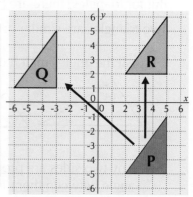

2) Rotations

To describe a <u>rotation</u>, you must give <u>3 details</u>:

1) The <u>angle of rotation</u> (usually 90° or 180°).

2) The <u>direction of rotation</u> (clockwise or anticlockwise). ◄

3) The <u>centre of rotation</u> (often, but not always, the origin).

For a rotation of 180°, it doesn't matter whether you go clockwise or anticlockwise.

EXAMPLE a) **Describe the transformation that maps triangle A onto B.**
b) **Describe the transformation that maps triangle A onto C.**

a) The transformation from A to B is a rotation of <u>90°</u> <u>anticlockwise</u> about the <u>origin</u>.

b) The transformation from A to C is a rotation of <u>180°</u> clockwise (or anticlockwise) about the <u>origin</u>.

If it helps, you can use tracing paper to help you find the centre of rotation.

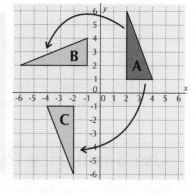

3) Reflections

For a <u>reflection</u>, you must give the <u>equation</u> of the <u>mirror line</u>.

EXAMPLE

a) **Describe the transformation that maps shape D onto shape E.**
b) **Describe the transformation that maps shape D onto shape F.**

a) The transformation from D to E is a reflection in the y-axis.

b) The transformation from D to F is a reflection in the line $y = x$.

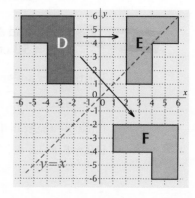

A rotation is specified by an angle, a direction and a centre

Shapes are <u>congruent</u> under translation, reflection and rotation — this is because their <u>size</u> and <u>shape</u> don't change, just their position and orientation. Now have a go at this Exam Practice Question:

Q1   On a grid, copy shape D above and rotate it 90° clockwise about the point (–1, –1).   [2 marks]

The Four Transformations

*One more transformation coming up — **enlargements**. They're the trickiest, but also the most interesting.*

4) Enlargements

For an <u>enlargement</u>, you must specify:

1) The <u>scale factor</u>. ◄——
2) The <u>centre of enlargement</u>.

$$\text{scale factor} = \frac{\text{new length}}{\text{old length}}$$

1) The <u>scale factor</u> for an enlargement tells you <u>how long</u> the sides of the new shape are compared to the old shape. E.g. a scale factor of 3 means you <u>multiply</u> each side length by 3.

2) If you're given the <u>centre of enlargement</u>, then it's vitally important <u>where</u> your new shape is on the grid.

> The <u>scale factor</u> tells you the **RELATIVE DISTANCE** of the
> old points and new points from the <u>centre of enlargement</u>.

So, a <u>scale factor of 2</u> means the corners of the enlarged shape are <u>twice</u>
<u>as far from the centre of enlargement</u> as the corners of the original shape.

Describing Enlargements

EXAMPLE   **Describe the transformation that maps Triangle A onto Triangle B.**

Use the formula to find the <u>scale factor</u>. (Just do this for one pair of sides.)

Old length of triangle base = 3 units
New length of triangle base = 6 units

$$\text{Scale factor} = \frac{\text{new length}}{\text{old length}} = \frac{6}{3} = 2$$

To find the <u>centre of enlargement</u>, draw <u>lines</u> that go through
<u>matching corners</u> of both shapes and see where they <u>cross</u>.

So the transformation is an enlargement of scale factor 2, centre (2, 6).

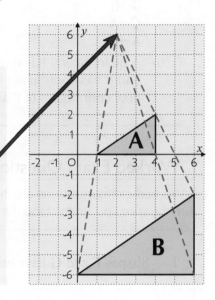

Fractional Scale Factors

1) If the scale factor is <u>bigger than 1</u> the <u>shape gets bigger</u>.

2) If the scale factor is <u>smaller than 1</u> (e.g. ½) it <u>gets smaller</u>.

EXAMPLE   **Enlarge the shaded shape by a scale factor of $\frac{1}{2}$, about centre 0.**

1) <u>Draw lines</u> going from the <u>centre</u> to <u>each corner</u> of the original shape. The corners of the new shape will be on these lines.

2) The scale factor is $\frac{1}{2}$, so make <u>each corner</u> of the new shape <u>half as far</u> from 0 as it is in the original shape.

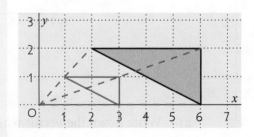

An enlargement is given by a scale factor and a centre of enlargement

Shapes are <u>similar</u> under enlargement — the position and the size change, but the angles and ratios of the sides don't (see p.107). A scale factor smaller than 1 means the shape gets smaller.

Q1   On a grid, draw triangle A with vertices (2, 1), (4, 1) and (4, 3), and triangle B with vertices (3, 1), (7, 1) and (7, 5). Describe the transformation that maps A to B.   [4 marks]

Q1 Video
Solution

Warm-up and Worked Exam Questions

Nothing too tricky so far in this section. Now it's time for some warm-up questions to get your brain ticking — before moving on to the exam-style questions. It's all good practice for the big day.

Warm-up Questions

1) Copy the letters, mark in their lines of symmetry and give their order of rotational symmetry:

2) Give all the properties of an equilateral triangle.

3) How many lines of symmetry does a kite have?

4) Which two of these shapes are: a) similar?   b) congruent?

5) Describe fully these 4 transformations, as shown on the grid:
   A→B
   B→C
   C→A
   A→D

6) A quadrilateral has vertices PQRS, where P has coordinates (3, 4) and R has coordinates (5, −1). The quadrilateral is translated, and the new coordinates of P are (7, 2). What are the new coordinates of R?

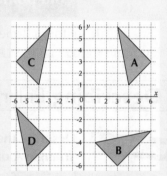

Worked Exam Question

Worked exam questions are the ideal way to get the hang of answering the real exam questions — make sure you understand the answer to this one.

1 Shapes **F** and **G** have been drawn on the grid below. ③

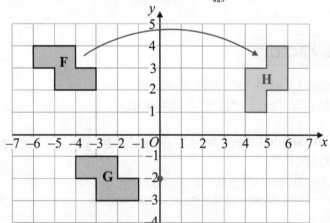

a) Write down the vector which describes the translation that maps **F** onto **G**.

To get from F to G, the shape is moved 2 units to the right and 5 units down.

$\begin{pmatrix} 2 \\ -5 \end{pmatrix}$

[2 marks]

b) Rotate shape **F** by 90° clockwise about the point (0, −2).
Label your image **H**.

See the grid above — you might find it easiest to use tracing paper to draw rotations.

[2 marks]

Exam Questions

2   An isosceles triangle has vertices A(1, 1), B(3, 7) and C(5, 1).
    Give the equation of its line of symmetry.   (2)

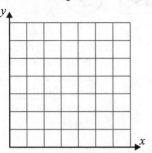

....
[1 mark]

3   Triangle **A** has been drawn on the grid below.
    Reflect triangle **A** in the line $x = -1$. Label your image **B**.   (3)

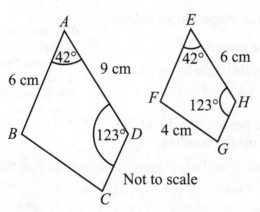

[2 marks]

4   The shapes *ABCD* and *EFGH* are mathematically similar.   (4)

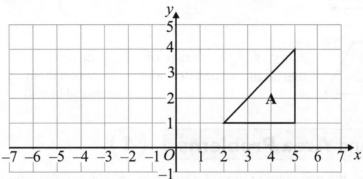

Not to scale

a) Find the length of *EF*.

.... cm
[2 marks]

b) Find the length of *BC*.

.... cm
[1 mark]

5   On the grid enlarge the triangle by a scale factor of 3, centre (–4, 0).   (4)

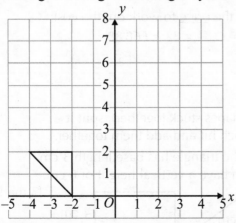

[3 marks]

Perimeter and Area

*Perimeter is the **distance** around the outside of a shape. **Area** is a bit trickier — you need to learn some formulas. You should already know that the area of a **rectangle** is A = l × w and the area of a **square** is A = l².*

Area Formulas for Triangles and Quadrilaterals

<u>Learn</u> these formulas:

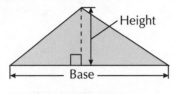

<u>Area of triangle</u> = ½ × base × vertical height

$$A = ½ × b × h$$

Note that in each case the height must be the <u>vertical height</u>, not the sloping height.

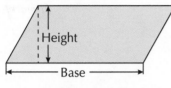

<u>Area of parallelogram</u> = base × vertical height

$$A = b × h$$

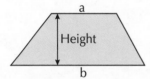

<u>Area of trapezium</u> = average of parallel sides × distance between them (vertical height)

$$A = ½(a + b) × h$$

Perimeter and Area Problems

You might have to <u>use</u> the perimeter or area of a shape to answer a <u>slightly more complicated</u> question (e.g. find the area of a wall, then work out how many rolls of wallpaper you need to wallpaper it).

EXAMPLE **Huda is making a stained-glass window in the shape shown below.**

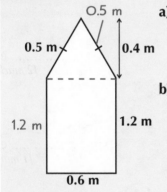

a) **Find the perimeter of the window.**

<u>Label</u> all the side lengths, then <u>add</u> them up:
0.5 m + 1.2 m + 0.6 m + 1.2 m + 0.5 m = 4 m

When you're adding side lengths it's a good idea to <u>mark them off</u> as you go along to make sure you don't repeat or miss any.

b) **Coloured glass costs £82 per m². Work out the cost of the glass needed for the window.**

Split the shape into a <u>triangle</u> and a <u>rectangle</u> (as shown) to find the area:
Area of rectangle = length × width = 0.6 × 1.2 = 0.72 m²
Area of triangle = $\frac{1}{2}$ × base × height = $\frac{1}{2}$ × 0.6 × 0.4 = 0.12 m²
Total area of shape = 0.72 + 0.12 = <u>0.84 m²</u>

Then <u>multiply</u> the <u>area</u> by the <u>price</u> to work out the cost:
Cost = area × price per m² = 0.84 × 82 = £68.88

Learn the area formulas

If you have a composite shape (a shape made up of different shapes stuck together), split it into triangles and quadrilaterals. Then, work out the area of each bit and add them together.

Q2 Video Solution

Q1 A shape is made up of a triangle and a parallelogram. The triangle has base length 3 cm and the parallelogram has base length 11 cm. They both have a vertical height of 6 cm. Find the total area of the shape.
[3 marks] (3)

Q2 The triangle and rectangle shown on the right have the same area. Find the value of *x*.
[2 marks] (4)

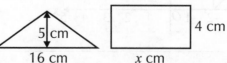

Perimeter and Area — Circles

Another page of formulas, this time on circles. You know the drill — learn all the formulas in boxes on this page.

Area and **Circumference** of **Circles**

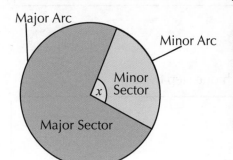

Area of circle = π × (radius)²
Remember that the radius is half the diameter.

Circumference = π × diameter
= 2 × π × radius

Diameter

$$A = \pi r^2$$

$$C = \pi D = 2\pi r$$

For these formulas, use the π button on your calculator. For non-calculator questions, use π ≈ 3.142.

Arc Lengths and Areas of Sectors

These next ones are a bit more tricky — before you try and learn the formulas, make sure you know what a sector and an arc are (I've helpfully labelled the diagram below — I'm nice like that).

Major Arc
Minor Arc
Minor Sector
x
Major Sector

$$\underline{\text{Area of Sector}} = \frac{x}{360} \times \textbf{Area of full Circle}$$

$$\underline{\text{Length of Arc}} = \frac{x}{360} \times \textbf{Circumference of full Circle}$$

You also need to know what a segment, a chord and a tangent are.

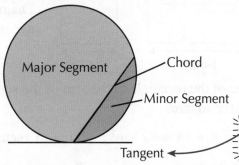

Major Segment
Chord
Minor Segment
Tangent

A tangent just touches one point of the circle.

EXAMPLE **In the diagram on the right, a sector with angle 60° has been cut out of a circle with radius 3 cm. Find the exact area of the shaded shape.**

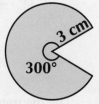

3 cm
300°

Use the formula to find the area of the shaded sector:

area of sector $= \frac{x}{360} \times \pi r^2 = \frac{300}{360} \times \pi \times 3^2$

$= \frac{5}{6} \times \pi \times 9 = \frac{15}{2}\pi$ cm²

'Exact area' means leave your answer in terms of π.

Make sure you know all of these circle terms

One more thing — if you're asked to find the perimeter of a semicircle or quarter circle, don't forget to add on the straight edges too. It's an easy mistake to make, and it'll cost you marks. Now, have a go at this question:

Q1 a) For sector A, find:
     (i) the area. Give your answer in terms of π.   [2 marks]
     (ii) the arc length, to 2 d.p.   [2 marks]
   b) Show that area of sector A is the
     same as the area of sector B.   [2 marks]

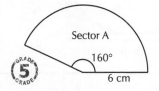

Sector A
160°
6 cm

Sector B
8 cm

Warm-up and Worked Exam Questions

There are lots of formulas in this section. The best way to find out what you know is to practise these questions. If you find you keep forgetting the formulas, you need more practice.

Warm-up Questions

1) Find the perimeter of the shape shown on the right.

2) Give the formulas for:
   a) the area of a rectangle
   b) the circumference of a circle
   c) the area of a parallelogram

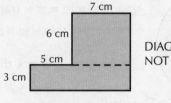

DIAGRAM NOT TO SCALE

7 cm
6 cm
5 cm
3 cm

3) A triangle has a base of 3 m and a vertical height of 7 m. Calculate its area.

4) A woodworking template has the shape shown on the right:
   Calculate the area of the template.

8 cm

5) a) What is a tangent?
   b) Draw a circle and label a tangent.

Worked Exam Questions

Here are two juicy worked exam questions for you. Work through each one step by step.

1   The diagram below shows a rectangle and a square. **④**

 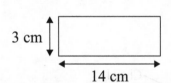

3 cm

14 cm

? cm

Diagram not accurately drawn

The ratio of the area of the rectangle to the area of the square is 6:7.
What is the area of the square?

Area of rectangle = 3 × 14 = 42 cm²

See p.79 for more on scaling up ratios.

area of rectangle : area of square
                    6:7
(×7)   42:49   (×7)
So area of the square = 49 cm²

..........49.......... cm²
[2 marks]

2   The diagram below shows a square with a circle inside. The circle touches each of the four sides of the square. Calculate the shaded area. Give your answer to 2 d.p. **④**

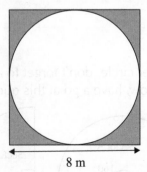

8 m

Area of square = 8 × 8 = 64 m²
Area of circle = π × 4² = 50.2654... m²
Shaded area = 64 − 50.2654...
            = 13.7345... m²

..........13.73.......... m²
[3 marks]

Exam Questions

3   A shape is made up from an isosceles triangle and a trapezium.

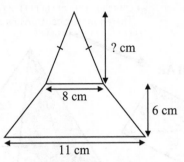

? cm

8 cm

6 cm

11 cm

Diagram not
accurately drawn

The area of the trapezium is 3 times as big as
the area of the triangle.

a)   Find the total area of the shape.

.... cm²
[3 marks]

b)   Find the height of the triangle.

.... cm
[2 marks]

4   The diagram below shows a rectangle with a right-angled triangle inside.

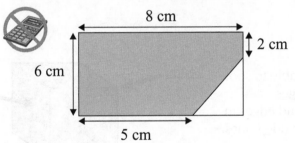

8 cm

2 cm

6 cm

5 cm

Calculate the area of the shaded part.

.... cm²
[4 marks]

5   Look at the sector shown in the diagram below.

Diagram not
accurately drawn

30°

6 cm

Find the perimeter and the area of the sector.
Give your answers to 3 significant figures.

Don't forget to add
the two radii to the
arc length when
finding the perimeter.

Perimeter = ... cm

Area = ... cm²
[5 marks]

3D Shapes

*First up are some **3D shapes** for you to learn, closely followed by a look at the **different parts of solids**.*

Eight **Solids** to Learn

3D shapes are solid shapes. These are the ones you need to know:

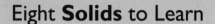

There's more about prisms on p.118.

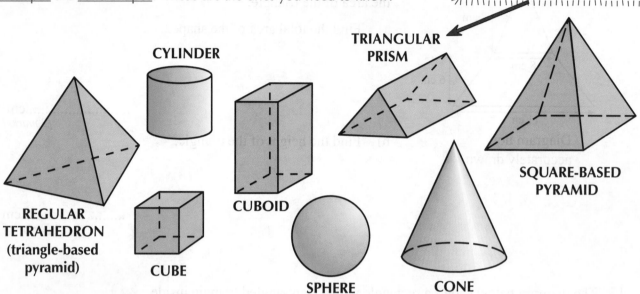

CYLINDER

TRIANGULAR PRISM

SQUARE-BASED PYRAMID

REGULAR TETRAHEDRON (triangle-based pyramid)

CUBE

CUBOID

SPHERE

CONE

Different Parts of Solids

There are different parts of 3D shapes you need to be able to spot. These are <u>vertices</u> (corners), <u>faces</u> (the flat bits) and <u>edges</u>. You might be asked for the <u>number</u> of vertices, faces and edges in the exam — just <u>count</u> them up, and don't forget the <u>hidden</u> ones.

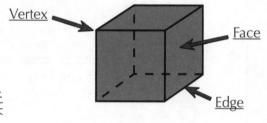

<u>Vertex</u>

<u>Face</u>

<u>Edge</u>

Faces (especially curved faces) are sometimes called surfaces.

EXAMPLE

For the triangular prism on the right, write down the number of faces, the number of edges and the number of vertices.

A triangular prism has **5 faces** (there are three rectangular faces and two triangular ones).

It has **9 edges** (there are 3 hidden ones — the dotted lines in the diagram).

It has **6 vertices** (there's one hidden at the back).

Make sure you can spot the vertices, faces and edges of 3D shapes

Remember — 1 vertex, 2 vertices. They're funny words, designed to confuse you, so don't let them catch you out. You need to know the names of all the solid shapes above too.

Q1   a)   Write down the mathematical name of the shape on the right.   [1 mark]

      b)   Write down: (i)   the number of faces   [1 mark]

                 (ii)   the number of edges   [1 mark]

                 (iii)   the number of vertices   [1 mark]

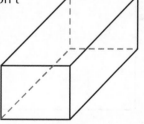

3D Shapes — Surface Area

*Surface area is like normal area but for 3D shapes — for some shapes you can use **2D areas** and add them up, for others there are special **formulas** you'll need to use.*

Surface Area using Nets

1) <u>SURFACE AREA</u> only applies to 3D objects — it's just the <u>total area</u> of all the <u>faces</u> added together.

2) <u>SURFACE AREA OF A SOLID = AREA OF THE NET</u> (remember that a <u>net</u> is just a <u>3D shape</u> folded out flat). So if it helps, imagine (or sketch) the net and add up the area of <u>each bit</u>.

EXAMPLE **Find the surface area of the square-based pyramid below.**

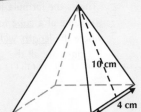

Sketch the net — a square-based pyramid has <u>1 square face</u> and <u>4 triangular faces</u>.

Area of square face = 4 × 4 = 16 cm²
Area of triangular face = ½ × 4 × 10 = 20 cm²
Total surface area = 16 + (4 × 20) = 16 + 80 = 96 cm²

Surface Area Formulas

1) <u>SPHERES, CONES AND CYLINDERS</u> have surface area formulas that you need to be able to use.

2) Luckily you <u>don't</u> need to memorise the <u>sphere</u> and <u>cone</u> formulas — you'll be given them in your exam.

3) But you must get <u>lots of practice</u> using them, or you might slip up when it comes to the exam.

Surface area of a SPHERE = $4\pi r^2$

curved area of cone (l is the slant height)   area of circular base

Surface area of a CONE = $\pi r l + \pi r^2$

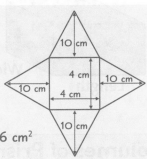

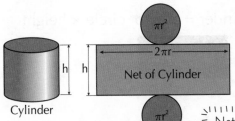

Net of Cylinder

Cylinder

Surface area of a CYLINDER = $2\pi rh + 2\pi r^2$

Note that the <u>length of the rectangle</u> is equal to the <u>circumference</u> of the circular ends.

EXAMPLE **Find the surface area of the cylinder on the right to 1 d.p.**

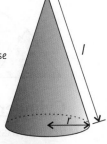

Just put the <u>measurements</u> into the <u>formula</u> and work it out very carefully in stages:

Surface area of cylinder = $2\pi rh + 2\pi r^2$
= (2 × π × 1.5 × 5) + (2 × π × 1.5²)
= 47.123... + 14.137... = 61.261... = 61.3 cm²

To find the surface area of a solid, add up the area of each face

Use nets to find surface area — they make it easier to see each face and work out the area.
Once you're familiar with the formulas on this page, get some practice with these questions.

Q1   Find the surface area of the cone on the right.   [3 marks]

Q2   Find the radius of a sphere with surface area of 196π cm².   [2 marks]

3D Shapes — Volume

*You've already had a couple of pages on 3D shapes — now it's time to work out their **volumes**.*

LEARN these volume formulas...

Volumes of Cuboids

A <u>cuboid</u> is a <u>rectangular block</u>. Finding its volume is dead easy:

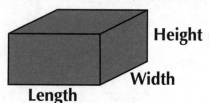

Height
Width
Length

Volume of Cuboid = length × width × height

$$V = L \times W \times H$$

This is the formula for the volume of a <u>cube</u> too — where the <u>length</u>, <u>width</u> and <u>height</u> are all the <u>same</u>.

Volumes of Prisms

A <u>PRISM</u> is a solid (3D) object which is the <u>same shape</u> all the way through — i.e. it has a <u>CONSTANT AREA OF CROSS-SECTION</u>.

Triangular Prism

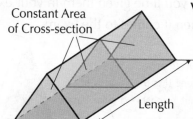

Constant Area of Cross-section

Length

Volume of Prism = cross-sectional area × length

$$V = A \times L$$

This formula works for <u>any</u> prism.

Cylinder
(circular prism)

h

Constant Area of Cross-section

r

Volume of Cylinder = area of circle × height

$$V = \pi r^2 h$$

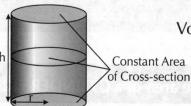

EXAMPLE **Honey comes in cylindrical jars with radius 4.5 cm and height 12 cm. Dan has a recipe that needs 1 litre of honey. How many jars should he buy?**

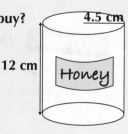

4.5 cm

12 cm

Honey

First, work out the <u>volume</u> of the jar — just use the <u>formula</u> above:

$V = \pi r^2 h = \pi \times 4.5^2 \times 12$
$= 763.4070... \text{ cm}^3$

1 litre = 1000 cm³ (see p.95), so he needs to buy **2 jars of honey**.

You have to remember what a prism is

You might get a question where you're given a shape made up of 1 cm cubes and asked for its volume. All you have to do here is count up the cubes (not forgetting any hidden ones at the back of the shape). Have a go at this Exam Practice Question — you'll need your area formulas from p.112.

Q1 Find the volume of the triangular prism on the right. [3 marks]

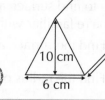

10 cm
12 cm
6 cm

3D Shapes — Volume

Another page on volumes now — my generosity knows no limits.

Volumes of **Spheres**

$$\text{Volume of Sphere} = \frac{4}{3}\pi r^3$$

A <u>hemisphere</u> is half a sphere. So the volume of a hemisphere is just half the volume of a full sphere, $V = \frac{2}{3}\pi r^3$.

Volumes of **Pyramids** and **Cones**

A pyramid is a shape that goes from a <u>flat base</u> up to a <u>point</u> at the top. Its base can be any shape at all.

 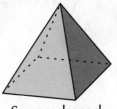

Cone   Square-based Pyramid

$$\text{Volume of Pyramid} = \frac{1}{3} \times \text{Base Area} \times \text{Vertical Height}$$
$$\text{Volume of Cone} = \frac{1}{3} \times \pi r^2 \times h$$

Make sure you use the <u>vertical height</u> in these formulas — don't get confused with the <u>slant height</u>, which you used to find the <u>surface area</u> of a cone.

Volumes of **Frustums**

A <u>frustum of a cone</u> is what's left when the top part of a cone is cut off parallel to its circular base. You'll be given the formula for the <u>volume</u> of a <u>cone</u> in your exam, but you'll need to remember:

This bit is the frustum

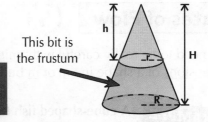

$$\begin{array}{ccc} \text{VOLUME OF} & = & \text{VOLUME OF} & - & \text{VOLUME OF} \\ \text{FRUSTUM} & & \text{ORIGINAL CONE} & & \text{REMOVED CONE} \end{array}$$

EXAMPLE

A waste paper basket is the shape of a frustum formed by removing a cone of height 10 cm from a cone of height 50 cm and radius 35 cm. Find the volume of the waste paper basket to 3 significant figures.

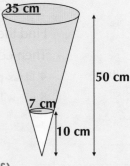

Use the <u>formula</u> for the <u>volume of a cone</u> above:

Volume of original cone = $\frac{1}{3} \times \pi \times 35^2 \times 50 = 64140.850...\ \text{cm}^3$

Volume of removed cone = $\frac{1}{3} \times \pi \times 7^2 \times 10 = 513.126...\ \text{cm}^3$

Volume of frustum = $64140.850... - 513.126... = 63627.723... = 63\,600\ \text{cm}^3$ (3 s.f.)

Remember, a frustum is just a cone with the top chopped off

The frustum formula makes sense when you think about it — if you subtract the volume of the removed cone from the original volume, you're left with the volume of the bit at the bottom. Try it on this question:

Q1   A cone has radius 12 m and vertical height 18 m. A cone 3 m high with a radius of 2 m is cut off the cone to make a frustum. Find the volume of the frustum, leaving your answer in terms of π.   [4 marks]

Q1 Video Solution

Trickier Volume Problems

*You might get a question asking you something a little more challenging than just finding the volume — this page will talk you through a couple of **trickier types** of volume question.*

Ratios of Volumes

1) You might need to look at how the <u>volumes</u> of different shapes are linked.

2) So you could be given two shapes and have to show <u>how many times bigger</u> one volume is than the other, or you might need to show the <u>ratio</u> of their volumes:

> 1) Work out each volume <u>separately</u> — make sure the <u>units</u> are the <u>same</u>.
> 2) Write the volumes as a <u>ratio</u> and <u>simplify</u>.

EXAMPLE **The cone in the diagram has a radius of 5 cm and a height of 12 cm. The sphere has a radius of 15 cm. Find the ratio of their volumes in its simplest form.**

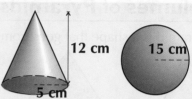

Put the numbers into the <u>volume formulas</u> (see p.119):

Volume of cone $= \frac{1}{3} \times \pi r^2 \times h = \frac{1}{3} \times \pi \times 5^2 \times 12 = \frac{1}{3} \times \pi \times 300 = 100\pi$ cm^3

Volume of sphere $= \frac{4}{3} \pi r^3 = \frac{4}{3} \times \pi \times 15^3 = \frac{4 \times 3375}{3} \times \pi = 4500\pi$ cm^3

When comparing volumes, it's usually best to leave your answers in terms of π.

Find the <u>ratio</u> of the volumes and <u>simplify</u>:   volume of cone : volume of sphere

$$\div 100\pi \underbrace{\overset{100\pi : 4500\pi}{1:45}} \div 100\pi$$

Rates of Flow

You need to be really careful with <u>units</u> in rates of flow questions. You might be given the <u>dimensions</u> of a shape in <u>cm</u> or <u>m</u> but the <u>rate of flow</u> in <u>litres</u> (e.g. litres per minute).

EXAMPLE **A cube-shaped fish tank with sides of length 30 cm is being filled with water at a rate of 4 litres per minute. How long will it take to fill the fish tank? Give your answer in minutes and seconds. 1 litre = 1000 cm^3**

Find the <u>volume</u> of the fish tank: V = (side length)^3 = 30^3 = 27 000 cm^3

Then convert the <u>rate of flow</u> into cm^3/minute — <u>multiply</u> by 1000:

4 litres per minute = 4 × 1000 = 4000 cm^3/min

So it will take 27 000 ÷ 4000 = 6.75 minutes

= 6 minutes and 45 seconds to fill the fish tank.

Leave volumes in terms of π when comparing them

Sorry, this page is a rotten one. When dealing with rates of flow, you might need to convert the rate of flow so its units match the volume (e.g. m^3/s), then use this to find your answer.

Q1   A sphere has a radius of 3 cm. A cylinder has a radius of 6 cm and a height of 10 cm. Show that the volume of the cylinder is 10 times as big as the volume of the sphere.   [3 marks]

Q2   A square-based pyramid with base sides of length 60 cm and height 110 cm is being filled with water at a rate of 100 cm^3 per second. Does it take longer than 20 minutes to fill?   [3 marks]

Projections

Projections are just different **views** of a 3D solid shape — looking at it from the **front**, the **side** and the **top**.

The Three Different **Projections**

There are three different types of projections — front elevations, side elevations and plans (elevation is just another word for projection).

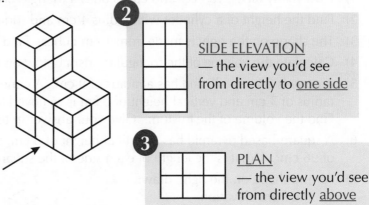

1 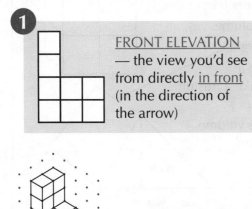 FRONT ELEVATION — the view you'd see from directly in front (in the direction of the arrow)

2 SIDE ELEVATION — the view you'd see from directly to one side

3 PLAN — the view you'd see from directly above

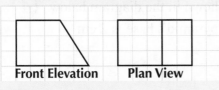 Don't be thrown if you're given a diagram on isometric (dotty) paper like this — it works in just the same way. If you have to draw shapes on isometric paper, just join the dots. You should only draw vertical and diagonal lines (no horizontal lines).

Drawing Projections

EXAMPLES

1. The front elevation and plan view of a shape are shown below. Sketch the solid shape.

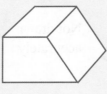
Front Elevation   **Plan View**

Just piece together the original shape from the information given — here you get a prism in the shape of the front elevation.

2. a) On the cm square grid, draw the side elevation of the prism from the direction of the arrow.

b) Draw a plan of the prism on the grid.

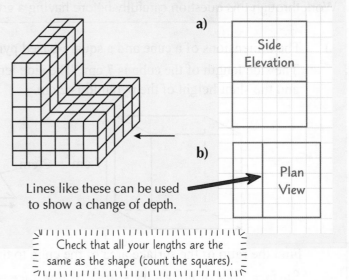

Lines like these can be used to show a change of depth.

a) Side Elevation

b) Plan View

Check that all your lengths are the same as the shape (count the squares).

You need to know the three different types of projection

Projection questions aren't too bad — just take your time and sketch the diagrams carefully. Watch out for questions on isometric paper — they may look confusing, but can actually be easier than other questions.

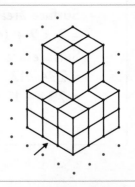

Q1 For the shape on the right, draw:
a) The front elevation (from the direction of the arrow),   [1 mark]
b) The side elevation,   [1 mark]
c) The plan view.   [1 mark]

Warm-up and Worked Exam Questions

Turns out there's lots to know about 3D shapes. If you have any problems doing these warm-up questions, look back over anything you're unsure of before tackling the exam questions.

Warm-up Questions

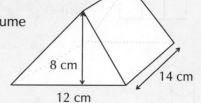

1) How many faces, vertices and edges does a triangle-based pyramid have?
2) Find the height of a cylinder with radius 4 cm and surface area 64π cm².
3) The shape on the right is made from 1 cm cubes. Find its volume.
4) Calculate the volume of the triangular prism below on the right.
5) A cone is 24 cm tall, and has a radius of 9 cm. A cone with a radius of 3 cm and vertical height of 8 cm is removed to make a frustum. Find the volume of the frustum. Give your answer in terms of π.
6) A square-based pyramid has a vertical height of 8 cm, and a volume of 96 cm³. What is the length of each side of the square base?
7) For the shape on the right, draw:
   a) the front elevation
      (from the direction of the arrow)
   b) the side elevation
   c) the plan view.

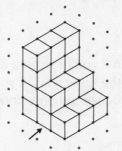

8 cm

12 cm

14 cm

Worked Exam Question

Work through this question carefully before having a go at the exam questions.

1   The dimensions of a cube and a square-based pyramid are shown in the diagram below. **(4)** **GRADE**
    The side length of the cube is 7 cm. The side length of the pyramid's base is 2 cm
    and the slant height of the pyramid is 2 cm.

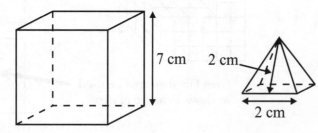

7 cm   2 cm

Not drawn accurately

2 cm

Find the ratio of the surface area of the cube to the surface area of the pyramid in the form $n:1$.

Surface area of cube = 6 × area of one face = 6 × 7 × 7 = 294 cm²

Surface area of square-based pyramid = area of base + (4 × area of one triangular face)

= 2 × 2 + (4 × ½ × 2 × 2) = 4 + 8 = 12 cm²

Surface area of cube : surface area of pyramid

= 294 : 12

= 294 ÷ 12 : 12 ÷ 12 = 24.5 : 1

Once you've found the surface area of each, set them as a ratio then divide to get the ratio in the form n:1.

24.5 : 1
....
[4 marks]

Exam Questions

2   The diagram below shows the plan view, and the front and side elevations of a shape made from identical cubes.

   Plan view

How many cubes make up the shape?

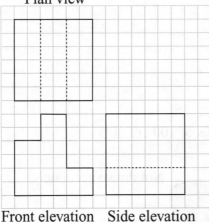

Front elevation   Side elevation

....

[2 marks]

3   The diagram below shows the plan, the front elevation and the side elevation of a prism.

Plan view

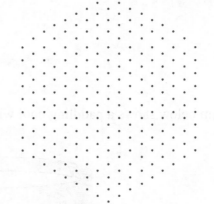

Front elevation   Side elevation

Draw a sketch of the solid prism on the grid below.

[2 marks]

4   Volume of sphere = $\frac{4}{3}\pi r^3$.
Find the volume of the sphere on the right.
Give your answer to 3 significant figures.

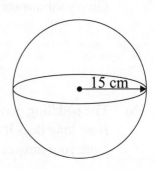

15 cm

.... cm³
[2 marks]

Exam Questions

5   The tank shown in the diagram below is completely filled with water.

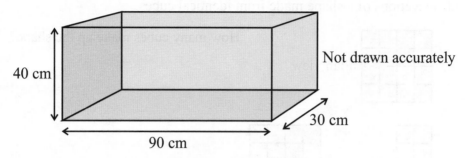

Not drawn accurately

40 cm

90 cm

30 cm

a)   Calculate the volume of water in the tank. ②

.... cm³
[2 marks]

b)   The water from this tank is then poured into a second tank with length 120 cm. ④
The depth of the water is 18 cm. What is the width of the second tank?

.... cm
[2 marks]

6   The diagram below shows a paddling pool with a radius of 100 cm. ⑤

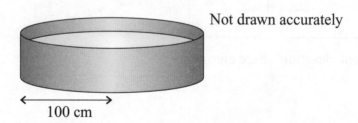

Not drawn accurately

100 cm

a)   What is the volume of water in the paddling pool when it is filled to a depth of 40 cm?
Give your answer in terms of π.

.... cm³
[2 marks]

b)   The paddling pool is filled at a rate of 300 cm³ per second.
How long does it take to fill the pool to a depth of 40 cm?
Give your answer to the nearest minute.

.... minutes
[2 marks]

Revision Questions for Section Five

Now you've finished Section Five, try out your new <u>shape skills</u>...
- Try these questions and <u>tick off each one</u> when you <u>get it right</u>.
- When you're <u>completely happy</u> with a topic, tick that off too.

For even more practice, try the Sudden Fail Quiz for Section Five — just scan this QR code!

Section Five Quiz

2D Shapes (p103-107) ☐

1) For each of the letters shown, write down how many lines of symmetry they have and their order of rotational symmetry. **H Z T N E X S** ☐

2) Write down four properties of an isosceles triangle. ☐

3) How many lines of symmetry does a rhombus have? What is its order of rotational symmetry? ☐

4) What are congruent and similar shapes? ☐

5) Look at the shapes A-G on the right and write down the letters of:
   a) a pair of congruent shapes,
   b) a pair of similar shapes.

6) These two triangles are similar. Write down the values of *b* and *y*. ☐

(A) B (C) (D)
(E) (F) (G)

b° 6 cm   89° 3 cm
8 cm   54°   4 cm   54°
       y cm
37°   10 cm   37°

Transformations (p108-109) ☐

7) Describe the transformation that maps:
   a) Shape A onto shape B
   b) Shape A onto shape C

8) Carry out the following transformations on the triangle X, which has vertices (1, 1), (4, 1) and (2, 3):
   a) a rotation of 90° clockwise about (1, 1)   b) a translation by the vector $\begin{pmatrix} -3 \\ -4 \end{pmatrix}$
   c) an enlargement of scale factor 2, centre (1, 1) ☐

Perimeter and Area (p112-113) ☐

9) Write down the formula for finding the area of a trapezium. ☐
10) Find the area of a parallelogram with base 9 cm and vertical height 4 cm. ☐
11) Find the area of the shape on the right. ☐
12) Find, to 2 decimal places, the area and circumference of a circle with radius 7 cm. ☐
13) Draw a circle and label an arc, a sector, a chord and a segment. ☐
14) Find, to 2 decimal places, the area and perimeter of a quarter circle with radius 3 cm. ☐

3 cm   8 cm
5 cm

3D Shapes — Surface Area, Volume and Projections (p116-121) ☐

15) Write down the number of faces, edges and vertices for the following 3D shapes:
    a) a square-based pyramid   b) a cone   c) a triangular prism ☐

16) Find the surface area of a cube with side length 5 cm. ☐
17) Find, to 1 decimal place, the surface area of a cylinder with height 8 cm and radius 2 cm. ☐
18) Write down the formula for the volume of a cylinder with radius *r* and height *h*. ☐
19) A pentagonal prism has a cross-sectional area of 24 cm² and a length of 15 cm. Find its volume. ☐

20) a) Find the volume of the cylinder on the right (to 2 d.p.).
    b) How long will it take to fill the cylinder with water if the water is flowing at 1.5 litres per minute? Give your answer in seconds to 1 d.p.

9 cm
2 cm

21) On squared paper, draw the front elevation (from the direction of the arrow), side elevation and plan view of the shape on the right. ☐

Angle Basics

*Before we really get going with the thrills and chills of angles and geometry, there are a few things you need to know. Nothing too scary — just some **special angles** and some **fancy notation**.*

Fancy **Angle Names**

Some angles have special names. You might have to <u>identify</u> these angles in the exam.

ACUTE angles

Sharp pointy ones
(less than 90º)

RIGHT angles

Square corners
(exactly 90º)

OBTUSE angles

Flatter ones
(between 90º and 180º)

REFLEX angles

Ones that bend
back on themselves
(more than 180º)

Measuring Angles with a **Protractor**

1) <u>ALWAYS</u> position the protractor with the <u>base line</u> of it along one of the lines as shown here:

2) Count the angle in <u>10° STEPS</u> from the <u>start line</u> right round to the other line over there.

Start line

Check your measurement by looking at it. If it's between a right angle and a straight line, it's between 90° and 180°.

Made in England

<u>DON'T JUST READ A NUMBER OFF THE SCALE</u> — chances are it'll be the wrong one because there are <u>TWO scales</u> to choose from.

The answer here is 135° (NOT 45°) which you will only get right if you start counting 10°, 20°, 30°, 40° etc. from the <u>start line</u> until you reach the <u>other line</u>.

Three-Letter Angle Notation

The best way to say which angle you're talking about in a diagram is by using <u>THREE letters</u>.

For example in the diagram, angle ACB = 25°.

1) The <u>middle letter</u> is where the angle is.
2) The <u>other two letters</u> tell you which two lines enclose the angle.

angle ACD = 20°

You might see angles written in other ways as well — ∠ABC and AB̂C are both the same as angle ABC.

Four fancy angle names to learn — acute, right, obtuse and reflex

In the exams, it's pretty likely that angles will be referred to using three-letter notation — so make sure you know how to use it. And learn the four special angles too. Now have a go at this Exam Practice Question.

Q1　a) An angle measures 66°. What type of angle is this? 　　　　　　　　　[1 mark]
　　　b) Measure ∠ADC on the diagram above. 　　　　　　　　　　　　　　[1 mark]

Five Angle Rules

If you know all these rules thoroughly, you'll at least have a fighting chance of working out problems with lines and angles. If you don't — you've no chance. Sorry to break it to you like that.

5 Simple Rules — that's all

1) Angles in a <u>triangle</u> add up to <u>180°</u>.

$$a + b + c = 180°$$

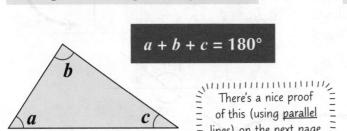

There's a nice proof of this (using <u>parallel lines</u>) on the next page.

2) Angles on a <u>straight line</u> add up to <u>180°</u>.

$$a + b + c = 180°$$

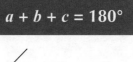
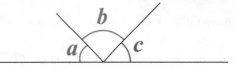

3) Angles in a <u>quadrilateral</u> add up to <u>360°</u>.

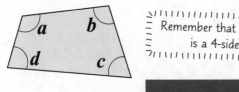

Remember that a quadrilateral is a 4-sided shape.

$$a + b + c + d = 360°$$

4) Angles <u>round a point</u> add up to <u>360°</u>.

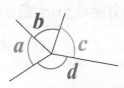

$$a + b + c + d = 360°$$

You can <u>see why</u> this is if you split the quadrilateral into <u>two triangles</u> along a <u>diagonal</u>. Each triangle has angles adding up to 180°, so the two together have angles adding up to 180° + 180° = 360°.

5) <u>Isosceles triangles</u> have <u>2 sides the same</u> and <u>2 angles the same</u>.

In an isosceles triangle, you only need to know <u>one angle</u> to be able to find the other two.

These dashes indicate two sides the same length.

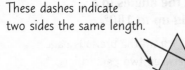
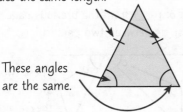

These angles are the same.

EXAMPLE **Find the size of angle x.**

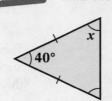

180° − 40° = 140°

<u>The two angles on the right are the same</u> (they're both *x*) and they must add up to 140°, so 2*x* = 140°, which means *x* = 70°.

Five simple rules, make sure you LEARN THEM...

The basic facts are pretty easy really, but examiners like to combine them in questions to confuse you. There are some examples of questions like these on p.129, but have a go at this one as a warm-up.

Q1   Find the size of the angle marked *x*.   [2 marks]

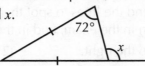

Parallel Lines

*Parallel lines are always the **same distance apart**. This page is all about them.*

Angles Around **Parallel Lines**

You also need to know what <u>perpendicular lines</u> are — they meet at <u>90°</u>.

When a line crosses two <u>parallel lines</u>...

> 1) The two bunches of angles are <u>the same</u>.
> 2) There are <u>only two different angles</u>: <u>a small one</u> and <u>a big one</u>.
> 3) These <u>ALWAYS ADD UP TO 180°</u>. E.g. 30° and 150° below.

The two lines with the <u>arrows</u> on are <u>parallel</u>:

These are <u>vertically opposite</u> angles.
They're equal to each other.

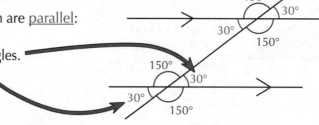

Alternate, **Allied** and **Corresponding** Angles

Watch out for these '<u>Z</u>', '<u>C</u>', '<u>U</u>' and '<u>F</u>' shapes popping up.
They're a dead giveaway that you've got a pair of <u>parallel lines</u>.

Don't call them Z, C, U and F angles in the exam — you'll need to use their proper names.

ALTERNATE ANGLES

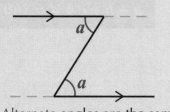

<u>Alternate</u> angles are the <u>same</u>.
They are found in a <u>Z-shape</u>.

ALLIED ANGLES

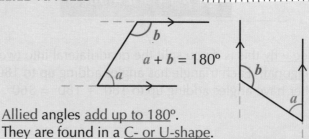

$a + b = 180°$

<u>Allied</u> angles <u>add up to 180°</u>.
They are found in a <u>C-</u> or <u>U-shape</u>.

CORRESPONDING ANGLES

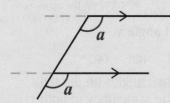

<u>Corresponding</u> angles are the <u>same</u>.
They are found in an <u>F-shape</u>.

EXAMPLE **Prove that the angles in a triangle add up to 180°.**

This is the proof of <u>rule 1</u> from the previous page.
First, draw a <u>triangle</u> between two <u>parallel lines</u>:

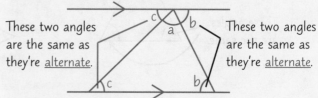

These two angles are the same as they're <u>alternate</u>.

These two angles are the same as they're <u>alternate</u>.

Angles on a straight line add up to 180°,
so $a + b + c = 180°$.

Parallel lines are key things to look out for in geometry

Watch out for Z, C, U and F shapes — extend the lines to spot them more easily.
Learn the proper names — you'll need them in the exam, and in this question here.

Q1 Find the value of x in the diagram to the right. [2 marks]

112°

Q1 Video Solution

Geometry Problems

*As if geometry wasn't enough of a problem already, here's a page dedicated to geometry problems.
Make sure you learn the five angle rules on p.127 — they'll help a lot on these questions.*

Using the **Five Angle Rules**

The best method is to find <u>whatever angles you can</u> until you can work out the ones you're looking for.
It's a bit trickier when you have to use <u>more than one</u> rule, but writing them all down is a big help.

EXAMPLES

1. **Find the value of x.**

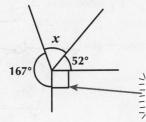

Use rule 4 from p.127:

Angles round a point add up to 360°,

so $x + 52° + 90° + 167° = 360°$

$x = 360° - 52° - 90° - 167° = 51°$

Remember — this little square means that it's a <u>right angle</u> (90°).

2. **Find the size of angle CDE.**

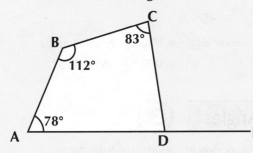

First use rule 3 from p.127:

Angles in a quadrilateral add up to 360°, so the fourth angle in the quadrilateral is
$360° - 78° - 112° - 83° = 87°$

Then use rule 2:
Angles on a straight line add up to 180°.
So $\angle CDE = 180° - 87° = 93°$

Parallel Lines and **Angle Rules**

Sometimes you'll come across questions <u>combining</u> parallel lines and the five angle rules. These look
pretty tricky, but like always, just work out all the angles you can find until you get the one you want.

EXAMPLE   **Find the value of angle x on the diagram below.**

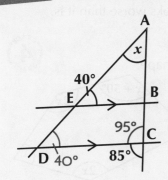

$\angle AEB$ and $\angle ADC$ are corresponding angles, so they are equal. $\angle ADC = 40°$

It's always a good idea to <u>label</u> your diagram as you work out each angle.

Use rule 2 from p.127 to find $\angle ACD$:

Angles on a straight line add up to 180°.
So $\angle ACD = 180° - 85° = 95°$

Use rule 1 to find x:

Angles in a triangle add up to 180°.
So $x = 180° - 95° - 40° = 45°$

The most important rule of all — don't panic

Geometry problems often look a lot worse than they are — don't panic,
just write down everything you can work out. Watch out for hidden parallel
lines and isosceles triangles — they can help you work out angles.

Q1   Find the size of missing angle x.   [2 marks]

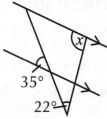

Q1 Video Solution

Polygons

*A polygon is a **many-sided shape**, and can be **regular** or **irregular**. A regular polygon (p.103) is one where all the sides and angles are the **same**. By the end of this page you'll be able to work out the angles in them.*

Exterior and Interior Angles

You need to know <u>what</u> exterior and interior angles are and <u>how to find them</u>.

For <u>ANY POLYGON</u> (regular or irregular):

> **SUM OF EXTERIOR ANGLES = 360°**

> **INTERIOR ANGLE = 180° – EXTERIOR ANGLE**

For <u>REGULAR POLYGONS</u> only:

> **Exterior angle = $\dfrac{360°}{n}$** (n is the number of sides)

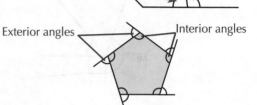

EXAMPLE **Find the exterior and interior angles of a regular octagon.**

Octagons have 8 sides: exterior angle = $\dfrac{360°}{n} = \dfrac{360°}{8} = 45°$

Use the exterior angle to find the interior angle: interior angle = 180° − exterior angle

= 180° − 45° = 135°

The Tricky One — Sum of Interior Angles

This formula for the <u>sum of the interior angles</u> works for <u>ALL</u> polygons, even irregular ones:

> **SUM OF INTERIOR ANGLES = (n – 2) × 180°**

EXAMPLE **Find the <u>sum of the interior angles</u> of the polygon on the right.**

The polygon is a hexagon, so n = 6: Sum of interior angles = (n − 2) × 180°

= (6 − 2) × 180° = 720°

Don't panic if the examiners put algebra in an interior angle question. It looks worse than it is.

EXAMPLE **Find the value of x in the diagram on the right.**

First, find the <u>sum of the interior angles</u> of the 5-sided shape:

Sum of interior angles = (n − 2) × 180°

= (5 − 2) × 180° = 540°

Now write an equation and solve it to find x:

$2x + x + 2x + x + (x + 50°) = 540°$

$7x + 50° = 540° \rightarrow 7x = 490° \rightarrow x = 70°$

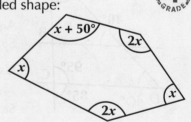

Learn these four important formulas

There are all manner of questions they can ask about angles in polygons, but they all come back to these four formulas — so make sure you've learnt them really well. Then try these lovely questions.

Q1   Find the size of the interior angle of a regular decagon.   [2 marks]

Q2   A regular polygon has exterior angles of 72°.
What is the name of the polygon?   [2 marks]

Warm-up and Worked Exam Questions

Oh look at all those lovely diagrams. But don't just look at them — you need to work through the questions one by one and polish all those geometry skills.

Warm-up Questions

1) Write down one example of:
   a) an acute angle
   b) an obtuse angle
   c) a reflex angle
   d) a right angle.

2) Measure these angles accurately with a protractor:

a)   b)

3) Use a protractor to accurately draw these angles:
   a) 35°   b) 150°   c) 80°

4) Work out angles x and y in the diagram below.

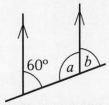

5) The diagram shown below has one angle given as 60°. Find the other two marked angles.

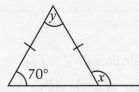

6) Find the sum of the interior angles in a pentagon.

Worked Exam Questions

There'll probably be a question in the exams that asks you to find angles. That means you have to remember all the different angle rules and practise using them in the right places...

1   The diagram to the right is wrong. **(3)** Explain why.

Diagram not accurately drawn

$110° + 170° + 50° + 40° = 370°$

......Angles round a point add up to 360°, so these angles do not fit round the point......

[2 marks]

2   BCD is a triangle. **(3)**
    AD is a straight line.

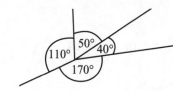

Diagram not accurately drawn

a) Find the value of x.

Angles in a triangle add up to 180°

$2x + 3x + 4x = 180$

So $9x = 180$ and $x = 20$

......$x = 20$......
[2 marks]

b) Find the value of y.

Angles on a straight line add up to 180°

$2x + y = 180$

$40 + y = 180$, so $y = 180 - 40 = 140$

......$y = 140$......
[2 marks]

Exam Questions

3 Find the size of the angle marked *a*. **(3)**
   Give a reason for your answer.

a / 75° Diagram not accurately drawn

....
[2 marks]

4 *ABCD* is a quadrilateral. **(3)**
   Work out the size of angle *ADC*.

A 70° / B / 97° C / D Diagram not accurately drawn

.............................°
[2 marks]

5 Part of a regular polygon is on the right. Each interior angle is 150°. **(3)**

   Calculate the number of sides of the polygon.

150° Diagram not accurately drawn

....
[3 marks]

6 *BD* and *EF* are parallel straight lines. **(4)**
   AH is a straight line.

   Work out the size of angle *x*.

A / D / E / C / 78° / B / *x* / G / H / F Diagram not accurately drawn

.............................°
[2 marks]

7 The irregular polygon below has been divided into triangles as shown. **(4)**

   Use the triangles to show that the sum of the interior angles of the polygon is 900°.

[3 marks]

Triangle Construction

*How you construct a triangle depends on what **info you're given** about the triangle...*

Three sides — Use a **Ruler and Compasses**

EXAMPLE **Construct the triangle ABC where AB = 6 cm, BC = 4 cm and AC = 5 cm.**

1 First, sketch and label a triangle so you know roughly what's needed. It doesn't matter which line you make the base line.

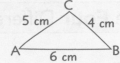

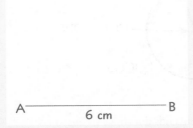

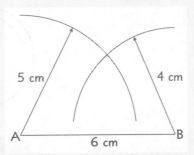

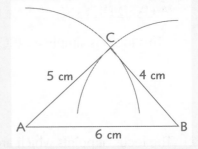

2 Draw the base line. Label the ends A and B.

3 For AC, set the compasses to 5 cm, put the point at A and draw an arc.
For BC, set the compasses to 4 cm, put the point at B and draw an arc.

4 Where the arcs cross is point C. Now you can finish your triangle.

Sides and Angles — use a **Ruler and Protractor**

EXAMPLE **Construct triangle DEF, where DE = 5 cm, DF = 3 cm, and angle EDF = 40°.**

1 Roughly sketch and label the triangle.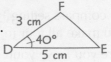

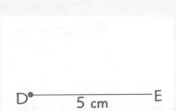

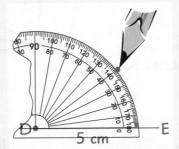

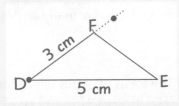

2 Draw the base line.

3 Draw angle EDF (the angle at D) — place the centre of the protractor over D, measure 40° and put a dot.

4 Measure 3 cm towards the dot and label it F. Join up D and F. Now you've drawn the two sides and the angle. Just join up F and E to complete the triangle.

Don't forget your compasses, ruler and protractor for the exam

Constructing a triangle isn't difficult — learn the methods on this page and then try these questions.

Q1 Construct an equilateral triangle with sides of 5 cm. [2 marks]

Q2 Construct a triangle with sides of 3 cm, 4 cm and 6 cm.
Leave visible constructions marks. [2 marks]

Loci and Construction

A **LOCUS** (another ridiculous maths word) is simply:

> ## A LINE or REGION that shows all the points which fit a given rule.

*Make sure you learn how to do these **PROPERLY** using a **ruler** and **compasses** as shown on the next few pages.*

The **Four** Different Types of **Loci**

Loci is just the plural of locus.

1) The locus of points which are '<u>A FIXED DISTANCE from a given POINT</u>'.

   This locus is simply a <u>CIRCLE</u>.

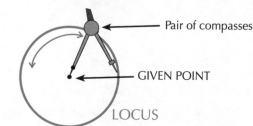

Pair of compasses
GIVEN POINT
LOCUS

2) The locus of points which are '<u>A FIXED DISTANCE from a given LINE</u>'.

   This locus is a <u>SAUSAGE SHAPE</u>.

   It has <u>straight sides</u> (drawn with a <u>ruler</u>) and <u>ends</u> which are <u>perfect semicircles</u> (drawn with compasses).

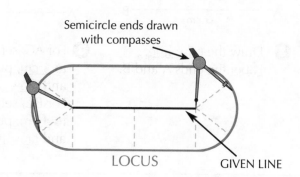

Semicircle ends drawn with compasses
LOCUS
GIVEN LINE

3) The locus of points which are '<u>EQUIDISTANT from TWO GIVEN LINES</u>'.

   1) Keep the compass setting <u>THE SAME</u> while you make <u>all four marks</u>.
   2) Make sure you <u>leave</u> your compass marks <u>showing</u>.
   3) You get <u>two equal angles</u> — i.e. this <u>LOCUS</u> is actually an <u>ANGLE BISECTOR</u>.

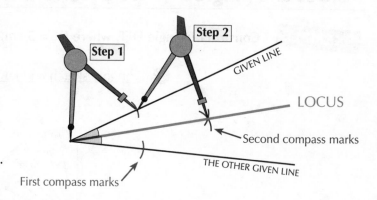

Step 1
Step 2
GIVEN LINE
LOCUS
Second compass marks
THE OTHER GIVEN LINE
First compass marks

4) The locus of points which are '<u>EQUIDISTANT from TWO GIVEN POINTS</u>'.

   <u>This LOCUS</u> is all points which are the <u>same distance</u> from A as they are from B.

   This time the locus is actually the <u>PERPENDICULAR BISECTOR</u> of the line joining the two points.

(In the diagram below, A and B are the two given points.)

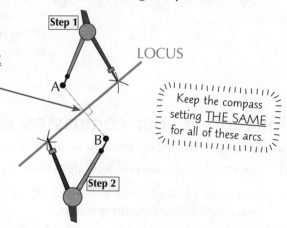

Step 1
LOCUS
A
B
Step 2
Keep the compass setting <u>THE SAME</u> for all of these arcs.

The perpendicular bisector of line segment AB is a line at <u>right angles</u> to AB, passing through the <u>midpoint</u> of AB. This is the method to use if you're asked to draw it.

Loci and Construction

Don't just read the page through once and hope you'll remember it — work through each example and see if you can do each one. It's the only way of testing whether you really know this stuff.

Constructing Accurate **60°** Angles

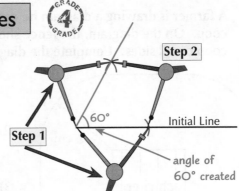

1) They may well ask you to draw an <u>accurate 60° angle</u> without a protractor.

2) <u>Follow the method</u> shown in this diagram (make sure you leave the compass settings the <u>same</u> for each step).

> You can construct 30° angles and 45° angles by <u>bisecting</u> 60° and 90° angles (see previous page).

Step 2

Step 1

60°

Initial Line

angle of 60° created

Constructing Accurate **90°** Angles

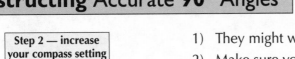

1) They might want you to construct an <u>accurate 90° angle</u>.

2) Make sure you can <u>follow the method</u> shown in this diagram.

Step 2 — increase your compass setting a bit for this step

90° angle created

A specific point

Initial Line

Step 1

> The examiners <u>WON'T</u> accept any of these constructions done 'by eye' or with a protractor. You've got to do them the <u>PROPER WAY</u>, with <u>compasses</u>.
>
> <u>DON'T</u> rub out your compass marks, or the examiner won't know you used the proper method.

Drawing the **Perpendicular** from a **Point** to a **Line**

1) This is similar to the one above but <u>not quite the same</u> — make sure you can do <u>both</u>.

2) You'll be given a line and a point, like this:

A ——————— B

•

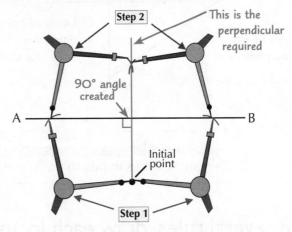

Step 2

This is the perpendicular required

90° angle created

A ——————————— B

Initial point

Step 1

Get out your ruler, pencil and compasses...

...because you'll need them to answer this practice question. And in your exam too, of course.

Q1 Use a ruler and compasses to construct an accurate 60° angle at T.
   Make sure you show all your construction lines.

T ————————————————

[2 marks]

Loci and Construction — Worked Examples

It's not break time just yet — first you should learn how to put those constructions to good use.

EXAMPLES

1. A farmer is drawing a diagram he can use to place a fence around his chicken coop. On the diagram, the fence should be exactly 2 cm from the edge of the coop on all sides. Complete the diagram below using a ruler and compass:

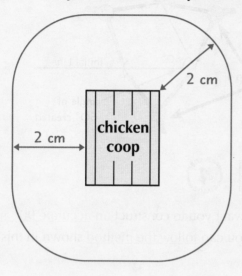

1) Set your compasses to 2 cm.

2) Place the point on each <u>corner</u> and draw a <u>quarter-circle</u> at each one.

3) Draw lines <u>parallel</u> to each edge of the chicken coop 2 cm away, joining up the ends of the quarter-circles.

2. Point P lies somewhere in triangle ABC. Using the following information, a ruler and a compass, shade the area that P could lie in:

   P is at least 4 cm away from A.
   P is closer to B than C.

1) Set your compasses to 4 cm. Place the point on A and draw an <u>arc</u>.

2) Draw the <u>perpendicular bisector</u> of line BC using the method given on page 134.

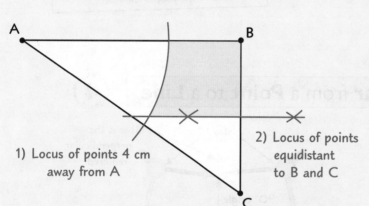

1) Locus of points 4 cm away from A

2) Locus of points equidistant to B and C

3) <u>Shade</u> the area that's at least 4 cm away from A and closer to B than C.

> Always <u>leave your construction lines showing</u>.
> They show the examiner that you used the proper method.

If there are several rules, draw each locus then find the bit you want

Don't panic if you get a wordy loci question — just deal with one condition at a time and work out which bit you need to shade at the end.

Q1 In a stately home, visitors must stay at least 2 m away from the portrait and at least 2 m away from the statue. Make a copy of the diagram using a scale of 1 cm = 1 m and indicate the area where visitors can go. **[4 marks]**

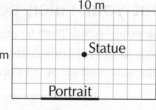

Bearings

Bearings. They'll be useful next time you're off sailing. Or in your Maths exam.

Bearings

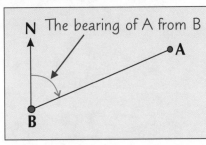

The bearing of A from B

1) A bearing is just a <u>direction</u> given as an <u>angle</u> in degrees.

2) All bearings are measured <u>clockwise</u> from the <u>North line</u>.

3) All bearings are given as <u>3 figures</u>:
e.g. 060° rather than just 60°, 020° rather than 20° etc.

The **3 Key** Words

To find or draw a bearing you must remember <u>three key words</u>:

1) **'FROM'**   <u>Find the word 'FROM' in the question</u>, and put your pencil on the diagram at the point you are going '<u>from</u>'.

2) **NORTH LINE**   At the point you are going <u>FROM</u>, draw in a <u>NORTH LINE</u>.

3) **CLOCKWISE**   Now draw in the angle <u>CLOCKWISE</u> from the <u>NORTH LINE</u> to the <u>line joining the two points</u> — this angle is the <u>bearing</u>.

EXAMPLES

1. Find the bearing of Q from P.

1) 'From P'

2) North line at P

3) <u>Clockwise</u>, from the N-line. This angle is the bearing of <u>Q from P</u>. Measure it with your protractor — **241°**.

2. The bearing of Z from Y is 110°. Find the bearing of Y from Z.

See page 128 for allied angles.

First sketch a diagram so you can see what's going on. Angles a and b are <u>allied</u>, so they add up to <u>180°</u>.

Angle b = 180° − 110° = 70°
So bearing of Y from Z = 360° − 70° = **290°**.

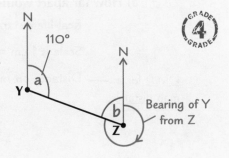

Bearing of Y from Z

From a point draw a North line then draw the angle clockwise

Make sure you've learnt the three key words above and the method for using them — scribble them out from memory to check you know them. You might need to use some of the geometry rules here too.

Q1   Measure the bearing of T from H.   [1 mark] **3**

Q2   A man walks in a straight line from A to B on a bearing of 210°. What bearing should he travel on to walk straight from B to A?   [2 marks] **4**

Maps and Scale Drawings

Scales tell you what a *distance* on a *map* or *drawing* represents in *real life*. *They can be written in various ways, but they all boil down to something like "**1 cm represents 5 km**".*

Map Scales

<u>1 cm = 3 km</u> — "<u>1 cm represents 3 km</u>"

<u>1 : 2000</u> — 1 cm on the map means 2000 cm in real life.
Converting to m gives "<u>1 cm represents 20 m</u>".

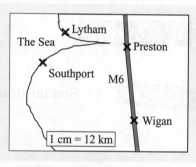 — Use a ruler. The line's 2 cm long, so 2 cm means 1 km.
Dividing by 2 gives "<u>1 cm represents 0.5 km</u>".

To <u>convert</u> between <u>maps</u> and <u>real life</u>, <u>learn</u> these rules:

- Make sure your map scale is of the form "<u>1 cm = ...</u>"
- To find <u>REAL-LIFE</u> distances, <u>MULTIPLY</u> by the <u>MAP SCALE</u>.
- To find <u>MAP</u> distances, <u>DIVIDE</u> by the <u>MAP SCALE</u>.
- Always check your answer looks <u>sensible</u>.

Converting from Map Distance to Real Life — Multiply

EXAMPLE

This map shows the original Roman M6 motorway built by the Emperor Hadrian in the year AD 120. Work out the length of the section of the M6 between Wigan and Preston in km.

1) Measure with a <u>ruler</u>:   Distance on map = 2 cm

2) Read off the <u>scale</u>:   Scale is 1 cm = 12 km

3) For <u>real life</u>, multiply: Real distance is: 2 × 12 = 24 km

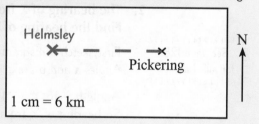

This looks <u>sensible</u> ✓

Converting from Real Life to Map Distance — Divide

EXAMPLE   **Helmsley is 18 km west of Pickering.**

a) How far apart would they be on this map?

Real-life distance = 18 km

Scale is 1 cm = 6 km

<u>Divide</u> for a —— Distance on map = 18 ÷ 6 = 3 cm
<u>map distance</u>.

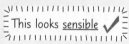
This looks <u>sensible</u> ✓

b) Mark Helmsley on the map.

<u>Measure</u> 3 cm to the <u>west</u> (left) of Pickering:

Helmsley   Pickering

1 cm = 6 km   N ↑

Practise reading scales on any maps you can find

Give these practice questions a go once you're happy with the two formulas and know when to use them.

Q1   Use this map to find the distance between Broughton and Coniston in miles.   [2 marks]

Coniston×   1 cm = 6 miles

×Broughton

Q2   Sarah's house is 2.25 km away from Luke's house. How far apart in cm would they be on a map where 1 cm represents 500 m?   [2 marks]

Q2 Video Solution

Maps and Scale Drawings

Scale Drawings

Scale drawings work just like maps. To convert between real life and scale drawings, just replace the word 'map' with 'drawing' in the rules on the previous page.

EXAMPLE

This is a scale drawing of a room in Ciara's house.
1 cm represents 1.5 m.

a) Find the real length and width of the sofa in m.

1 Measure with a ruler.

Length on drawing = 2 cm

Width on drawing = 0.5 cm

2 Multiply to get real-life length.

Real length = 2 × 1.5 = 3 m

Real width = 0.5 × 1.5 = 0.75 m

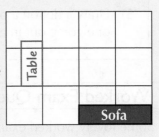

Scale drawings will often be shown on a grid.

b) Ciara's dining table is 90 cm wide and 180 cm long. Draw the table on the scale drawing.

1 Scale uses m, so convert cm to m.

Width = 90 cm = 0.9 m

Length = 180 cm = 1.8 m

2 Divide to get scale drawing length.

Width on drawing = 0.9 ÷ 1.5 = 0.6 cm

Length on drawing = 1.8 ÷ 1.5 = 1.2 cm

3 Draw with a ruler in any sensible position and label.

Map Questions Using Bearings

EXAMPLE

Liam walks 1.2 km from the car park on a bearing of 120°.

a) Mark his position on the map.

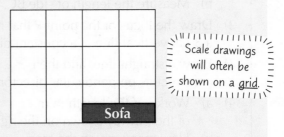

Scale = 1 : 20 000

1 Work out how many km 1 cm represents.

1 cm = 20 000 cm = 200 m = 0.2 km.

So 1 cm = 0.2 km

2 Divide to get distance on map.

Distance walked on map = 1.2 ÷ 0.2

= 6 cm

3 Mark a point 6 cm away, 120° clockwise from the North line.

b) How far is he from the farm in km?

1 Measure distance between Liam and farm.

Distance between Liam and farm = 4 cm

2 For real life, multiply:

Real distance = 4 × 0.2 = 0.8 km

Bearings can crop up in map questions too

You could come across questions which ask you to use maps and bearings. Just remember to measure your angle from the North line. Take a look back at page 137 if you get a bit stuck.

Q1 This is a scale drawing of a park. What does 1 cm represent? Mark on an area of woodland with dimensions 250 m × 300 m. **[3 marks]**

400 m

600 m

Q2

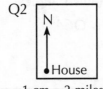

1 cm = 2 miles

A cinema is on a bearing of 035° from Ellie's house and is 3 miles away. Mark the cinema on this map. **[3 marks]**

Warm-up and Worked Exam Questions

Have a go at these warm-up questions to prepare yourself for the exam-style questions coming up.

Warm-up Questions

1) a) Construct a triangle ABC with side AB = 15 cm, side AC = 9 cm and angle BAC = 45°.
    b) Measure the length of side BC.

2) Draw the locus of the point P that moves around
   a 3 cm vertical line at a constant distance of 1 cm.

3) Draw a straight line, and then
   construct its perpendicular bisector.

4) a) Work out the length in m
       of the runway shown on the right:
    b) How many cm on the map
       would a 500 m runway be?

Scale: 1 cm to 200 m

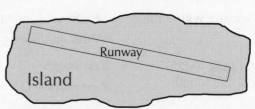

5) Draw a dot on a piece of paper to represent home, and then draw 2 lines,
   one going out in a south-westerly direction and the other on a bearing of 080°.

Worked Exam Questions

Some lovely worked exam questions here before you get into doing the questions yourself.

1   *EFG* is an isosceles triangle. Sides *EG* and *FG* are both 4.5 cm long. **(3)**
    Side *EF* has been drawn on the right.

    a) Complete the construction of triangle *EFG*
       by drawing sides *EG* and *FG*.

       Set the <u>compasses</u> to <u>4.5 cm</u>, put the point at E and
         <u>draw an arc</u>, then do another with the point at F.
            Point G is where they intersect.
                                              [2 marks]

    b) Construct the bisector of angle *EGF*.

       Put the point at G, then <u>draw arcs</u> intersecting EG and FG.
         Keeping the compasses <u>the same</u>, use these intersections to draw
       another two arcs, then join their intersection to G with a <u>straight line</u>.
                                              [2 marks]

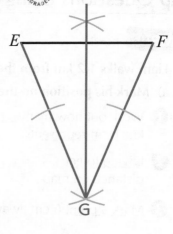

2   Find the bearing of *B* from *A*. **(3)**

       Figure out which angle you need to
       find before starting any calculations.

    360° − 162° − 82° = 116° **(angles round
                               a point)**

    180° − 116° = 64° **(allied angles)**
    Bearing of B from A is 064°.

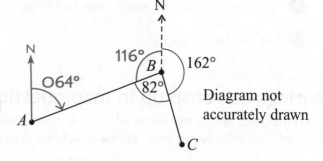

Diagram not
accurately drawn

......064......°

[2 marks]

Exam Questions

3   Zofia drew a scale drawing of one of the rooms in her house.   (2)

a)   Her dining table is 2 m long. What is the scale of this drawing?

1 cm to .... m
[1 mark]

b)   Work out the real distance from the dining table to the shelves.

.... m
[1 mark]

c)   Zofia wants to put a chair measuring 1 m × 1.5 m in the room so that there is a space of at least 0.5 m around it. Is this possible? Give a reason for your answer.

....
[2 marks]

4   Using the diagram below, find the three-figure bearing of Blackburn from Burnley.   (3)

.... °
[1 mark]

5   Ishita cycles in a straight line from *V* to *U*. (3)

Find the bearing on which she travels to get from *V* to *U*.

Diagram not accurately drawn

.... °
[2 marks]

Exam Questions

6   The instructions on a treasure map say "start at the cross and walk 400 metres on a bearing of 150°. Then walk 500 metres on a bearing of 090° to find the treasure."

Using a scale of 1 cm = 100 m, accurately draw the path that must be taken to find the treasure on the map below.

Make sure you draw the North line accurately for the second bearing.

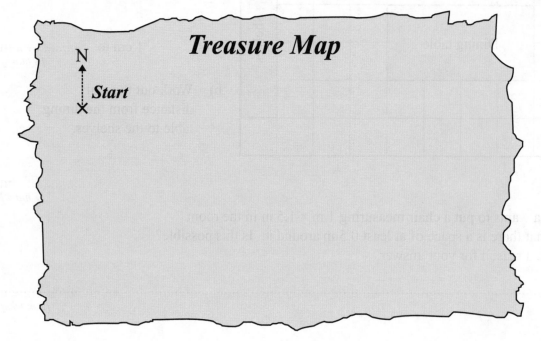

Treasure Map

N

Start

[3 marks]

7   *ABC* is a triangle. (4)

 Find and shade the region inside the triangle which is **both** closer to the line *AB* than the line *BC*, **and** more than 6.5 cm from the point *C*.

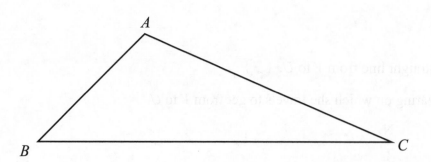

[4 marks]

Pythagoras' Theorem

Pythagoras' Theorem is dead important — make sure you learn how to use it.

Pythagoras' Theorem is Used on Right-Angled Triangles

Pythagoras' theorem only works for <u>RIGHT-ANGLED TRIANGLES</u>.
It uses <u>two sides</u> to find the <u>third side</u>.

The formula for Pythagoras' theorem is:

$$a^2 + b^2 = c^2$$

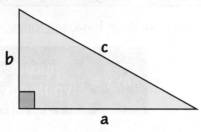

short sides   long side
(hypotenuse)

The trouble is, the formula can be quite difficult to use. <u>Instead</u>, it's a lot better to just <u>remember</u> these <u>three simple steps</u>, which work every time:

1) SQUARE THEM   <u>SQUARE THE TWO NUMBERS</u> that you are given
(use the x^2 button if you've got your calculator).

2) ADD or SUBTRACT   To find the <u>longest side</u>, <u>ADD</u> the two squared numbers. $a^2 + b^2 = c^2$
To find <u>a shorter side</u>, <u>SUBTRACT</u> the smaller from the larger. $c^2 - b^2 = a^2$

3) SQUARE ROOT   Once you've got your answer, take the <u>SQUARE ROOT</u> $c = \sqrt{a^2 + b^2}$
(use the $\sqrt{}$ button on your calculator). $a = \sqrt{c^2 - b^2}$

EXAMPLES

1. Find the length of side PQ in this triangle.

1) <u>Square</u> them: $a^2 = 12^2 = 144$, $b^2 = 5^2 = 25$

2) You want to find the <u>longest side</u>, so <u>ADD</u>: $a^2 + b^2 = c^2$
   $144 + 25 = 169$

3) <u>Square root</u>: $c = \sqrt{169} = 13$ cm

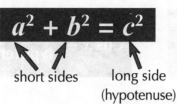

Always check the answer's sensible — 13 cm is longer than the
other two sides, but not too much longer, so it seems OK.

2. Find the length of SU to 1 decimal place.

1) <u>Square</u> them: $b^2 = 3^2 = 9$, $c^2 = 6^2 = 36$

2) You want to find <u>a shorter side</u>, so <u>SUBTRACT</u>: $c^2 - b^2 = a^2$
   $36 - 9 = 27$

3) <u>Square root</u>: $a = \sqrt{27} = 5.196...$
            $= 5.2$ m (to 1 d.p.)

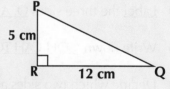

Check the answer is <u>sensible</u> — yes,
it's a bit shorter than the longest side.

Use Pythagoras' theorem to find lengths in right-angled triangles

This is one of the most famous of all maths theorems and it'll probably be in your exam at some point.
You really need to learn the method and practise plenty of questions. So here are two to get you started.

Q1   Look at triangle ABC on the right.
Find the length of side AC correct to 1 decimal place.   [3 marks]

Q2   A 4 m long ladder leans against a wall. Its base is 1.2 m
from the wall. How far up the wall does the ladder reach?
Give your answer to 1 decimal place.   [3 marks]

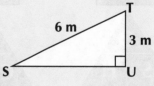

Q2 Video
Solution

Trigonometry — Sin, Cos, Tan

Trigonometry — it's clever stuff. The three trig formulas are used on right-angled triangles to:
a) find an unknown side if you know a side and an angle, or b) find an angle if you know two lengths.

The **3 Trigonometry Formulas**

There are three basic <u>trig formulas</u> — each one links <u>two sides and an angle</u> of a <u>right-angled triangle</u>.

$$\text{Sin } x = \frac{\text{Opposite}}{\text{Hypotenuse}}$$

$$\text{Cos } x = \frac{\text{Adjacent}}{\text{Hypotenuse}}$$

$$\text{Tan } x = \frac{\text{Opposite}}{\text{Adjacent}}$$

- The <u>Hypotenuse</u> is the <u>LONGEST SIDE</u>.
- The <u>Opposite</u> is the side <u>OPPOSITE</u> the angle <u>being used</u> (x).
- The <u>Adjacent</u> is the (other) side <u>NEXT TO</u> the angle <u>being used</u>.

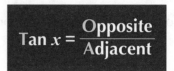

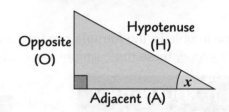

There's more about formula triangles on p.98 if you need to jog your memory.

Formula Triangles Make Things Easier

A great way to tackle trig questions is to convert the formulas into <u>formula triangles</u>.
Then you can use the <u>same method every time</u>, no matter which side or angle is being asked for.

1) <u>Label</u> the three sides <u>O, A and H</u> (Opposite, Adjacent and Hypotenuse).

2) Write down '<u>SOH CAH TOA</u>'.

3) Decide which <u>two sides</u> are <u>involved</u>: O,H A,H or O,A and choose <u>SOH</u>, <u>CAH</u> or <u>TOA</u> accordingly.

4) Turn the one you choose into a <u>FORMULA TRIANGLE</u>:

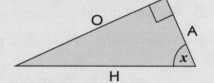

In the formula triangles, S represents sin x, C is cos x, and T is tan x.

5) <u>Cover up</u> the thing you want to find with your finger, and write down whatever is left showing.

6) <u>Stick in the numbers</u> and work it out using the [sin], [cos] and [tan] buttons on your <u>calculator</u>.

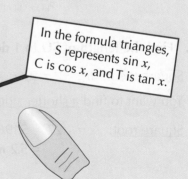

If you're finding an <u>angle</u>, you'll need to add an extra step to find the <u>inverse</u>. See next page.

H = longest, O = opposite, A = next to, and remember SOH CAH TOA

You really need to know all of this stuff off by heart — so go over this page a few more times.
Make sure you've got those formulas firmly lodged in your mind and all ready to reel off in the exam.

Trigonometry — Examples

Here are some lovely examples using the method from the previous page to help you through the trials of trig.

Examples:

1 **Find the length of x in the triangle to the right.**

1) <u>Label</u> the sides

2) <u>Write down</u> — (SOH) CAH TOA

3) <u>O</u> and <u>H</u> involved

4) Write down the <u>formula triangle</u>

5) <u>You want H</u> so <u>cover it up</u> to give — $H = \dfrac{O}{S}$

6) <u>Put in</u> the <u>numbers</u>

 15 ÷ sin 30 =

$x = \dfrac{15}{\sin 30°} = \dfrac{15}{0.5} = 30 \text{ m}$

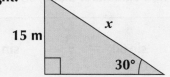

2 **Find the angle x in the triangle to the right.**

1) <u>Label</u> the sides

2) <u>Write down</u> — SOH (CAH) TOA

3) <u>A</u> and <u>H</u> involved

4) Write down the <u>formula triangle</u>

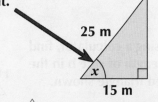

5) You want the <u>angle</u> so <u>cover up C</u> to give — $C = \dfrac{A}{H}$

6) Put in the numbers

 15 ÷ 25 =

$\cos x = \dfrac{15}{25} = 0.6$

7) Find the <u>inverse</u>.

 shift cos 0.6 =

$\Rightarrow x = \cos^{-1}(0.6) = 53.1301...°$
$= 53.1° \text{ (1 d.p.)}$

> When you're finding an <u>angle</u> you'll have to find the <u>INVERSE</u> at the end. Press **SHIFT** or **2ndF**, followed by sin, cos or tan — your calculator will display $\sin^{-1}$, $\cos^{-1}$ or $\tan^{-1}$.

You need to have learnt all seven steps

In example 2 you can see the six steps from the previous page, plus an extra one put into action. Remember — you only need to do step 7 if you're finding an angle. Now use the seven steps to answer these questions.

Q1 Find the length of y and give your answer to 2 decimal places.

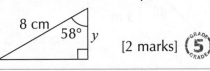

8 cm 58° y

[2 marks]

Q2 Find the value of x and give your answer to 1 decimal place.

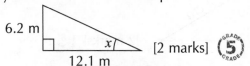

6.2 m x 12.1 m

[2 marks]

Q2 Video Solution

Trigonometry — Common Values

Now that you're in the swing of trigonometry questions it's time to put those calculators away. Sorry.

Learn these **Common Trig Values**

The tables below contain a load of <u>useful trig values</u>. You might get asked to work out some <u>exact</u> trig answers in your non-calculator exam, so having these in your brain will come in handy.

$$\sin 30° = \frac{1}{2} \qquad \sin 60° = \frac{\sqrt{3}}{2} \qquad \sin 45° = \frac{1}{\sqrt{2}}$$

$$\cos 30° = \frac{\sqrt{3}}{2} \qquad \cos 60° = \frac{1}{2} \qquad \cos 45° = \frac{1}{\sqrt{2}}$$

$$\tan 30° = \frac{1}{\sqrt{3}} \qquad \tan 60° = \sqrt{3} \qquad \tan 45° = 1$$

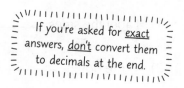
If you're asked for <u>exact</u> answers, <u>don't</u> convert them to decimals at the end.

$$\sin 0° = 0 \qquad \cos 0° = 1 \qquad \tan 0° = 0$$

$$\sin 90° = 1 \qquad \cos 90° = 0$$

Have a look at the <u>examples</u> below —
they might help cement a few values into your head.

EXAMPLES

1. Without using a calculator, find the exact length of side b in the right-angled triangle shown.

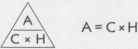

1) It's a right-angled triangle so use SOH CAH TOA to pick the correct <u>trig formula</u> to use.

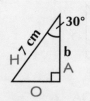 $A = C \times H$

2) Put in the <u>numbers</u> from the diagram in the question.

$$b = \cos 30° \times 7$$

3) You know the <u>value</u> of <u>cos 30°</u>, so <u>substitute</u> this in.

$$b = \frac{\sqrt{3}}{2} \times 7 = \frac{7\sqrt{3}}{2} \text{ cm}$$

2. Without using a calculator, show that $\cos 60° + \sin 30° = 1$

Put in the right values for $\cos 60°$ and $\sin 30°$, then do the sum.

$$\cos 60° = \frac{1}{2} \qquad \sin 30° = \frac{1}{2}$$

$$\cos 60° + \sin 30° = \frac{1}{2} + \frac{1}{2} = 1$$

Learn these common trig values off by heart

There are a lot of angles to learn on this page but you need to know them all. If a trigonometry question asks for an <u>exact</u> answer, you'll need to use them. When you're ready, try this Exam Practice Question.

Q1   Find the exact length of side *x*.   Q2   Find the exact length of side *y*.

[2 marks]

[2 marks]

Vectors — Theory

*Vectors represent a movement of a certain **size** in a certain **direction**.*
They might seem a bit weird at first, but there are really just a few facts to get to grips with...

The Vector **Notations**

There are several ways to <u>write</u> vectors...

They're shown on a diagram by an <u>arrow</u>.

1) <u>Column</u> vectors: $\begin{pmatrix} 2 \\ -5 \end{pmatrix}$ —— 2 units right
—— 5 units down $\begin{pmatrix} -7 \\ 4 \end{pmatrix}$ —— 7 units left
—— 4 units up

2) **a** —— <u>exam questions</u> use <u>bold</u> like this

3) a̰ —— <u>you</u> should always <u>underline</u> them

4) $\overrightarrow{AB}$ —— this means the vector <u>from point A to point B</u>

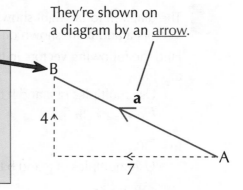

Multiplying a Vector **by a Number**

1) Multiplying a vector by a <u>positive</u> number <u>changes</u> the vector's <u>size</u> but <u>not its direction</u>.

2) If the number's <u>negative</u> then the <u>direction gets switched</u>.

Vectors that are <u>multiples</u> of each other are <u>parallel</u>.

a   2**a**   −1.5**a**

Adding and **Subtracting** Vectors

You can describe movements between points by <u>adding and subtracting known vectors</u>.

"a̰ + b̰" means 'go along a̰ then b̰'.

In the diagrams,
$\overrightarrow{PR}$ = a̰ + b̰ and
$\overrightarrow{XZ}$ = c̰ − d̰.

"c̰ − d̰" means 'go along c̰ then backwards along d̰' (the <u>minus</u> sign means go the <u>opposite</u> way).

When adding <u>column vectors</u>, add the top to the top and the bottom to the bottom. The same goes when subtracting.

$$\begin{pmatrix} 3 \\ -1 \end{pmatrix} + \begin{pmatrix} 5 \\ 3 \end{pmatrix} = \begin{pmatrix} 3+5 \\ -1+3 \end{pmatrix} = \begin{pmatrix} 8 \\ 2 \end{pmatrix}$$

That's three vital vector facts done

But they're only really 'done' if you've learnt them. So be sure you know how vectors can be written, can multiply a vector by a number and can add and subtract vectors. Now have a go at these lovely questions.

Q1   Calculate $\begin{pmatrix} 4 \\ 7 \end{pmatrix} - \begin{pmatrix} 3 \\ 2 \end{pmatrix}$.   [1 mark]

Q2   Find $\overrightarrow{LN}$ on the diagram to the right.   [1 mark]

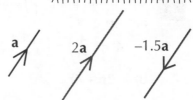

Vectors — Examples

Here's a full page of worked examples to get you in the mood for some tasty vector questions of your own.

Examples

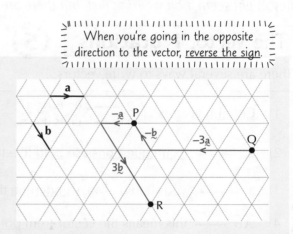

1 The diagram to the right shows an isometric grid. Vectors **a** and **b** are shown on the grid.

Find the following vectors in terms of **a** and **b**:

a) $\overrightarrow{PR}$

Use multiples of $\underset{\sim}{a}$ and $\underset{\sim}{b}$ to get from <u>P to R</u>.

$\overrightarrow{PR} = -\underset{\sim}{a} + 3\underset{\sim}{b}$

b) $\overrightarrow{QP}$

Use multiples of $\underset{\sim}{a}$ and $\underset{\sim}{b}$ to get from <u>Q to P</u>.

$\overrightarrow{QP} = -3\underset{\sim}{a} - \underset{\sim}{b}$

2 Given that $\mathbf{p} = \begin{pmatrix} 4 \\ -1 \end{pmatrix}$ and $\mathbf{r} = \begin{pmatrix} -3 \\ 2 \end{pmatrix}$ find:

a) $4\mathbf{p}$

$4 \times \begin{pmatrix} 4 \\ -1 \end{pmatrix} = \begin{pmatrix} 4 \times 4 \\ 4 \times -1 \end{pmatrix} = \begin{pmatrix} 16 \\ -4 \end{pmatrix}$

b) $-2\mathbf{p} + 4\mathbf{r}$

$-2 \times \begin{pmatrix} 4 \\ -1 \end{pmatrix} + 4 \times \begin{pmatrix} -3 \\ 2 \end{pmatrix} = \begin{pmatrix} -2 \times 4 \\ -2 \times -1 \end{pmatrix} + \begin{pmatrix} 4 \times -3 \\ 4 \times 2 \end{pmatrix}$

$= \begin{pmatrix} -8 \\ 2 \end{pmatrix} + \begin{pmatrix} -12 \\ 8 \end{pmatrix} = \begin{pmatrix} -20 \\ 10 \end{pmatrix}$

3 The diagram to the right shows the vectors $\overrightarrow{BA}$ and $\overrightarrow{AC}$.

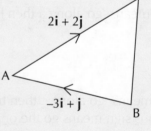

a) Find $\overrightarrow{BC}$ in terms of **i** and **j**.

You need to go from <u>B to A</u>, then from <u>A to C</u>.

$\overrightarrow{BA} = -3\underset{\sim}{i} + \underset{\sim}{j}$

$\overrightarrow{AC} = 2\underset{\sim}{i} + 2\underset{\sim}{j}$

$\overrightarrow{BC} = -3\underset{\sim}{i} + \underset{\sim}{j} + 2\underset{\sim}{i} + 2\underset{\sim}{j}$

$= -\underset{\sim}{i} + 3\underset{\sim}{j}$

b) Alison adds a new line, BD, to the diagram. Given that $\overrightarrow{BD}$ is in the opposite direction to $\overrightarrow{BC}$ and is twice the length of $\overrightarrow{BC}$, find $\overrightarrow{BD}$ in terms of **i** and **j**.

$\overrightarrow{BD}$ is in the <u>opposite</u> direction to $\overrightarrow{BC}$, so <u>reverse</u> the sign. $\longrightarrow \underset{\sim}{i} - 3\underset{\sim}{j}$

$\overrightarrow{BD}$ is also <u>twice</u> the length of $\overrightarrow{BC}$, so <u>multiply by 2</u>. $\longrightarrow 2\underset{\sim}{i} - 6\underset{\sim}{j}$

So $\overrightarrow{BD} = 2\underset{\sim}{i} - 6\underset{\sim}{j}$

You could get similar questions to these on the exam

So learn how to do these types of questions — just use the vectors you're given to find what you're asked for. Test out your vector skills on this practice question.

Q1 Find $\overrightarrow{EF}$ in terms of **p** and **q**. [2 marks]

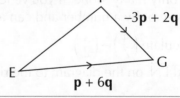

Q1 Video Solution

Warm-up and Worked Exam Questions

There are a lot of different ideas to take in from this mini-section, so here's a bit of a warm-up to get you into the swing of things before the exam questions on the next page.

Warm-up Questions

1) Find the length of the side AB. Give your answer to 1 decimal place.

2) Find the length of z correct to 2 decimal places.

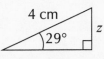

3) Without using a calculator, find the exact length of side x in this triangle.

4) Without a calculator, find the value of $\tan 45° - \cos 60°$.

5) Given that $\mathbf{b} = \begin{pmatrix} -5 \\ 3 \end{pmatrix}$ and $\mathbf{c} = \begin{pmatrix} 1 \\ 6 \end{pmatrix}$ find:

   a) $3\mathbf{b}$ b) $-2\mathbf{c}$ c) $3\mathbf{c} - \mathbf{b}$

6) For the diagram on the right, find $\overrightarrow{EF}$ in terms of $\mathbf{a}$ and $\mathbf{b}$.

Worked Exam Questions

Some more exam questions with the answers written in — just what the doctor ordered.

1   A rectangle has a height of 3 cm and a diagonal length of 5 cm. **(4)**

Calculate the area of the rectangle.

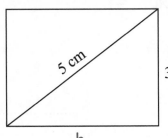

Not to scale

$5^2 = 3^2 + b^2$ ——— Use Pythagoras'
$b^2 = 25 - 9 = 16$ Theorem
$b = \sqrt{16}$
$b = 4$ cm
Area of rectangle = 3 cm × 4 cm
             = 12 cm²

......12..... cm²
[4 marks]

2   The diagram shows a right-angled triangle. **(5)**

Work out the exact length of the side marked y.

You want to find the opposite length, so cover up O.

$y = \tan 60° \times 4$

$y = \sqrt{3} \times 4 = 4\sqrt{3}$ m

 60°   Not drawn accurately

4 m

y

......$4\sqrt{3}$..... m
[2 marks]

Exam Questions

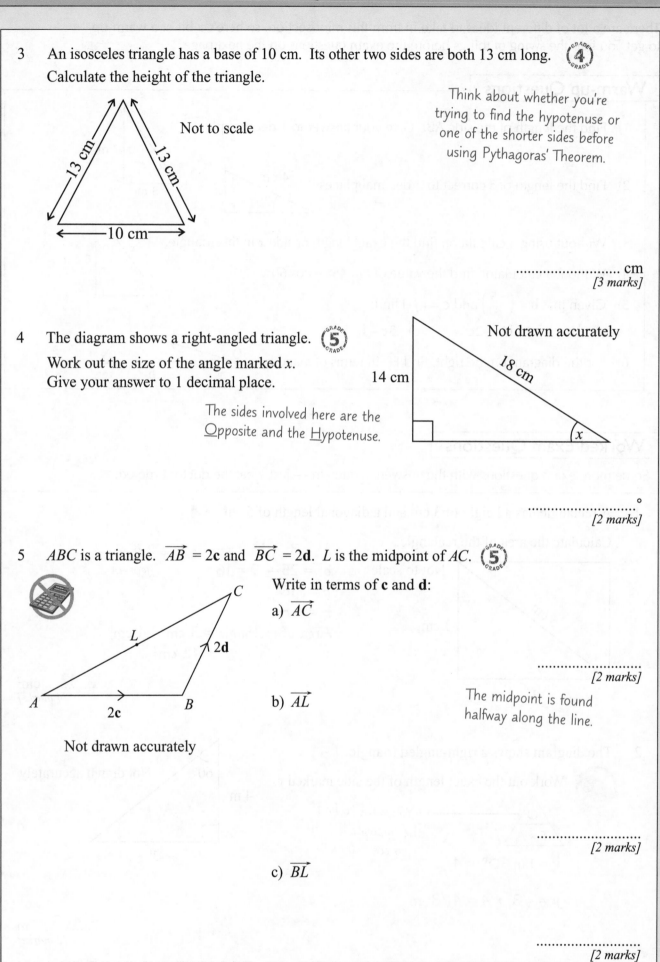

3   An isosceles triangle has a base of 10 cm. Its other two sides are both 13 cm long. **(4)**
Calculate the height of the triangle.

Not to scale

13 cm

13 cm

←——10 cm——→

Think about whether you're trying to find the hypotenuse or one of the shorter sides before using Pythagoras' Theorem.

.... cm
[3 marks]

4   The diagram shows a right-angled triangle. **(5)**

Work out the size of the angle marked *x*.
Give your answer to 1 decimal place.

The sides involved here are the Opposite and the Hypotenuse.

Not drawn accurately

14 cm

18 cm

x

........................°
[2 marks]

5   *ABC* is a triangle. $\overrightarrow{AB}$ = 2**c** and $\overrightarrow{BC}$ = 2**d**. *L* is the midpoint of *AC*. **(5)**

Write in terms of **c** and **d**:

a) $\overrightarrow{AC}$

C

L

2**d**

A   2**c**   *B*

....
[2 marks]

b) $\overrightarrow{AL}$

The midpoint is found halfway along the line.

Not drawn accurately

....
[2 marks]

c) $\overrightarrow{BL}$

....
[2 marks]

Revision Questions for Section Six

Look — a chance to use your artistic skills while doing maths...

- Try these questions and <u>tick off each one</u> when you <u>get it right</u>.
- When you're <u>completely happy</u> with a topic, tick that off too.

For even more practice, try the Sudden Fail Quiz for Section Six — just scan this QR code!

Section Six Quiz

Angles and Geometry Problems (p126-129) ☑

1) What is the name for an angle larger than 90° but smaller than 180°?

2) What do angles in a quadrilateral add up to?

3) Find the missing angles in the diagrams below.

a)

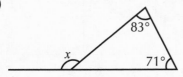

b)

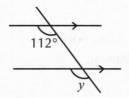

c)

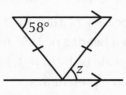

4) Given that angle DAC = 70°, work out angle CED.

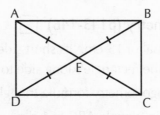

Angles in Polygons (p130) ☑

5) Find the exterior angle of a regular hexagon.

6) Find the sum of interior angles in a regular octagon.

7) Find the interior angle of a regular 20-sided polygon.

Constructions and Loci (p133-136) ☑

8) Construct triangle XYZ, where XY = 5.6 cm, XZ = 7.2 cm and angle YXZ = 55°.

9) What shape does the locus of points that are a fixed distance from a given point make?

10) Draw a horizontal line with a length of 8 cm.
    Draw the locus of points exactly 2 cm away from the line.

11) Construct an accurate 90° angle.

12) Draw a square with sides of length 6 cm and label it ABCD. Shade the region
    that is nearer to AB than CD and less than 4 cm from vertex A.

Bearings (p137) ☑

13) Using the diagram on the right, find the bearing of Y from X.

14) Look at the diagram to the right.
    Tom wants to travel from point A to point B.
    Find the bearing he should travel on.

Revision Questions for Section Six

Maps and Scale Drawings (p138-139) ☑

15) The scale on a map is 1 cm = 4 km. On the map, Leadz is 6.5 cm away from Horrowgate. How far is this in real life? ☑

16) The garden plan on the right has a scale of 1:200. Allen wants to build a square shed in the top right corner of the garden and a rectangular pond in the bottom right. The shed will measure 4 m × 4 m and the pond will measure 6 m × 2 m. Draw these accurately on the plan. ☑

17) John travels on a bearing of 180° for 3 km. He then travels on a bearing of 145° from his new position for 6 km. Using a scale of 1 cm = 1.5 km, draw an accurate diagram to represent this. ☑

Pythagoras and Trigonometry (p143-146) ☑

18) A rectangle has a diagonal of 15 cm. Its short side is 4 cm. Calculate the length of the rectangle's long side to 1 d.p. ☑

19) Write down the three trigonometry formula triangles. ☑

20) Find the size of angle x in triangle ABC to 1 d.p. ☑

21) Work out the value of x in triangle PQR to 1 d.p.

22) Find the exact length of side XZ in triangle XYZ without using your calculator. ☑

23) Without using your calculator, show that $\tan 45° + \sin 60° = \dfrac{2+\sqrt{3}}{2}$ ☑

Vectors (p147-148) ☑

24) $\underset{\sim}{a}$ and $\underset{\sim}{b}$ are column vectors, where $\underset{\sim}{a} = \begin{pmatrix} 4 \\ -2 \end{pmatrix}$ and $\underset{\sim}{b} = \begin{pmatrix} 7 \\ 6 \end{pmatrix}$.
   a) Find $\underset{\sim}{a} - \underset{\sim}{b}$
   b) Find $5\underset{\sim}{a}$ ☑

25) The diagram to the right shows a grid of unit squares. Find the vector $\underset{\sim}{c}$ in terms of $\underset{\sim}{a}$ and $\underset{\sim}{b}$.

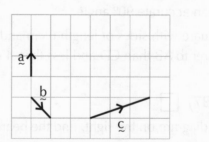

26) Find the vector that describes $\overrightarrow{XY}$ in the form $m\underset{\sim}{a} + n\underset{\sim}{b}$. ☑

27) Find the vector that describes $\overrightarrow{RS}$ in the form $m\underset{\sim}{i} + n\underset{\sim}{j}$.

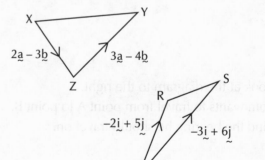

Probability Basics

*A lot of people think **probability** is tough. But learn the **basics** well, and it'll all make sense.*

All **Probabilities** are **Between 0 and 1**

1) Probabilities are <u>always</u> between 0 and 1.
2) The <u>higher</u> the probability of something, the <u>more likely</u> it is.
3) A probability of <u>ZERO</u> means it will <u>NEVER HAPPEN</u>.
4) A probability of <u>ONE</u> means it <u>DEFINITELY WILL HAPPEN</u>.

You can show the probability of something happening on a <u>scale</u> from 0 to 1.
Probabilities can be given as <u>fractions</u>, <u>decimals</u> or <u>percentages</u>.

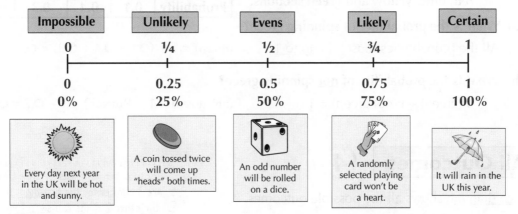

Impossible	Unlikely	Evens	Likely	Certain
0	¼	½	¾	1
0	0.25	0.5	0.75	1
0%	25%	50%	75%	100%

Every day next year in the UK will be hot and sunny.	A coin tossed twice will come up "heads" both times.	An odd number will be rolled on a dice.	A randomly selected playing card won't be a heart.	It will rain in the UK this year.

Use This **Formula** When **All Outcomes** are **Equally Likely**

Use this formula to find probabilities for a <u>fair</u> spinner, coin or dice.
A spinner/coin/dice is 'fair' when it's <u>equally likely</u> to land on <u>any</u> of its sides.

$$\text{Probability} = \frac{\text{Number of ways for something to happen}}{\text{Total number of possible outcomes}}$$

<u>Outcomes</u> are just 'things that could happen'.

EXAMPLE   **The picture on the right shows a fair, 8-sided spinner.**

a) **Work out the probability of this spinner landing on green.**

There are <u>8 sides</u> so there are <u>8 possible outcomes</u>.
There are <u>3 ways</u> for it to land on <u>green</u>.

P(green) means 'The probability of the spinner landing on green'.

$$P(\text{green}) = \frac{\text{number of ways for 'green' to happen}}{\text{total number of possible outcomes}} = \frac{3}{8} \text{ (or } 0.375\text{)}$$

b) **Which of its four colours is the spinner <u>least likely</u> to land on?**

It's least likely to land on the colour that 'can happen in the <u>fewest ways</u>' — this is the one on the <u>fewest sections</u>.   White

A probability of 1 means it's certain to happen

A probability of 0 means it definitely won't happen — the higher the probability, the more likely it is.

Q1   Calculate the probability of the fair spinner on the right:
       a) landing on a 4.   [2 marks]   b) landing on an even number.   [2 marks]
Q2   Show the probabilities in Q1 on a scale from 0 to 1.   [1 mark]

More Probability

Probabilities **Add Up To 1**

1) If <u>only one</u> possible result can happen at a time, then the probabilities of <u>all</u> the results <u>add up to 1</u>.

Probabilities always ADD UP to 1

2) So since something must either <u>happen</u> or <u>not happen</u> (i.e. <u>only one</u> of these can happen at a time):

P(event happens) + P(event doesn't happen) = 1

EXAMPLE A spinner has different numbers of red, blue, yellow and green sections.

Colour	red	blue	yellow	green
Probability	0.1	0.4	0.3	

a) **What is the probability of spinning green?**

All the probabilities must <u>add up to 1</u>. P(green) = 1 – (0.1 + 0.4 + 0.3) = 0.2

b) **What is the probability of <u>not</u> spinning green?**

P(green) + P(not green) = 1 P(not green) = 1 – P(green) = 1 – 0.2 = 0.8

Listing **All Outcomes**

A <u>sample space diagram</u> shows all the possible outcomes.

> Try to order your lists — here there are <u>3</u> choices for the <u>first digit</u>, then the other <u>2</u> digits can <u>swap round</u>.

1) It can just be a <u>simple list</u>...
   E.g. Find all the 3-digit numbers that include the digits 1, 2 and 3. 1<u>23</u>, 1<u>32</u>, 2<u>13</u>, 2<u>31</u>, 3<u>21</u>, 3<u>12</u>

2) Or you can draw a <u>two-way table</u> if there are <u>two activities</u> going on (e.g. two coins being tossed, or a dice being thrown and a spinner being spun).

EXAMPLE The spinner on the right is spun twice, and the scores added together.

a) **Complete this sample space diagram showing all the possible outcomes.**

+	1	2	3
1	2	3	4
2	3	4	5
3	4	5	6

There are <u>9 possible outcomes</u> here — even though some of the actual scores are repeated.

b) **Find the probability of spinning a total of 3.**

$$P(\text{total of 3}) = \frac{\text{ways to score 3}}{\text{total number of possible outcomes}} = \frac{2}{9}$$

> There are <u>2 ways</u> to score 3.

c) **Find the probability of spinning a total of 4 or more.**

$$P(\text{total of 4 or more}) = \frac{\text{ways to score 4 or more}}{\text{total number of possible outcomes}} = \frac{6}{9} = \frac{2}{3}$$

> There are <u>6 ways</u> to score either 4, 5 or 6.

List all possible outcomes in a methodical way

Be careful when you're listing outcomes — you don't want to lose easy marks by missing one out.

Q1 Two fair dice are thrown, and the scores added together. By drawing a sample space diagram,
   a) find the probability of throwing a total of 7, [3 marks]
   b) find the probability of throwing any total except 7. [1 mark]

Q1 Video Solution

Probability Experiments

*The formula on page 153 only works when the outcomes are equally likely. If they're **not equally likely**, you can use the results from experiments to **estimate** the probability of each outcome.*

Do the Experiment **Again** and **Again**...

You need to do an experiment <u>over and over again</u> and count how many times each outcome happens (its <u>frequency</u>). Then you can calculate the <u>relative frequency</u> using this formula:

$$\text{Relative frequency} = \frac{\text{Frequency}}{\text{Number of times you tried the experiment}}$$

An experiment could just mean rolling a dice.

You can use the <u>relative frequency</u> of a result as an <u>estimate</u> of its <u>probability</u>.

EXAMPLE The spinner on the right was spun 100 times. Use the results in the table below to estimate the probability of getting each of the scores.

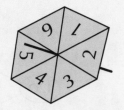

Score	1	2	3	4	5	6
Frequency	3	14	41	20	18	4

<u>Divide</u> each of the frequencies by 100 to find the <u>relative frequencies</u>.

Score	1	2	3	4	5	6
Relative Frequency	$\frac{3}{100}$ = 0.03	$\frac{14}{100}$ = 0.14	$\frac{41}{100}$ = 0.41	$\frac{20}{100}$ = 0.2	$\frac{18}{100}$ = 0.18	$\frac{4}{100}$ = 0.04

The <u>MORE TIMES</u> you do the experiment, the <u>MORE ACCURATE</u> your estimate of the probability should be. E.g. if you spun the above spinner <u>1000 times</u>, you'd get a <u>better</u> estimate of the probability for each score.

Fair or **Biased**?

'Fair' means all the outcomes are <u>equally likely</u>. If something is unfair, it's called <u>biased</u>.

1) If the dice/spinner/coin/etc. is <u>fair</u>, then the relative frequencies of the results should <u>roughly match</u> the probabilities you'd get using the formula on p.153.

2) If the relative frequencies are <u>far away</u> from those probabilities, you can say it's probably <u>biased</u>.

EXAMPLE

Do the above results suggest that the spinner is biased?

Yes, because the relative frequency of 3 is much higher than you'd expect, while the relative frequencies of 1 and 6 are much lower.

For a <u>fair</u> 6-sided spinner, you'd expect all the relative frequencies to be about 1 ÷ 6 = 0.17(ish).

More experiments mean a more accurate probability estimate

Remember that relative frequency can only be used to <u>estimate</u> the probability of a result. You can increase the <u>accuracy</u> of your estimate by increasing the number of times you do the experiment.

Q1 This table shows how many times Sekai and Sandro got a free biscuit on their visits to a coffee shop.

	Sekai	Sandro
Visits to coffee shop	20	150
Got a free biscuit	13	117

a) Based on Sekai's results, estimate the probability of getting a free biscuit at the shop. [2 marks]
b) Whose results will give a better estimate of the probability? Explain your answer. [1 mark]

Probability Experiments

*OK, I'll admit it, probability experiments aren't as fun as science experiments but they are **useful**.*

Record Results in **Frequency Trees**

When an experiment has two or more steps, you can record the results using a <u>frequency tree</u>.

EXAMPLE   120 GCSE maths students were asked if they would go on to do A-level maths.
- 45 of them said they would go on to do A-level maths.
- 30 of the students who said they would do A-level maths actually did.
- 9 of the students who said they wouldn't do A-level maths actually did.

a)   Complete the frequency tree below.

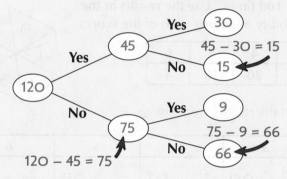

Will they take
A-level maths?

Did they take
A-level maths?

Yes   30
45
45 − 30 = 15
Yes
No   15

120

No
75
Yes   9
75 − 9 = 66
No   66

120 − 45 = 75

b)   A student who said they wouldn't do A-level maths is chosen at random. What is the probability that they <u>did</u> do A-level maths?

9 out of the <u>75 students</u> who said they wouldn't do A-level maths actually did.

So the probability is $\frac{9}{75}$ = 0.12

Use Probability to Find an "**Expected Frequency**"

1)   You can <u>estimate</u> how many times you'd <u>expect</u> something to happen if you do an experiment n <u>times</u>.

2)   This <u>expected frequency</u> is based on the <u>probability</u> of the result happening.

> **Expected frequency of a result = probability × number of trials**

A <u>trial</u> is a single experiment.

EXAMPLE   A person spins the fair spinner on the right 200 times. Estimate how many times it will land on 5.

1)   First calculate the probability of the spinner <u>landing on 5</u>.

$$P(\text{lands on 5}) = \frac{\text{ways to land on 5}}{\text{number of possible outcomes}} = \frac{1}{8}$$

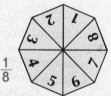

2)   Then <u>multiply</u> by <u>200</u> spins.

Expected number of 5's = P(lands on 5) × number of trials

$$= \frac{1}{8} \times 200 = 25 \text{ times}$$

If you don't know the probability of a result, fear not...
... you can estimate the probability using the <u>relative frequency</u> of the result in <u>past</u> experiments.

Expected frequency is how many times you'd expect something to happen

Make sure you can remember the formula for expected frequency in the box above. Try to get your head around where you can use frequency trees — they're really useful for experiments with two or more steps.

Q1   Using the frequency tree above, find the probability that a randomly chosen student said they were going to do A-level maths but didn't actually do it.   [2 marks]

Q2   The spinner above is spun 300 times.
Estimate how many times it will land on an even number.   [2 marks]

Warm-up and Worked Exam Questions

These probability basics aren't that difficult, but it's easy to throw away marks by being a little slap-dash with your calculations. So it's important to get loads of practice. Try these questions.

Warm-up Questions

1) Calculate the probability of the fair spinner on the right landing on a red triangle.

2) The probability of rolling a double from two dice rolls is $\frac{1}{6}$.
What is the probability of not rolling a double?

3) Two fair coins are tossed: a) List all the possible outcomes.
b) Find the probability of getting exactly 1 head.

4) Elsa rolled a dice 1000 times and got the results shown in the table below.

Score	1	2	3	4	5	6
Frequency	140	137	138	259	161	165

Find the relative frequencies for each of the scores 1-6.

5) Using the frequency tree on page 156, find the probability that a randomly chosen student said they were going to do A-level maths and actually did.

6) The spinner on page 156 is spun 500 times.
Estimate how many times it will land on a factor of 6.

Worked Exam Questions

Take a look at these worked exam questions. They should give you a good idea of how to answer similar questions. You'll usually get at least one probability question in the exam.

1 Sophie records the positions of all the members of her football team. The table on the right shows her results.

A member of the team is chosen at random.
What is the probability they're a midfielder?
Give your answer as a decimal.

Position	Frequency
Attacker	6
Midfielder	9
Defender	4
Goalkeeper	1

There are 6 + 9 + 4 + 1 = 20 people on the team

P(midfielder) = $\frac{9}{20}$ = 0.45 ⟶ 9 out of the 20 people on the team are midfielders.

.........0.45.........
[2 marks]

2 George has a biased 5-sided spinner numbered 1-5.
The table below shows the probabilities of the spinner landing on numbers 1-4.

Number	1	2	3	4	5
Probability	0.3	0.15	0.2	0.25	

He spins the spinner 100 times. Estimate the number of times it will land on 5.

P(landing on a 5) = 1 − (0.3 + 0.15 + 0.2 + 0.25) = 0.1

In 100 spins, you'd estimate: 0.1 × 100 = 10 fives

Expected frequency = probability × no. of trials

.........10.........
[2 marks]

Exam Questions

3   There are 10 counters in a bag. 4 of the counters are blue and the rest are red. ②
     One counter is picked out at random. On the scale below,
     mark with an arrow (↓) the probability that a red counter is picked.

```
   ┬──┬──┬──┬──┬──┬──┬──┬──┬──┬──┬
   0              0.5              1
```

[2 marks]

4   Katie decides to attend two new after-school activities. She can do one on Monday ③
     and one on Thursday. Below are lists of the activities she could do on these days.

Monday	**Thursday**
Hockey	Netball
Orchestra	Choir
Drama	Orienteering

   a)   List all nine possible combinations of two activities Katie could try in one week.

[2 marks]

Katie randomly picks an activity to do on each day.
Use your answer to part a) to find:

   b)   the probability that she does hockey on Monday and netball on Thursday,

....

[1 mark]

   c)   the probability that she does drama on Monday.

....

[1 mark]

5   Mani has 3 pieces of homework, English (E), History (H) and Maths (M). ③
     He has to do all 3 pieces tonight but he can do them in any order.

   a)   List all the different orders in which he could do his pieces of homework.

....

....

[2 marks]

Mani randomly chooses the order in which to do his pieces of homework.

   b)   Use your answer to part a) to find the probability that he does his Maths homework
        before his English homework. Give your answer as a fraction in its simplest form.

....

[1 mark]

Exam Questions

6   Danielle flipped a coin 100 times and predicted the outcome before each flip.
     She predicted heads 47 times and got 25 correct.
     Of the times she predicted tails, she got 26 correct.

     a)   Complete the frequency tree below to show these results.

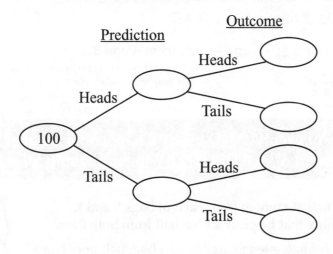

[2 marks]

     b)   Work out the relative frequency of Danielle predicting the outcome correctly.

     ....
     [2 marks]

7   Mel throws a ball at a target using her left and right hands.
     Her results are shown in the table on the right.

     a)   Estimate the probability that Mel will hit the
           target with her next throw if she uses her left hand.

	Left Hand	Right Hand
Throws	20	100
Hit target	12	30

     ....
     [2 marks]

     b)   Mel uses her results to estimate the probabilities of her hitting the target using
           each hand. Explain which of her estimated probabilities will be more reliable.

     ....

     ....
     [1 mark]

The AND / OR Rules

This page will show you two really important probability rules.

Combined Probability — Two or More Events

1) Always start by working out what different <u>SINGLE EVENTS</u> you're interested in.
2) Find the probability of <u>EACH</u> of these <u>SINGLE EVENTS</u>.
3) Apply the <u>AND/OR</u> rule.

And now for the rules. Say you have <u>two events</u> — call them A and B...

The **AND** Rule

This only works when the two events are <u>independent</u> — one event happening <u>does not affect</u> the chances of the other happening.

The probability of event A <u>AND</u> event B happening is equal to the probability of event A <u>MULTIPLIED BY</u> the probability of event B.

EXAMPLE   **Dave picks one ball at random from each of bags X and Y. Find the probability that he picks a blue ball from both bags.**

1) The <u>single events</u> you're interested in are 'picks a blue ball from bag X' and 'picks a blue ball from bag Y'.

2) Find the <u>probabilities</u> of the events.
   $P(\text{Dave picks a blue ball from bag X}) = \frac{4}{10} = 0.4$
   $P(\text{Dave picks a blue ball from bag Y}) = \frac{2}{8} = 0.25$

3) Use the <u>AND rule</u>. $P(\text{Dave picks a blue ball from bag X \underline{AND} bag Y}) = 0.4 \times 0.25 = 0.1$

The **OR** Rule

This rule only works when the two events <u>can't both happen</u> at the same time.

The probability of <u>EITHER</u> event A <u>OR</u> event B happening is equal to the probability of event A <u>ADDED TO</u> the probability of event B.

EXAMPLE   **A spinner with red, blue, green and yellow sections is spun — the probability of it landing on each colour is shown in the table. Find the probability of spinning either red or green.**

Colour	red	blue	yellow	green
Probability	0.25	0.3	0.35	0.1

1) The <u>single events</u> you're interested in are 'lands on red' and 'lands on green'.

2) Write down the <u>probabilities</u> of the events.
   $P(\text{lands on red}) = 0.25$
   $P(\text{lands on green}) = 0.1$

3) Use the <u>OR rule</u>. $P(\text{lands on \underline{either} red \underline{OR} green}) = 0.25 + 0.1 = 0.35$

Two rules to learn here

The way to remember this is that it's the wrong way round — you'd want AND to go with '+' but it doesn't. It's 'AND with ×' and 'OR with +'. Once you've got that, try these Exam Practice Questions.

Q1   Shaun is a car salesman. The probability that he sells a car on a Monday is 0.8. The probability that he sells a car on a Tuesday is 0.9.
What is the probability that he sells a car on both Monday and Tuesday?   [2 marks]

Q2   a) What is the probability of spinning blue OR yellow on the spinner above?   [2 marks]
      b) What is the probability of spinning blue THEN green?   [2 marks]

Tree Diagrams

*Tree diagrams can really help you work out probabilities when you have a **combination of events**.*

Remember These **Four** Key **Tree Diagram** Facts

1) On any set of branches which meet at a point, the probabilities must <u>add up to 1</u>.

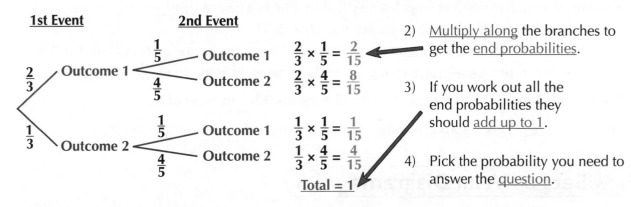

1st Event   **2nd Event**

$\frac{2}{3}$ Outcome 1

$\frac{1}{5}$ — Outcome 1 $\frac{2}{3} \times \frac{1}{5} = \frac{2}{15}$

$\frac{4}{5}$ — Outcome 2 $\frac{2}{3} \times \frac{4}{5} = \frac{8}{15}$

$\frac{1}{3}$ Outcome 2

$\frac{1}{5}$ — Outcome 1 $\frac{1}{3} \times \frac{1}{5} = \frac{1}{15}$

$\frac{4}{5}$ — Outcome 2 $\frac{1}{3} \times \frac{4}{5} = \frac{4}{15}$

Total = 1

2) <u>Multiply along</u> the branches to get the <u>end probabilities</u>.

3) If you work out all the end probabilities they should <u>add up to 1</u>.

4) Pick the probability you need to answer the <u>question</u>.

EXAMPLE

A box contains only red and green discs. A disc is taken at random and replaced. A second disc is then taken. The tree diagram below shows the probabilities of picking each colour.

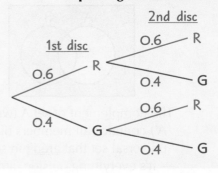

2nd disc

1st disc

0.6 R

0.6 R

0.4 G

0.4 G

0.6 R

0.4 G

a) **What is the probability that both discs are red?**

<u>Multiply</u> along the <u>branches</u> to find the probability you want:

P(both discs are red) = P(red, red) = 0.6 × 0.6 = 0.36

b) **What is the probability that you pick a green disc then a red disc?**

<u>Multiply</u> along the <u>branches</u> to find the probability you want:

P(green, red) = 0.4 × 0.6 = 0.24

Watch out for events that are affected by <u>what else has happened</u> — you'll get <u>different probabilities</u> on different sets of branches.

EXAMPLE

Florence either walks or drives to work. The probability that she <u>walks</u> is <u>0.3</u>. If she <u>walks</u>, the probability that she is <u>late</u> is <u>0.8</u>. If she <u>drives</u>, the probability that she is <u>late</u> is <u>0.1</u>. Complete the tree diagram below.

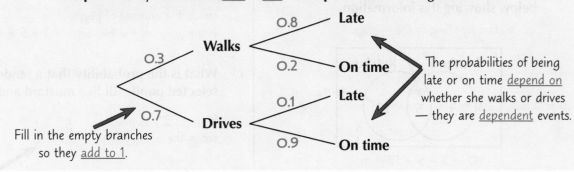

0.8 **Late**

Walks

0.3

0.2 **On time**

0.1 **Late**

0.7 **Drives**

0.9 **On time**

The probabilities of being late or on time <u>depend on</u> whether she walks or drives — they are <u>dependent</u> events.

Fill in the empty branches so they <u>add to 1</u>.

See how useful tree diagrams are

With probability questions that seem hard, drawing a tree diagram can be a good place to start.

Q1 Using the second tree diagram, find the probability of picking two green discs. [2 marks]

Q2 Using the third tree diagram, find the probability that Florence drives to work and is late. [2 marks]

Sets and Venn Diagrams

*Venn diagrams are a way of displaying sets in **intersecting circles**.*

A **Set** is a **Collection of Numbers** or **Objects**

1) Sets are just <u>collections of things</u> — we call these 'things' <u>elements</u>.

2) Sets can be written in different ways but they'll always be in a pair of <u>curly brackets</u> {}. You can:

Each of these describes the same set. → • <u>list the elements</u> in the set, e.g. {2, 3, 5, 7}.

→ • give a <u>description</u> of the elements in the set, e.g. {prime numbers less than 10}.

→ • use <u>formal notation</u>, e.g. {$x : x$ is a prime number less than 10}

3) The symbol $\in$ means '<u>is a member of</u>'. So $x \in$ A means 'x is a member of A'.

4) The <u>universal set</u> (ξ) is the group of things that the elements of the set are selected from.

Show **Sets** on **Venn Diagrams**

1) On a <u>Venn diagram</u>, each <u>set</u> is represented by a <u>circle</u>.
The <u>universal set</u> is everything <u>inside</u> the <u>rectangle</u>.

2) The diagram can show either the <u>actual elements</u> of each set, or the <u>number of elements</u> in each set.

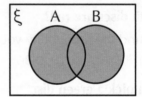

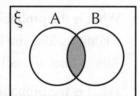

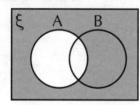

The <u>union</u> of sets A and B (written A $\cup$ B) contains all the elements in <u>either</u> set A <u>or</u> set B — it's everything <u>inside the circles</u>.

The <u>intersection</u> of sets A and B (written A $\cap$ B) contains all the elements in <u>both</u> set A <u>and</u> set B — it's where the <u>circles overlap</u>.

The <u>complement</u> of set A (written A') contains all members of the universal set that <u>aren't</u> in set A — it's everything <u>outside circle A</u>.

EXAMPLE

In a class of 30 pupils, 8 of them like mustard, 24 of them like ketchup and 5 of them like both mustard and ketchup.

a) **Complete the Venn diagram below showing this information.**

Start by filling in the <u>overlap</u>.

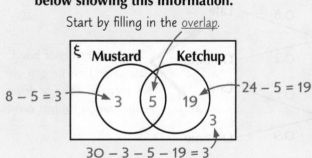

$8 - 5 = 3$

$24 - 5 = 19$

$30 - 3 - 5 - 19 = 3$

b) **How many pupils like mustard or ketchup?**

This is the number of pupils in the <u>union</u> of the two sets. $3 + 5 + 19 = 27$

c) **What is the probability that a randomly selected pupil will like mustard and ketchup?**

<u>5 out of 30</u> pupils are in the <u>intersection</u>. $\frac{5}{30} = \frac{1}{6}$

This is P(M $\cap$ K).

Learn what each bit of a Venn diagram represents

Once you've got your head round the new words to learn, test your skills with this Exam Question.

Q1 50 birdwatchers were looking for pigeons and seagulls. 28 of them saw a pigeon, 15 saw both birds and 10 didn't see either bird. Show this information on a Venn diagram and use it to find the probability that a randomly selected birdwatcher saw a seagull.   **[4 marks]**

Q1 Video Solution

Warm-up and Worked Exam Questions

Probability can be tricky to get your head around so it's important to get loads of practice.
Try these warm-up questions and take a look back at anything you're unsure about.

Warm-up Questions

1) What is the probability of rolling a six three times in a row with a six-sided dice?

2) Dmitri is practising front flips. The probability that he lands correctly on his first try is 0.5.
   The probability that he lands correctly on his second try is 0.7.
   What is the probability that he lands correctly on both his first and second tries?

3) For bags X and Y on page 160, find the probability of picking:
   a) an orange ball from both bags
   b) an orange ball from bag X OR bag Y.

4) A bag contains 6 red balls and 4 black ones. If one ball is picked at random, placed back into
   the bag, then another ball is drawn at random, find the probability that they're both red.

5) There are 40 people at a pet owners convention. 13 of them own a cat,
   21 of them own a dog and 5 of them own a cat and a dog.
   a) Show this information on a Venn diagram.
   b) Find the probability that a randomly selected pet owner owns a cat but not a dog.

Worked Exam Question

Look through this worked exam question and make sure you understand it — don't leave it to chance.

1 A couple are both carriers of a gene that causes a disease.
   If they have a child, the probability that the child will carry the gene is 0.25.

   a) The couple have two children. Draw a tree diagram to show the probabilities of each child
      carrying or not carrying the gene.

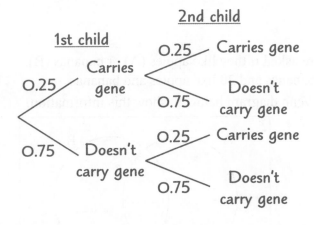

   [1 mark]

   b) Find the probability that both children will carry the gene.

   P(both children carry the gene) = 0.25 × 0.25 = 0.0625

   0.0625
   ....
   [2 marks]

Exam Questions

2   A biased 5-sided spinner is numbered 1-5.
    The probability that the spinner will land on each of the numbers 1 to 5 is given in this table.

Number	1	2	3	4	5
Probability	0.3	0.15	0.2	0.25	0.1

a)   What is the probability of the spinner landing on a 4 or a 5?

....
[2 marks]

b)   The spinner is spun twice. What is the probability that it will land
     on a 1 on the first spin and a 3 on the second spin?

....
[2 marks]

3   Chelsea is playing the game 'hook-a-duck'. The probability that she wins a prize is 0.3.

a)   What is the probability that she does not win a prize?

....
[1 mark]

b)   If she plays two games, what is the probability that she doesn't win a prize in either game?

....
[2 marks]

4   100 Year 7 students were asked if they like apples (A) or bananas (B).
    70 like apples, 40 like bananas and 20 like apples and bananas. (5)

   a)   Complete the Venn diagram below to show this information.

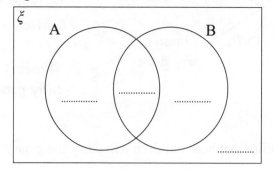

It's a good idea to start by filling in the intersection.

[3 marks]

b)   One of the students is selected at random.
     Find P(A ∪ B).

....
[2 marks]

Sampling and Bias

Sampling is about using what you know about **smaller** groups to tell you about **bigger** groups.

Use a **Sample** to **Find Out About** a **Population**

1) For any statistical project, you need to find out about a <u>group</u> of people or things. E.g. all the pupils in a school, or all the trees in a forest. This <u>whole group</u> is called the <u>POPULATION</u>.

2) Often you <u>can't</u> collect information about <u>every member</u> of the population because there are <u>too many</u>. So you <u>select a smaller group</u> from the population, called a <u>SAMPLE</u>, instead.

3) It's really <u>important</u> that your <u>sample fairly represents</u> the <u>WHOLE population</u>. This allows you to <u>apply</u> any <u>conclusions</u> about your sample to the <u>whole population</u>.

E.g. if you find that ¾ of the people in your <u>sample</u> like cheese, you can <u>estimate</u> that ¾ of the people in the <u>whole population</u> like cheese.

You Need to **Spot Problems** with **Sampling Methods**

A <u>BIASED sample</u> (or survey) is one that <u>doesn't properly represent</u> the <u>whole population</u>.

To <u>SPOT BIAS</u>, you need to <u>think about</u>:

> 1) <u>**WHEN**</u>, <u>**WHERE**</u> and <u>**HOW**</u> the sample is taken.
> 2) <u>**HOW MANY**</u> members are in it.

If certain groups are <u>left out</u> of the sample, there can be <u>BIAS</u> in things like <u>age</u>, <u>gender</u>, or different <u>interests</u>. If the <u>sample</u> is <u>too small</u>, it's also likely to be <u>biased</u>. *Bigger populations need bigger samples to represent them.*

EXAMPLE

Samir's school has 800 pupils. Samir is interested in whether these pupils would like to have more music lessons. For his sample he selects 5 members of the school orchestra to ask.
Explain why the opinions Samir collects from his sample might not represent the whole school.

Only members of the orchestra are included, so the opinions are likely to be biased in favour of more music lessons. And a sample of 5 is too small to represent the whole school.

If possible, the best way to <u>AVOID BIAS</u> is to select a <u>large</u> sample at <u>random</u> from the <u>whole population</u>.

Simple Random Sampling — choosing at **Random**

One way to get a <u>random</u> sample is to use '<u>simple random sampling</u>'.

To SELECT a SIMPLE RANDOM SAMPLE...

1) <u>Assign a number</u> to <u>every member</u> of the population.
2) Create a <u>list</u> of <u>random numbers</u>.
3) <u>Match</u> the random numbers to members of the population

 E.g. by using a computer, calculator or picking numbers out of a bag.

Before you begin collecting data, think about your sampling method

You want to make sure that you choose a sample that represents your population. Make sure you know how to spot poor sampling methods too. Then you'll be ready to take on this Exam Practice Question.

Q1 Tina wants to find out how often people in the UK travel by train. She decides to ask 20 people waiting for trains at her local train station one morning. Comment on whether Tina can use the results of her survey to draw conclusions about the whole population. [2 marks]

Collecting Data

*Data you **collect yourself** is called **primary** data. If you use data that **someone else has collected**, e.g. you get it from a website, it's called **secondary** data. You need to **record** primary data in a way that's **easy to analyse** and **suitable** for the **type** of data you've got.*

There are **Different Types** of **Data**

QUALITATIVE DATA is <u>descriptive</u>. It uses <u>words</u>, not numbers.	E.g. <u>pets' names</u> — Smudge, Snowy, Dave, etc. <u>Favourite flavours of ice cream</u> — 'vanilla', 'caramel-marshmallow-ripple', etc.
QUANTITATIVE DATA measures <u>quantities</u> using <u>numbers</u>.	E.g. <u>heights</u> of people, <u>times taken</u> to finish a race, <u>numbers of goals</u> scored in football matches, and so on.

There are two types of <u>quantitative</u> data.

DISCRETE DATA
1) It's <u>discrete</u> if the numbers can only take certain <u>exact</u> values.
2) E.g. the number of customers in a shop each day has to be a whole number — you can't have half a person.

CONTINUOUS DATA
1) If the numbers can take <u>any value</u> in a range, it's called <u>continuous</u> data.
2) E.g. heights and weights are continuous measurements.

You can **Organise** your **Data** into **Classes**

1) To record data in a <u>table</u>, you often need to <u>group</u> it into <u>classes</u> to make it more manageable. <u>Discrete</u> data classes should have '<u>gaps</u>' between them, e.g. '<u>0-1 goals</u>', '<u>2-3 goals</u>' (it jumps from 1 to 2 because there are no values in between). <u>Continuous</u> data classes should have <u>no 'gaps'</u>, so are often written using <u>inequalities</u> (see p.177).

2) Whatever the data you have, make sure <u>none of the classes overlap</u> and that they <u>cover all the possible values</u>.

When you <u>group</u> data you <u>lose</u> <u>some accuracy</u> because you don't know the exact values any more.

EXAMPLE
Jonty wants to find out about the ages (in whole years) of people who use his local library. Design a table he could use to collect his data.

Include <u>columns</u> for: the <u>data values</u>, '<u>Tally</u>' to count the data and '<u>Frequency</u>' to show the totals.

Use <u>non-overlapping</u> classes — with <u>gaps</u> because the data's <u>discrete</u>.

Include classes like '<u>...or over</u>', '<u>...or less</u>' or '<u>other</u>' to <u>cover all options</u> in a sensible number of classes.

Age (whole years)	Tally	Frequency
0-19		
20-39		
40-59		
60-79		
80 or over		

Questionnaires should be **Designed Carefully**

Another way to record data is to ask people to fill in a <u>questionnaire</u>. Your <u>questions</u> should be:

<u>Watch out</u> for <u>response boxes</u> that could be <u>interpreted</u> in <u>different</u> ways, that <u>overlap</u>, or that <u>don't</u> <u>allow</u> for <u>all</u> possible answers.

1) **Clear** and **easy to understand**
2) **Easy** to **answer**
3) **Fair** — not leading or biased

A question is '<u>leading</u>' if it guides you to picking a particular answer.

Tables are a really good way to record data

You need to know what type of data you've got so you can record and display it in a suitable way.

Q1 Penny asks some students how many times they went to the cinema in the last year. Say whether this data is discrete or continuous and design a table to record it in. [2 marks]

Mean, Median, Mode and Range

Mean, median, mode and *range* pop up all the time in exams — make sure you know what they are.

MODE = MOST common

MEDIAN = MIDDLE value (when values are in order of size)

MEAN = TOTAL of items ÷ NUMBER of items

RANGE = Difference between highest and lowest

REMEMBER:

Mode = most (emphasise the 'mo' in each when you say them)

Median = mid (emphasise the m*d in each when you say them)

Mean is just the average, but it's mean 'cos you have to work it out.

There's one Golden Rule for finding the median that lots of people forget:

Always REARRANGE the data in ASCENDING ORDER (and check you have the same number of entries!)

You must do this when finding the median, but it's also really useful for working out the mode too.

EXAMPLE Find the **median**, **mode**, **mean**, and **range** of these numbers: **2, 5, 3, 2, 0, 1, 3, 3**

1 Rearrange the numbers into ascending order. 0, 1, 2, (2, 3) 3, 3, 5
The **MEDIAN** is the middle value.
← 4 numbers either side →

When there are two middle numbers, the median is halfway between the two.

Median = 2.5

To find the position of the median of n values, you can use the formula (n + 1) ÷ 2. Here, (8 + 1) ÷ 2 = position 4.5 — that's halfway between the 4th and 5th values.

2 MODE (or modal value) is the most common value = 3

3 MEAN = $\frac{\text{total of items}}{\text{number of items}}$ = $\frac{0+1+2+2+3+3+3+5}{8}$ = $\frac{19}{8}$ = 2.375

4 RANGE = difference between highest and lowest values = 5 − 0 = 5

A Trickier Example

EXAMPLE The heights (to the nearest cm) of 8 penguins at a zoo are 41, 43, 44, 44, 47, 48, 50 and 51. Two of the penguins are moved to a different zoo. If the mean height of the remaining penguins is 44.5 cm, find the heights of the two penguins that moved.

Mean = $\frac{\text{total height}}{\text{no. of penguins}}$

So total height = no. of penguins × mean

Total height of 8 penguins = 368 cm.
Total height of remaining 6 penguins = 6 × 44.5 = 267 cm.
Combined height of penguins that moved = 368 − 267 = 101 cm.
So the heights must be 50 cm and 51 cm.

Mean, median, mode, range — easy marks for learning 4 definitions

The maths involved in working these out is simple, so you'd be mad not to learn the definitions.

Q1 Find the mean, median, mode and range for these test scores:
6, 15, 12, 12, 11 [4 marks]

Q2 A set of 8 heights has a mean of 1.6 m. A new height of 1.5 m is added.
Explain whether the mean of all 9 heights will be higher or lower than 1.6 m. [1 mark]

Q1 Video Solution

Warm-up and Worked Exam Questions

By the time the big day comes you need to know all the facts in these warm-up questions — and how to use them to answer exam questions. It's not easy, but it's the only way to get good marks.

Warm-up Questions

1) An investigation into the average number of people in households in Britain was done by surveying 100 households in one city centre. Give two reasons why this is a poor sampling technique.

2) Carl records the weights of 30 beavers for his biology project. Say whether this data is discrete or continuous and design a table to record it in.

3) Give one criticism of each of these questions:
   a) Do you watch a lot of television?
   b) Do you agree that maths is the most important subject taught in schools?
   c) What is your favourite drink? Answer A, B or C.   A) Tea   B) Milk   C) Coffee

4) Find the mean, median, mode and range for this set of data:
   1, 3, 14, –5, 6, –12, 18, 7, 23, 10, –5, –14, 0, 25, 8

5) Three different numbers have a mean of 4 and a range of 4. What are the numbers?

Worked Exam Question

There's no better preparation for exam questions than doing, err... practice exam questions.
Hang on, what's this I see...

1   Lee has 6 pygmy goats. Their weights, in kg, are listed below.

     32   23   31   28   36   26

a) Which three weights from the list above would have a range which is half the value of the median of the three weights? Also write the range and median of the three weights. **(3)**

> Use trial and error to find the three weights
> that work — 23, 26 and 36 have a range
> of 36 − 23 = 13 and a median of 26.

.....23....., ...26....., ...36.....

range = ...13....., median = ...26.....

[2 marks]

b) Two of the goats wander off and don't return. The mean weight of the herd is now 27.25 kg. Find the weights of the two goats who wandered off. **(4)**

Total weight of all 6 goats = 32 + 23 + 31 + 28 + 36 + 26 = 176 kg

Weight of 4 remaining goats = 4 × 27.25 = 109 kg

> Find the total
> weight of the goats
> that wandered off.

The goats that wandered off weigh: 176 kg − 109 kg = 67 kg

so the goats weigh 31 kg and 36 kg

> Use trial and error to find which
> two weights add up to 67 kg.

.....31..... kg and .....36..... kg

[3 marks]

Exam Questions

2 Faye is investigating how many chocolate bars teenagers buy each week.
She is going to collect data by asking her teenage friends how many they buy.

a) Design a table that Faye could use to record her data. (**3**)

[2 marks]

b) Comment on whether she can use her results
to draw conclusions about teenagers in the UK. (**4**)

....

....
[2 marks]

3 A bakery records the number of cookies it sells each day for ten days. (**4**)
The mean number is 17 and the median number is 15.

The next day the bakery sells 18 cookies.

a) Is the mean number sold over all eleven days higher than 17? Explain your answer.

....
[1 mark]

b) Is the median number sold over all eleven days higher than 15? Explain your answer.

....
[1 mark]

4 25 people were asked how many holidays they went on last year.
The vertical line graph below shows the results.

a) Write down the modal number of holidays. (**3**)

....
[1 mark]

b) Find the median number of holidays. (**4**)

Imagine the data in a list — O, O, O, O, 1…
Find the position of the median and count
up through the bars till you get there.

....
[2 marks]

Simple Charts and Graphs

*Pictograms and bar charts both show **frequencies**. (Remember... frequency = '**how many** of something'.)*

Pictograms Show Frequencies Using **Symbols**

Every pictogram has a key telling you what one symbol represents.

With pictograms, you __MUST__ use the __KEY__.

EXAMPLE **This pictogram shows how many peaches were sold by a greengrocer on different days.**

a) **How many peaches were sold on Tuesday?**
Each circle represents 4 peaches. 2 × 4 = 8 peaches

Key:
● represents 4 peaches

b) **How many peaches were sold on Wednesday?**
Three-quarters of a circle = 3 peaches. (3 × 4) + 3 = 15 peaches

Monday	●
Tuesday	●●
Wednesday	●●●◖
Thursday	●◖
Friday	

c) **43 peaches were sold altogether. Work out how many peaches were sold on Friday and show this information on the diagram.**

1) Add up the peaches for Mon-Thurs. 4 + 8 + 15 + (4 + 2) = 33

2) Subtract this from the total. Friday = 43 − 33 = 10

Half a circle = 2 peaches.

3) You need 2 whole circles (= 8), plus another half a circle (= 2).

Friday	●●◖

Bar Charts Show Frequencies Using **Bars**

1) Frequencies on bar charts are shown by the heights of the different bars.
2) Dual bar charts show two things at once — they're good for comparing different sets of data.

EXAMPLE **This dual bar chart shows the number of men and women visiting a coffee shop on different days.**

a) **How many men visited the coffee shop altogether?**
Add up the numbers shown by the heights of the dark red bars. 4 + 3 + 6 + 2 = 15 men

b) **On which day did the most women visit the coffee shop?**
Find the tallest purple bar. Tuesday

c) **On which day was there the biggest difference between the numbers of men and women?**
Count up from the smaller to the larger bar for each day to find the differences. Wednesday

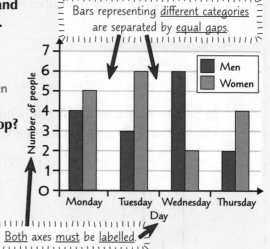

Bars representing different categories are separated by equal gaps.

Both axes must be labelled.

Pictograms and bar charts are good for comparing data

The most important part of a pictogram is the key — it tells you what the symbols represent.

Q1 This pictogram shows the different types of CDs Javier owns, but the key is missing. Javier owns 20 blues CDs.
a) How many jazz CDs does Javier own? [2 marks]
b) He owns 5 opera CDs. Complete the pictogram. [1 mark]

Rock	●
Blues	●●
Opera	
Jazz	●◖

Q1 Video Solution

Simple Charts and Graphs

*Here are **two-way tables**, **stem and leaf diagrams** and **line graphs**. Make sure you can draw and interpret them.*

Two-Way Tables Show How Many in each Category

EXAMPLE   This table shows the number of cakes and pies a bakery sold on Friday and Saturday.

a)   **How many pies were sold on Saturday?**

Read across to 'Pies' and down to 'Saturday'.   **14 pies**

b)   **How many items were sold in total on Friday?**

Add the number of cakes for
Friday to the number of pies.   12 + 10 = **22**

	Cakes	Pies	Total
Friday	12	10	
Saturday	4	14	18
Total	16	24	40

Or you could subtract the total for Saturday
from the overall total: 40 – 18 = 22.

Stem and Leaf Diagrams put data in Order

An ordered stem and leaf diagram shows a set of data in order of size.
This makes it easy to find things like the median and range (see p.167).

EXAMPLE   This stem and leaf diagram shows the ages of some school teachers.

a)   **How old is the oldest teacher?**

Use the key to help you read off the diagram.   6 | 3 = **63 years old**

b)   **What is the median age?**

The median is the middle value.
Find its position, then read off the value.

There are 11 values, so the median is the 6th value.
So median age is 4 | 8 = **48 years**

```
3 | 3  5
4 | 0  5  7  8
5 | 1  4  9
6 | 1  3
```
Key: 5 | 4 = 54 years

Line Graphs can show Time Series

1)   A time series is when you measure the same thing at different times. A line graph of
the data has 'time' along the bottom and the thing being measured down the side.

2)   A basic pattern often repeats itself — this is called seasonality (but it doesn't have to match the seasons).

3)   You can also see the overall trend by looking at the peaks and troughs.

EXAMPLE   The table shows how much Jamie spent
on heating during Spring/Summer and
Autumn/Winter over 4 years.

6-month period	Spr / Sum	Aut / Win	Spr / Sum	Aut / Win	Spr / Sum	Aut / Win	Spr / Sum	Aut / Win
Amount spent (£)	250	350	300	375	290	400	300	425

a)   **Draw a line graph of this data
on the grid opposite.**

Put 'Time' along the bottom and
'Amount spent' down the side.

Label your axes at equal intervals.

Plot the points and
join them up with
straight lines.
The pattern repeats
itself every 2 points.

b)   **Describe the trend in the data.**

Look at the trend in the peaks.   **The data shows an upward trend in the amount Jamie spent.**

Time series often show a repeating pattern

To see the overall trend of a time series graph just look at the peaks and troughs of the graph.

Q1   This data shows how many times Khalid goes rock-climbing in different quarters over 2 years.

    a)   Draw a line graph to show this data.   [2 marks]

    b)   In which quarter, each year, does Khalid
go rock climbing most often?   [1 mark]

Quarter	1	2	3	4	1	2	3	4
Climbing	2	4	10	6	1	4	11	7

Pie Charts

*Unlike other charts, **pie charts DON'T tell you numbers** of things, they show the **proportion in each category**. Remember that. And here's another thing to remember... the **Golden Pie Chart Rule**...*

The TOTAL of Everything = 360°

1) **Fraction** of the Total = **Angle ÷ 360°**

EXAMPLE

This pie chart shows the colour of all the cars sold by a dealer. What fraction of the cars were red?

Fraction of red cars = $\dfrac{\text{angle of red cars}}{\text{angle of everything}} = \dfrac{72°}{360°} = \dfrac{1}{5}$

2) Find a **Multiplier** to Calculate Your **Angles**

EXAMPLE

Draw a pie chart to show this information about the types of animal in a petting zoo.

Animal	Geese	Hamsters	Guinea pigs	Rabbits	Ducks
Number	12	20	17	15	26

1) Find the <u>total</u> by <u>adding</u>.   12 + 20 + 17 + 15 + 26 = 90

2) 'Everything = 360°' — so find the <u>multiplier</u> that turns your total into 360°.   Multiplier = 360 ÷ 90 = 4

3) <u>Multiply every number</u> by 4 to get the <u>angle</u> for each sector.

Angle	12 × 4 = 48°	20 × 4 = 80°	17 × 4 = 68°	15 × 4 = 60°	26 × 4 = 104°

4) Draw your pie chart accurately using a <u>protractor</u>.

3) Find **How Many** by Using the Angle for **1 Thing**

EXAMPLE

The pie chart on the right shows information about the types of animals liked most by different students. There were 90 students altogether.

a) **Work out the number of students who liked dogs most.**

1) 'Everything = 360°', so... ➞ 90 students = 360°

2) <u>Divide by 90</u> to find... ➞ 1 student = 4°

3) <u>Divide</u> the <u>angle for dogs</u> by the <u>angle for 1 student</u> to get: ➞ 160° ÷ 4° = 40 — 40 students liked dogs most

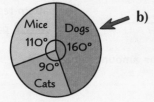

b) **The pie chart on the left shows information about the types of animals liked most by a different group of students. Dave says, "This means that 40 students in this group like dogs most." Explain why Dave is not correct.**

We don't know how many students in total the pie chart represents, so we can't work out how many students liked dogs most.

Pie charts are all about angles

Remember, the angles of each sector in a pie chart will add up to 360°.

Q1   Draw an accurate pie chart to show the information about Rahul's DVD collection given in this bar chart.   **[4 marks]**

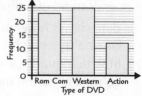

Q1 Video Solution

Scatter Graphs

*A **scatter graph** tells you **how closely** two things are **related** — the fancy word is **CORRELATION**.*

Scatter Graphs Show **Correlation**

1) If you can draw a <u>line of best fit</u> pretty close to <u>most</u> of your data points, the two things are <u>correlated</u>. If the points are <u>randomly scattered</u>, and you <u>can't draw</u> a line of best fit, then there's <u>no correlation</u>.

2) <u>Strong correlation</u> is when your points make a <u>fairly straight line</u> — the two things are <u>closely related</u>. <u>Weak correlation</u> is when your points <u>don't line up</u> so nicely, but you can still draw a line of best fit.

3) If the points form a line sloping <u>uphill</u> from left to right, then there is <u>positive correlation</u>. If the line slopes <u>downhill</u> from left to right, then there is <u>negative correlation</u>.

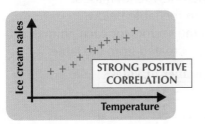
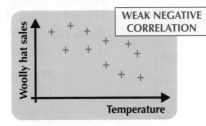
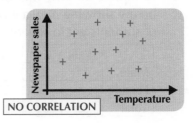

Use a **Line of Best Fit** to Make **Predictions**

1) Predicting a value <u>within the range</u> of data you have should be <u>fairly reliable</u>. But if you extend your line <u>outside</u> the range of data your prediction might be <u>unreliable</u>, because the <u>pattern might not continue</u>.

2) Also watch out for <u>outliers</u> — data points that <u>don't fit the general pattern</u>. Outliers can <u>drag</u> your <u>line of best fit</u> away from the other values, so it's best to <u>ignore</u> them when you're drawing the line.

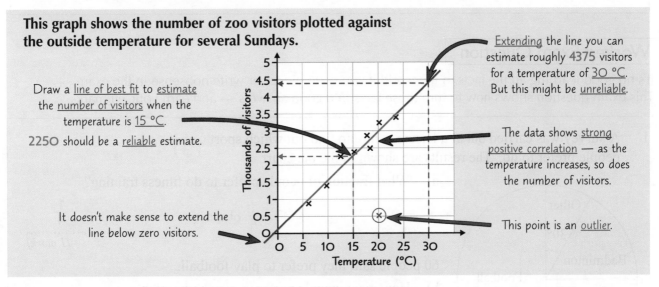

This graph shows the number of zoo visitors plotted against the outside temperature for several Sundays.

<u>Extending</u> the line you can estimate roughly **4375** visitors for a temperature of <u>30 °C</u>. But this might be <u>unreliable</u>.

Draw a <u>line of best fit</u> to <u>estimate</u> the <u>number of visitors</u> when the temperature is <u>15 °C</u>.
2250 should be a <u>reliable</u> estimate.

The data shows <u>strong positive correlation</u> — as the temperature increases, so does the number of visitors.

It doesn't make sense to extend the line below zero visitors.

This point is an <u>outlier</u>.

<u>BE CAREFUL</u> with <u>correlation</u> — if two things are correlated it <u>doesn't mean</u> that one causes the other. There could be a third factor affecting both, or it could just be a coincidence.

Correlation means that there's a relationship between two things

Make sure you know all the terms in case you have to describe a correlation.

Q1 This graph shows Sam's average speed on runs of different lengths.
   a) Describe the relationship between length of run and average speed. [1 mark]
   b) Circle the point that doesn't follow the trend. [1 mark]
   c) Estimate Sam's average speed for an 8-mile run. [1 mark]
   d) Comment on the reliability of your estimate in part c). [1 mark]

Warm-up and Worked Exam Questions

There's a nice selection of warm-up questions here covering tables, charts and graphs.
Now's the time to go back over any bits you're not sure of — in the exam it'll be too late.

Warm-up Questions

1) This pictogram shows the different colours of balloons stocked by a party shop, but there is no key. There are 40 red balloons.
   a) There are 16 purple balloons. Complete the pictogram.
   b) Ellen needs 37 blue balloons. Will she be able to buy them all from this party shop? Explain your answer.

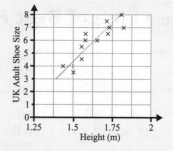

Red	● ● ● ● ●
Purple	
Blue	● ● ● ● ◗
Orange	● ● ● ◗

2) Complete the two-way table below showing how a group of students get to school.

	Walk	Car	Bus	Total
Male	15	21	13	49
Female	18	11	22	51
Total	33	32	35	100

3) 90 students vote for their new team mascot. The results are shown in the table below. Work out the angle of the sectors for each animal if a pie chart were to be created from the table.

Mascot	Number of Votes
Giraffe	31
Penguin	25
Lemur	34

4) This graph shows the heights and shoe sizes of students in a class.
   a) Describe the correlation between height and shoe size. *positive*
   b) Gina is 1.75 m tall. Estimate her shoe size. 7
   c) Comment on the reliability of your estimate in part b).
   d) Amal is 1.5 m tall and has a shoe size of 4. Does this follow the trend on the graph? *yes*

Worked Exam Question

It's no good learning all the facts in the world if you go to pieces or write nonsense in the exam.
This exam question shows how to turn those facts into good answers — and earn yourself marks.

1 A survey was carried out at a leisure centre to find out which sport people prefer to do. The results are shown in the pie chart. **(3)**

a) What fraction of people prefer to do fitness training?

$90° = \frac{1}{4}$ of a circle

$\frac{1}{4}$
....
[1 mark]

60 people said they prefer to play football.

b) How many people prefer to play badminton?

Badminton = 360° − 180° − 90° − 30° = 60°

Football = 180°, so 60 people = 180°

Find the angle that represents 1 person. → 1 person = 180° ÷ 60 = 3°

Number of people who prefer badminton = 60° ÷ 3°
= 20

Divide the angle of 'badminton' by the angle for '1 person'.

20
....
[2 marks]

Exam Questions

2   This table shows some information about the favourite sports of some students.

Sport	Students
Football	14
Swimming	5
Athletics	9
Netball	1
Hockey	6

Show this information as a bar chart on the grid below.

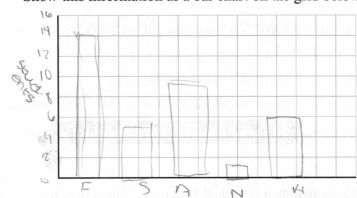

[4 marks]

3   50 people were asked if they've ever been skiing.
The table on the right shows the results.

	Have been skiing	Have not been skiing
Male	15	20
Female	5	10

a)   Write down the number of males who have
been skiing to the number of males who have
not been skiing as a ratio in its simplest form.

....

[1 mark]

b)   What percentage of all the people asked have been skiing?

.... %

[2 marks]

4   The scatter graph below shows the heights and weights of boys playing in a rugby team.

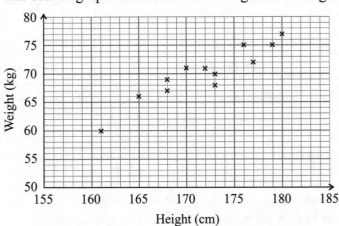

Height (cm)

Two more boys join the team.
Their heights and weights are
shown in this table.

Player	Height (cm)	Weight (kg)
13	169	70
14	183	76

a)   Add the information in the table to the scatter graph.

[1 mark]

b)   What fraction of the players have a height of less than 170 cm?

....

[1 mark]

c)   Describe the relationship between the height and weight of the players.

....

[1 mark]

Frequency Tables — Finding Averages

*You saw how to find **averages and range** on p.167 — the same applies here, but with the data in a table.*

Find **Averages** from **Frequency Tables**

1) The <u>MODE</u> is just the <u>CATEGORY with the MOST ENTRIES</u>.

2) The <u>RANGE</u> is found from the <u>extremes of the first column</u>.

3) The <u>MEDIAN</u> is the <u>CATEGORY</u> of the <u>middle value</u>.

4) To find the <u>MEAN</u>, you have to <u>WORK OUT A THIRD COLUMN</u> yourself.

The <u>MEAN</u> is then: | **3rd Column Total ÷ 2nd Column Total** |

Categories   How many

Number of cats	Frequency	
0	17	
1	22	
2	15	
3	7	

Mysterious 3rd column...

EXAMPLE

Some people were asked how many sisters they have. The table opposite shows the results.

Find the mode, the range, the mean and the median of the data.

Number of sisters	Frequency
0	7
1	15
2	12
3	8
4	4
5	0

1 The <u>MODE</u> is the <u>category</u> with the <u>most entries</u> — i.e. the one with the <u>highest frequency</u>:

The highest frequency is 15 for '1 sister', so <u>MODE</u> = 1

2 The <u>RANGE</u> is the <u>difference</u> between the highest and lowest numbers of sisters — that's 4 sisters (no one has 5 sisters) and no sisters, so:

<u>RANGE</u> = 4 – 0 = 4

3 To find the <u>MEAN</u>, <u>add a 3rd column</u> to the table showing 'number of sisters × frequency'. <u>Add up</u> these values to find the <u>total number of sisters</u> of all the people asked.

$$\text{MEAN} = \frac{\text{total number of sisters}}{\text{total number of people asked}} = \frac{79}{46} = 1.72 \text{ (3 s.f.)}$$

3rd column total · 2nd column total

Number of sisters	Frequency	No. of sisters × Frequency
0	7	0
1	15	15
2	12	24
3	8	24
4	4	16
5	0	0
Total	46	79

4 The <u>MEDIAN</u> is the <u>category</u> of the <u>middle</u> value. Work out its <u>position</u>, then <u>count through</u> the 2nd column to find it.

It helps to imagine the data set out in an ordered list:
0000000111111111111111222222222222223333333334444
median

The median is in position (n + 1) ÷ 2 = (46 + 1) ÷ 2 = 23.5 — halfway between the 23rd and 24th values. There are a total of (7 + 15) = 22 values in the first two categories, and another 12 in the third category takes you to 34. So the 23rd and 24th values must both be in the category '2 sisters', which means the <u>MEDIAN</u> is 2.

Remember — mode is most, median is middle

Learn the four key points about averages, then try this question.

Q1 50 people were asked how many times a week they play sport. The table opposite shows the results.
- a) Find the median. [2 marks]
- b) Calculate the mean. [3 marks]

No. of times sport played	Frequency
0	8
1	15
2	17
3	6
4	4
5 or more	0

Q1 Video Solution

Grouped Frequency Tables

Grouped frequency tables are like ordinary frequency tables, but they group the data into **classes**.

<u>NO GAPS</u> between classes for <u>CONTINUOUS</u> data.

Use <u>inequality symbols</u> to cover all possible values.

Height (*h* millimetres)	Frequency
$5 < h \leq 10$	12
$10 < h \leq 15$	15

See p.166 for grouped discrete data.

To find MID-INTERVAL VALUES:
- Add together the <u>end values</u> of the <u>class</u> and <u>divide by 2</u>.
- E.g. $(5 + 10) \div 2 = \underline{7.5}$

Find **Averages** from **Grouped Frequency Tables**

Unlike with ordinary frequency tables, you <u>don't know the actual data values</u>, only the <u>classes</u> they're in. So you have to <u>ESTIMATE THE MEAN</u>, rather than calculate it exactly — you do this by <u>adding columns</u>:

1) Add a <u>3RD COLUMN</u> and enter the <u>MID-INTERVAL VALUE</u> for each class.
2) Add a <u>4TH COLUMN</u> to show '<u>FREQUENCY × MID-INTERVAL VALUE</u>' for each class.

You'll be asked to find the <u>MODAL CLASS</u> and the <u>CLASS CONTAINING THE MEDIAN</u>, not exact values. And the <u>RANGE</u> can only be estimated too — using the class boundaries.

EXAMPLE

This table shows information about the weights, in kilograms, of 60 school children.

a) **Write down the modal class.**
b) **Write down the class containing the median.**
c) **Calculate an estimate for the mean weight.**
d) **Estimate the range of weights.**

Weight (*w* kg)	Frequency
$30 < w \leq 40$	8
$40 < w \leq 50$	16
$50 < w \leq 60$	18
$60 < w \leq 70$	12
$70 < w \leq 80$	6

a) The <u>modal class</u> is the one with the <u>highest frequency</u>.

Modal class is $50 < w \leq 60$

b) Work out the <u>position</u> of the <u>median</u>, then <u>count through</u> the <u>2nd column</u>.

The median is in position $(n + 1) \div 2 = (60 + 1) \div 2 = 30.5$, halfway between the 30th and 31st values. Both these values are in the third class, so the class containing the median is $50 < w \leq 60$.

c) Add extra columns for '<u>mid-interval value</u>' and '<u>frequency × mid-interval value</u>'. Add up the values in the 4th column to estimate the <u>total weight</u> of the 60 children.

Weight (*w* kg)	Frequency	Mid-interval value	Frequency × mid-interval value
$30 < w \leq 40$	8	35	280
$40 < w \leq 50$	16	45	720
$50 < w \leq 60$	18	55	990
$60 < w \leq 70$	12	65	780
$70 < w \leq 80$	6	75	450
Total	60	—	3220

Mean $\approx \dfrac{\text{total weight}}{\text{number of children}}$ ← 4th column total / 2nd column total

$= \dfrac{3220}{60} = 53.7$ kg (3 s.f.)

d) Find the <u>difference</u> between the <u>highest</u> and <u>lowest</u> class <u>boundaries</u>.

Estimated range = $80 - 30 = 50$ kg

This is the <u>largest possible</u> range. The actual range is likely to be smaller, but you can't tell with grouped data.

This time there are two columns to add

It's still easy enough — just make sure you know what to put in each one.

Q1 a) Find the modal class. **[1 mark]**
b) Estimate the mean of this data. Give your answer to 3 significant figures. **[4 marks]**

Length (*l* cm)	Frequency
$15.5 \leq l < 16.5$	12
$16.5 \leq l < 17.5$	18
$17.5 \leq l < 18.5$	23
$18.5 \leq l < 19.5$	8

Q1 Video Solution

Interpreting Data

*This page is about **getting information** from data and **recognising** when it might be **misleading**.*

You can **Find Averages** from **Diagrams**

EXAMPLE

This vertical line graph shows information on the number of pairs of penguin slippers a shop sells each day for 50 consecutive days. Calculate the mean number of pairs sold each day.

Fill in a <u>frequency table</u> and add a third column to find the total number of pairs sold — see p.176.

$$\text{Mean} = \frac{\text{total number of pairs sold}}{\text{total number of days}}$$
$$= \frac{118}{50} = 2.36$$

Number of pairs	Frequency	No. of pairs × Frequency
0	7	0
1	8	8
2	10	20
3	13	39
4	9	36
5	3	15
Total	50	118

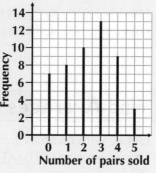

Watch Out for **Misleading Diagrams**

At first glance, a diagram might look perfectly fine. But at second glance, well, not so fine...

EXAMPLE

This bar chart shows the numbers of dogs of different breeds at a rescue centre.

a) **Write down <u>three</u> things that are wrong with the bar chart.**

1) The 'number of dogs' axis doesn't start at zero.
2) The 'number of dogs' axis has inconsistent numbering.
3) The 'breed of dog' axis has no label.

b) **The 'Husky' bar is twice as high as the 'Spaniel' bar. Explain why these bar heights could be misleading in the context of this data.**

The bar heights suggest that there are twice as many Huskies as Spaniels. But reading the scale, there are 6 Huskies and 5 Spaniels.

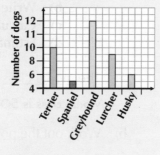

Be Careful with Measures of **Average** and **Range**

<u>Outliers</u> are data values that <u>don't fit</u> the <u>general pattern</u> — they're a long way from the rest of the data. Outliers can have a <u>big effect</u> on the <u>mean</u> or <u>range</u> of a data set, so you get a <u>misleading</u> value.

EXAMPLE

The data below shows the number of songs Fred downloads each week for ten weeks.

0, 1, 3, 3, 5, 6, 7, 8, 8, 20

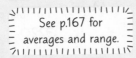

See p.167 for averages and range.

a) **Fred works out that the range of his data is 20. Comment on this value as a measure of the spread.**

A range of 20 isn't a true reflection of the spread of the whole data set, because most of the data is much closer together. The highest value of 20 has a big effect on increasing the range.

b) **Explain why the mode <u>isn't</u> a helpful measure of average for this data.**

The data has two modes, 3 and 8, so this doesn't give you a good idea of the average value.

Don't let the data give you the wrong idea...

Once you're happy with this stuff, use the data from the first example above to answer this Practice Question.

Q1 a) What is the modal number of pairs of penguin slippers sold? [1 mark]

 b) Use the data to estimate the probability that the shop will sell two pairs of penguin slippers on any given day. Comment on the reliability of your estimate. [3 marks]

Comparing Data Sets

*You can **compare** data sets using **averages** and **range**, or by **drawing suitable diagrams**.*

Compare Data Sets Using Averages and Range

Say which data set has the <u>higher/lower</u> value and what that means in the <u>context of the data</u>.

EXAMPLE

Some children take part in a 'guess the weight of the baby hippo' competition. Here is some information about the weights they guess.

Compare the distributions of the weights guessed by the boys and the girls.

Boys:	Girls:
Mean = 40 kg	Mean = 34 kg
Median = 43 kg	Median = 33 kg
Range = 42 kg	Range = 30 kg

1) Compare <u>averages</u>:
   The boys' mean and median values are higher than the girls', so the boys generally guessed heavier weights.

2) Compare <u>ranges</u>:
   The boys' guesses have a bigger range, so the weights guessed by the boys show more variation.

Compare Data Sets Using Diagrams

The <u>type</u> of diagram you should use depends on <u>what you want to show</u>.

EXAMPLE

Harry carried out a survey into whether or not people like olives. He draws these pie charts to show his results.

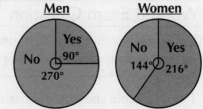

Men   **Women**

a) **Can you tell from the pie charts whether more women said 'yes' than men? Explain your answer.**

   No, you can't tell whether more women said 'yes'. You can see that a higher proportion of women said 'yes' but you don't know how many men and women the pie charts represent.

b) **Harry surveyed 20 men and 20 women. Draw a suitable diagram to compare the numbers of men and women giving each answer.**

   A <u>dual bar chart</u> is suitable — it shows the <u>numbers</u> of men and women <u>side by side</u>.

   Use the pie charts to work out the <u>frequency</u> of each answer.
   E.g. find the fraction of the total, then multiply by 20.

   Men: 'Yes' = $\frac{90}{360} \times 20 = 5$,   'No' = $\frac{270}{360} \times 20 = 15$

   Women: 'Yes' = $\frac{216}{360} \times 20 = 12$,   'No' = $\frac{144}{360} \times 20 = 8$

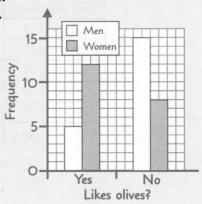

You could be asked to compare any type of chart or diagram

You might need to work out the values of average and range (see p.167), before comparing data sets.

Q1   The data below shows how many football matches two supporters attended in each of the last nine years. Compare the distributions of the number of matches attended.

       Hannah: 1, 5, 0, 7, 10, 8, 7, 4, 3
       Joseph: 13, 17, 16, 20, 32, 18, 14, 25, 25   [3 marks]

Warm-up and Worked Exam Questions

Think of the exam as a big race. In order to do your best, you should really warm up first. So give these questions a go and get your brain all ready for the big day.

Warm-up Questions

1) Ana recorded how many portions of fruit she ate every day for two months. Her results are shown in the table on the right.
   a) Find the mode.   b) Find the median.

No. of portions of fruit eaten	Frequency
0	3
1	8
2	11
3	19
4	14
5	6

2) Here are the heights of some adults to the nearest 0.1 cm.
   Design and fill in a grouped frequency table to record the data.
   150.4   163.5   156.7   164.1
   182.8   175.4   171.2   169.0
   173.3   185.6   167.0   162.6

3) The grouped frequency table below represents data from 79 random people.

Height (cm)	$145 \leq x < 155$	$155 \leq x < 165$	$165 \leq x < 175$	$175 \leq x < 185$
Frequency	18	22	24	15

   a) Estimate the range of heights.   b) Which group contains the median?
   c) State the modal group.

4) The following temperatures were recorded in a city at eight times during a year:
   12°C, 30°C, 30°C, 8°C, 17°C, 11°C, 4°C, 15°C
   Explain why the mode is not a good average to use for this data.

Worked Exam Question

This worked exam question is just like one that could come up in the exam.
But the one in the exam won't have the answers filled in so make the most of it now.

1   The table shows the times it took 32 pupils at a school to run a 200 m sprint. **(GRADE 5)**

   a)   Calculate an estimate for the mean time taken.

Time (t seconds)	Frequency	Mid-interval value	Frequency × Mid-interval value
$22 < t \leq 26$	4	24	4 × 24 = 96
$26 < t \leq 30$	8	28	8 × 28 = 224
$30 < t \leq 34$	13	32	13 × 32 = 416
$34 < t \leq 38$	6	36	6 × 36 = 216
$38 < t \leq 42$	1	40	1 × 40 = 40
Total:	32	Total:	992

   Estimate of mean = 992 ÷ 32 = 31

   ....31....... seconds
   [4 marks]

   All pupils with a time of 34 seconds or less qualified for the next round.

   b)   Anya says that fewer than 20% of the pupils failed to qualify for the next round.
         Comment on Anya's statement and show working to support your answer.

   6 + 1 = 7 people failed to qualify. 7 out of 32 = 7 ÷ 32 × 100 = 21.875%

   Over 20% of pupils failed to qualify, so Anya's statement is incorrect.
   [2 marks]

Exam Questions

2   A survey was carried out in a local cinema to find out which flavour 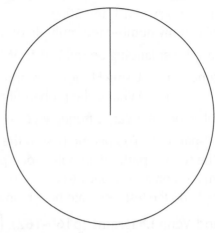 of popcorn people bought. The results are in the table below.

   a)   Draw and label a pie chart to represent the information.

Type of popcorn	Number sold
Plain	12
Salted	18
Sugared	9
Toffee	21

[4 marks]

Another survey was carried out to find out which flavour of ice cream people bought. The results are shown in the pie chart on the right.

Kim compares the two pie charts and says, "The results show that more people chose strawberry ice cream than toffee popcorn."

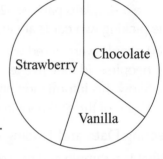

   b)   Explain whether or not Kim is right.

   ....

   ....

   ....

[1 mark]

3   This data shows the amount of rainfall in mm that fell on an island during a 12-day period in June.

```
0 | 8
1 | 7 9
2 | 3 6 9
3 | 0 1 4 7 8
6 | 3
```

Key
0 | 8 means
8 mm of rain

   a)   Work out the range of the rainfall and comment on this value as a measure of the spread of the data.

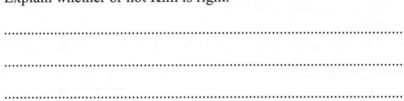

   Don't be put off by the way the data is displayed —
   look at the key to work out how to read off the values.

   ....

   ....

[3 marks]

In November the median amount of rainfall was 22 mm and the range was 20 mm.

   b)   Compare the rainfall in June with the rainfall in November.

   ....

   ....

   ....

[3 marks]

Section Seven — Probability and Statistics

Revision Questions for Section Seven

Here's the inevitable list of questions to test how much you know.
- <u>Tick off</u> each question when you've got it right.
- When you're <u>completely happy</u> with a topic, tick that off too.

For even more practice, try the Sudden Fail Quiz for Section Seven — just scan this QR code!

Section Seven Quiz

Probability (p153-156) ☑

1) I pick a random number between 1 and 50.
   Find the probability that my number is a multiple of 6. ☐

2) The probability of a spinner landing on red is 0.3. What is the probability it doesn't land on red? ☐

3) I flip a fair coin 3 times. a) Using H for heads and T for tails list all the possible outcomes.
   b) What is the probability of getting exactly one head? ☐

4) What are the formulas for: a) relative frequency? b) expected frequency? ☐

5) 160 people took a 2-part test. 105 people passed the first part and of these,
   60 people passed the second part. 25 people didn't pass either part.
   a) Show this information on a frequency tree.   b) Find the relative frequency of each outcome.
   c) If 300 more people do the test, estimate how many of them would pass both parts. ☐

Harder Probability and Venn Diagrams (p160-162) ☑

6) The table shows the probabilities of a biased dice landing on
   each number. What is the probability of it landing on 1 or 4? ☑

Number	1	2	3	4	5	6
Probability	0.2	0.15	0.1	0.3	0.15	0.1

7) I have a standard pack of 52 playing cards. Use a tree diagram to find the probability of
   me picking two cards at random and getting no hearts if the first card is replaced. ☑

8) 100 people were asked whether they like tea or coffee. Half the people said they like coffee,
   34 people said they like tea, 20 people said they like both.
   a) Show this information on a Venn diagram.
   b) If one of the 100 people is randomly chosen, find the probability of them liking tea or coffee. ☑

Collecting Data and Finding Averages (p165-167) ☑

9) What is a sample and why does it need to be representative? ☑

10) Is 'eye colour' qualitative, discrete or continuous data? ☑

Pet	Tally	Frequency

11) Complete this frequency table for the data below. ➡

   Cat, Cat, Dog, Dog, Dog, Rabbit, Fish, Cat, Rabbit, Rabbit, Dog, Dog, Cat, Cat, Dog, Rabbit, Cat, Fish, Cat, Cat ☑

12) Find the mode, median, mean and range of this data: 2, 8, 11, 15, 22, 24, 27, 30, 31, 31, 41 ☑

Graphs and Charts (p170-173) ☑

13) How do you find frequencies from a pictogram? ☑

14) The table opposite shows how some students rated a film.

Film rating	Terrible	Bad	OK	Good	Amazing
Students	40	30	40	45	25

   Draw a suitable diagram to show the number of students giving each rating. ☐

15) a) Draw a line graph to show the time series data in this table.
    b) Describe the repeating pattern in the data.

Quarter	1	2	3	4	1	2	3	4
Sales (1000's)	1	1.5	1.7	3	0.7	0.9	1.2	2.2

   ☑

16) Use data from Q14 to draw a suitable diagram showing the proportion of students giving each rating. ☑

17) Sketch graphs to show: a) weak positive correlation, b) strong negative correlation, c) no correlation ☑

Frequency Tables and Averages (p176-177) ☑

18) For this grouped frequency table showing the lengths of some pet alligators:
    a) find the modal class,   b) find the class containing the median,
    c) estimate the mean.

Length (y, in m)	Frequency
$1.4 \leq y < 1.5$	4
$1.5 \leq y < 1.6$	8
$1.6 \leq y < 1.7$	5
$1.7 \leq y < 1.8$	2

   ☑

Interpreting and Comparing Data Sets (p178-179) ☑

19) Explain the effect that outliers can have on the mean and range of data. ☑

20) These pie charts show the results of a survey on the colour of people's cars.
    Compare the popularity of each colour of car amongst men and women. ☑

Men
Red, Green, Black, Blue

Women
Silver, Green, Red, Blue

Section Seven — Probability and Statistics

Practice Paper 1: Non-calculator
Practice Paper 1: Non-calculator
As final preparation for the exams, we've included three full practice papers to really put your Maths skills to the test. Paper 1 is a non-calculator paper — Paper 2 and Paper 3 (on pages 196 and 209) require a calculator. There's a whole page on formulas on p.244. Good luck...

Candidate Surname		Candidate Forename(s)	
Centre Number	Candidate Number	Candidate Signature	

GCSE

Mathematics
Paper 1 (Non-Calculator)

Practice Paper
Time allowed: 1 hour 30 minutes

Foundation Tier

You must have:
Pen, pencil, eraser, ruler, protractor, pair of compasses.
You may use tracing paper.

You are **not allowed** to use a calculator.

Instructions to candidates
- Use **black** ink to write your answers.
- Write your name and other details in the spaces provided above.
- Answer **all** questions in the spaces provided.
- In calculations, show clearly how you worked out your answers.
- Do all rough work on the paper.

Information for candidates
- The marks available are given in brackets at the end of each question.
- You may get marks for method, even if your answer is incorrect.
- There are 26 questions in this paper. There are no blank pages.
- There are 80 marks available for this paper.

Answer ALL the questions.

Write your answers in the spaces provided.

You must show all of your working.

1   Write 0.113 as a fraction.
    Circle your answer.

$$\frac{113}{100} \qquad \frac{113}{10\,000} \qquad \frac{113}{1000} \qquad \frac{13}{100}$$

[Total 1 mark]

2   Write the ratio 40 : 25 in its simplest form.

....

[Total 1 mark]

3   Eight points are shown plotted on the grid.

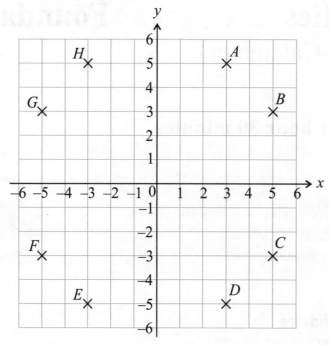

(a) Circle the point that has coordinates (−5, −3).

    C   *E*   *F*   *G*

[1]

(b) Circle the equation of the straight line that passes through points *A* and *D*.

    $x = 3$ $x + y = 3$ $y = 3x$ $y = 3$

[1]

[Total 2 marks]

4   Convert 3.97 km into m.

.... m

5   Karl has five number cards.

$$\boxed{-6} \quad \boxed{6} \quad \boxed{-8} \quad \boxed{-12} \quad \boxed{2}$$

(a)   Write Karl's number cards in order, starting with the lowest.

lowest   ...., ..., ..., ..., ...   highest

[1]

(b)   Use two of Karl's number cards to make this calculation correct.

.... − .... = 10

[1]

[Total 2 marks]

6   Beth has some 5p and 10p coins.

Coin	Number
5p	28
10p	41

She changes her coins for 50p coins at the bank.

How many 50p coins does she receive?

....

[Total 3 marks]

7   Calculate

$$\frac{1.2 - 0.2 \times 4}{0.05}$$

....

[Total 2 marks]

2

8

> If you add a multiple of 3 to a multiple of 6, you always get a multiple of 9.

Give an example to show that this statement is not true.

....

....

[Total 1 mark]

---

9 (a) Simplify $11a + 5b - 2a + 2b$

Circle your answer.

$13a + 3b$ $\qquad$ $9a + 7b$ $\qquad$ $13a + 7b$ $\qquad$ $16ab$

[1]

(b) Simplify $2a \times 3a$

Circle your answer.

$5a$ $\qquad$ $6a$ $\qquad$ $5a^2$ $\qquad$ $6a^2$

[1]

[Total 2 marks]

---

10 Chloe invests £300 in a bank account.
The account pays 2% simple interest each year.

Work out how much money she has in her account after 4 years.

£ ....

[Total 3 marks]

---

11 The dual bar chart below shows the favourite sports of the pupils in a class.

One bar is missing.

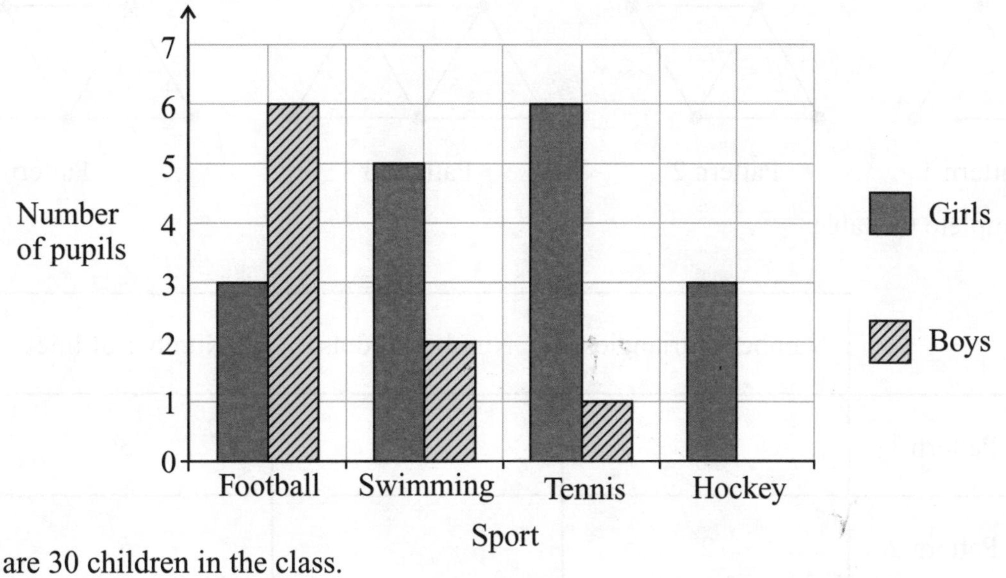

There are 30 children in the class.

(a) Draw the missing bar to show the number of boys whose favourite sport is Hockey.

[2]

(b) One child is chosen at random from the class.
Find the probability that their favourite sport is swimming.

....

[2]

(c) What is the ratio of the number of boys who chose swimming to the number of girls who chose tennis? Give your answer in its simplest form.

....

[2]

[Total 6 marks]

12 Decide whether the sequence is an arithmetic or geometric progression, and write down in words the rule to get from one term to the next.

2, 8, 32, 128...

Arithmetic ☐   Geometric ☐

Rule: ....

....

[Total 2 marks]

4

13 The diagram shows the first four patterns in a sequence.

 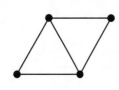 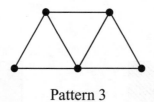 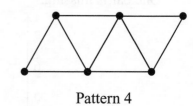

Pattern 1   Pattern 2   Pattern 3   Pattern 4

(a) Complete the table.

	Number of triangles	Number of dots	Number of lines
Pattern 1	1	3	3
Pattern 2	2	....	5
Pattern 3	....	5	....
Pattern 4	4	....	....

[1]

(b) Work out the number of lines in pattern 10.

....

[2]

(c) (i) Find a formula for the number of dots D in Pattern n.

....

[2]

(ii) Find the number of dots in pattern 200.

....

[1]

[Total 6 marks]

14 A theatre sells three types of tickets.

Ticket type	Cost
Adult	£9
Child	£5
Senior	£6.50

The pictogram shows the number of tickets of each type sold for one performance.

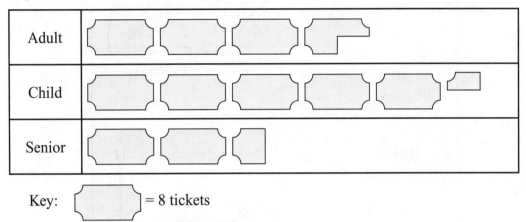

Key: = 8 tickets

How much money did the theatre make from all the ticket sales for this performance?

£ ....

[Total 6 marks]

15 The scale drawing shows the gardens of a country house.

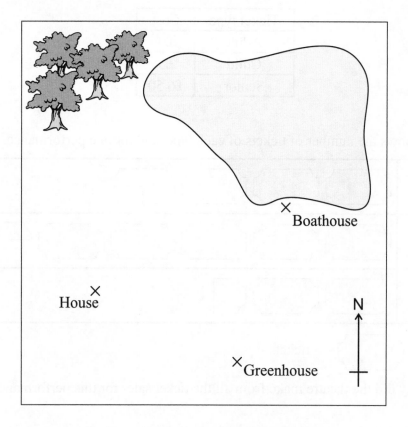

Scale: 1 cm = 100 metres

(a) Find the three-figure bearing of the boathouse from the house.

.... °

[1]

(b) Find the actual distance from the boathouse to the greenhouse.

.... metres

[2]

(c) A summerhouse is

             450 metres from the house
             700 metres from the greenhouse

Plot with a cross (×) the position of the summerhouse on the map.
Do not rub out your construction lines.

[2]

[Total 5 marks]

16 Angie makes wedding cakes with three tiers.

She needs 800 grams of sultanas to make the bottom tier of a cake.
The middle tier needs 75% of the ingredients required for the bottom tier.
The top tier needs 50% of the ingredients of the bottom tier.

Angie needs to make five wedding cakes. She has 8 kilograms of sultanas.

Does Angie have enough sultanas to make five cakes? Show your working.

[Total 5 marks]

---

17 Carrots cost 69p per kilogram.
Ahmed buys 2.785 kilograms of carrots.

(a) Estimate the cost, in pence, of his carrots.
Show the numbers you use to work out your estimate.

.... p
[2]

(b) Is your estimate in (a) bigger or smaller than the actual cost?
Tick the correct answer.

Bigger ☐   Smaller ☐

Explain your answer.

....

....
[1]

[Total 3 marks]

8

18 The graph can be used to convert between pounds (£) and Australian dollars ($).

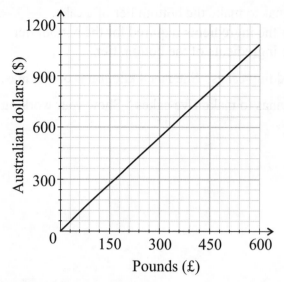

Jack goes on holiday to Australia and China.

(a) He changes £300 into Australian dollars ($).
    How many Australian dollars does he get for £300?

$ ....

[1]

(b) He spends $390 of his money while in Australia.
    He converts the rest of his Australian dollars into Chinese yuan using the exchange rate

        1 Australian dollar = 6 Chinese yuan

    How many Chinese yuan does Jack get?

.... yuan

[2]

[Total 3 marks]

19 Work out the value of k if

$$k \times 3^{-2} = 4$$

$k = $ ....

[Total 2 marks]

20 The diagram shows an isosceles triangle.

Three of these isosceles triangles fit together with three squares around a point O.

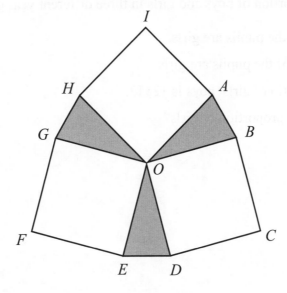

Show clearly that angle $OAB = 75°$.

21 Work out $1\frac{2}{3} \times 1\frac{5}{8}$. Give your answer as a mixed number.

....

[Total 3 marks]

194

22 Write 594 000 000 000 in standard form.

....

[Total 1 mark]

23 A school records the proportion of boys and girls in three different year groups.

In Year 9, $\frac{9}{20}$ of the pupils are girls.

In Year 10, 49% of the pupils are girls.

In Year 11, the ratio of girls : boys is 12 : 13.

Which year has the largest proportion of girls?

....

[Total 3 marks]

24 The diagram shows a circle A and a sector B.

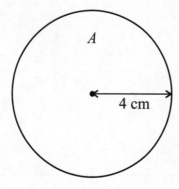
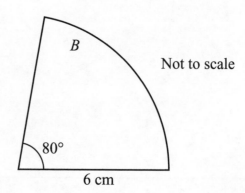

Not to scale

Show that the area of A is twice the area of B.

[Total 4 marks]

25 Quadrilateral *ABCD* is made up of two right-angled triangles, *ABC* and *ACD*.

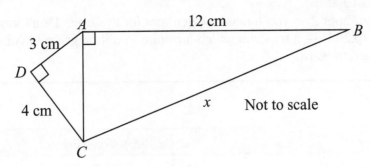

(a) Find the length of the side labelled *x*.

.... cm
[4]

(b) Find the area of quadrilateral *ABCD*.

.... cm²
[2]

[Total 6 marks]

26 Solve the simultaneous equations

$$3x + 2y = 17$$
$$2x + y = 10$$

x = ...

y = ...
[Total 3 marks]

[TOTAL FOR PAPER = 80 MARKS]

Practice Paper 2: Calculator
Right, here's Practice Paper 2 — you'll need a calculator for this one. Don't forget there's a page on formulas (p.244) — it tells you which formulas you'll be given in your exam and which you'll need to learn.

Candidate Surname		Candidate Forename(s)

Centre Number	Candidate Number	Candidate Signature

GCSE

Mathematics

Paper 2 (Calculator)

Foundation Tier

Practice Paper
Time allowed: 1 hour 30 minutes

You must have:
Pen, pencil, eraser, ruler, protractor, pair of compasses.
You may use tracing paper.

You **may use** a calculator.

Instructions to candidates
- Use **black** ink to write your answers.
- Write your name and other details in the spaces provided above.
- Answer **all** questions in the spaces provided.
- In calculations, show clearly how you worked out your answers.
- Do all rough work on the paper.
- Unless a question tells you otherwise, take the value of π to be 3.142, or use the π button on your calculator.

Information for candidates
- The marks available are given in brackets at the end of each question.
- You may get marks for method, even if your answer is incorrect.
- There are 28 questions in this paper. There are no blank pages.
- There are 80 marks available for this paper.

Answer ALL the questions.

Write your answers in the spaces provided.

You must show all of your working.

1   Write $\frac{3}{5}$ as a percentage.
Circle your answer.

6%   30%   15%   60%

[Total 1 mark]

2   A function is represented by this number machine.

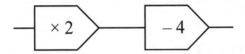

The **output** of the machine is 20. Circle the input.

8   12   14   36

[Total 1 mark]

3   Complete this bill.

Barbara's Café

Menu Item	Number Ordered	Cost per Item	Total
Tea	2	£1.25	£2.50
Coffee	....	£1.60	£9.60
Cake	4	£...............	£5.20
Tip			£2.50
		Total cost	£...............

[Total 3 marks]

1

4 (a) Draw a line to match each shape to its number of **surfaces**.

cone   4

                             3

sphere

                             2

cylinder
                             1

[2]

(b) Write down the number of **vertices** for a triangular prism.

....

[1]

[Total 3 marks]

5 (a) Calculate

$$\sqrt{12.2} + (1.1 + 3.6)^3$$

Write down all the digits on your calculator.

....

[1]

(b) Round your answer to (a) to two decimal places.

....

[1]

[Total 2 marks]

6 Kamil has these four number cards.

     3   5   4   6

List the eight even numbers greater than 4000 Kamil can make by rearranging all four cards.

[Total 2 marks]

7 Circle the number below that is both a square number and a cube number.

16   27   64   25   8   100

[Total 1 mark]

---

8 (a) Expand

$$4(a + 2)$$

....

[1]

(b) Factorise

$$y^2 + 5y$$

....

[1]

[Total 2 marks]

---

9 The ages (in years) of seven children are

6   12   9   6   5   7   11

(a) Find the mode of the ages.

....

[1]

(b) Find the median age.

....

[1]

(c) Find the mean age.

....

[2]

[Total 4 marks]

10 An equilateral triangle *T* is shown on the grid.

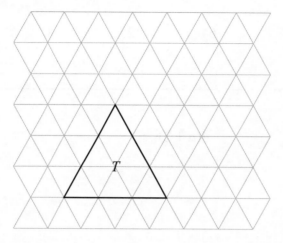

(a) Another triangle congruent to *T* is joined to *T* to form a quadrilateral.
Write down the number of lines of symmetry of the quadrilateral.

....

[1]

(b) Show on the grid how four triangles congruent to *T* can be joined together
to form a shape with rotational symmetry of order 3.

[1]

[Total 2 marks]

11 Work out 185% of £3500.

£ ....

[Total 2 marks]

4

12 Sandra attends a job interview at a school.
The school refunds her travelling expenses if she uses the cheapest possible method of transport.

There are two methods of transport that Sandra can use to attend the interview.

Method 1: By car	**Method 2: By car and train**
Sandra lives 27 miles from the school.	Sandra lives 4 miles from the station. The cost of a return train ticket is £17.60.

The school refunds car travel at a rate of 40p per mile.

Which method should Sandra use to travel to her interview and home again if she wants a refund for her expenses?

Show how you work out your answer.

[Total 3 marks]

13 A car park contains 28 cars and 16 motorbikes.

$\frac{3}{4}$ of the cars and $\frac{3}{8}$ of the motorbikes are red.
A red vehicle is chosen at random.

What is the probability that it is a car? Give your answer as a fraction in its simplest form.

....

[Total 3 marks]

Practice Paper 2

14 (a) Complete the table of values for $y = 7 - 2x$.

x	−2	−1	0	1	2	3	4
y		9	7			1	

[2]

(b) Draw the graph of $y = 7 - 2x$ for values of x between −2 and 4.

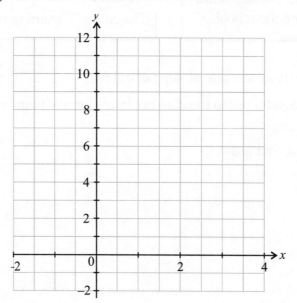

[2]

(c) What is the gradient of the line $y = 7 - 2x$?
Circle your answer.

−2   −1   2   7

[1]

[Total 5 marks]

15 Solve the equation $3(2x - 4) = 2x + 8$

x = ...

[Total 3 marks]

16 Kieron works out $5 \times \frac{2}{3}$ and gets the answer $\frac{10}{15}$.

Explain what mistake Kieron has made in calculating his answer.

....

....

[Total 1 mark]

17 The budget airline 'Fly By Us' produces this graph to show how their passenger numbers have increased.

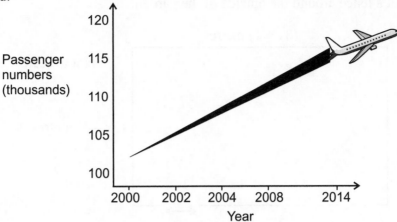

Give three different criticisms of the graph.

Criticism 1 ....

....

Criticism 2 ....

....

Criticism 3 ....

....

[Total 3 marks]

18 *AC* and *DG* are straight lines.

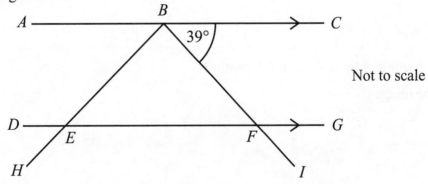

Not to scale

BH is perpendicular to *BI*.

Work out the size of angle *DEH*.
Show how you work out your answer.

..........................°

[Total 3 marks]

Practice Paper 2

19 Jimmy has a rectangular vegetable garden measuring $(3x + 1)$ metres by $(2x - 3)$ metres.

Jimmy wants to put a fence around the outside of the garden.

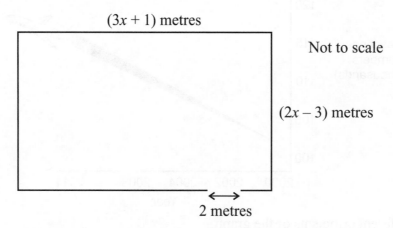

(3x + 1) metres

Not to scale

(2x – 3) metres

2 metres

He needs a 2 metre gap along one edge so that he can get in and out.

(a) Show that the length of the fence, L m, is given by the formula $L = 10x - 6$.

[2]

(b) Show that L is always an even number when x is a whole number.

[2]

[Total 4 marks]

20 Enlarge triangle A by scale factor 3, centre P.

Label the image B.

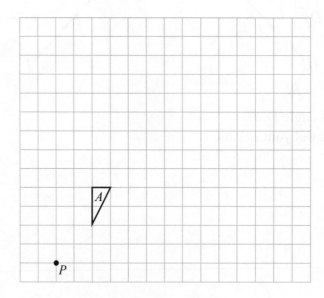

[Total 2 marks]

8

21 $\xi = \{1, 2, 3, \ldots, 10\}$
$A = \{x : 2 < x \leq 6\}$
$B = \{x : x \text{ is a factor of } 12\}$

Complete the Venn diagram to show the elements of each set.

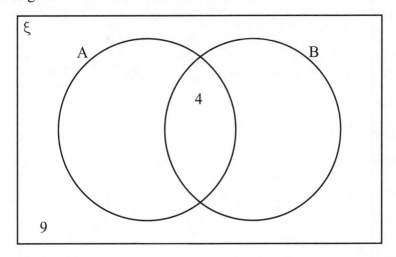

[Total 3 marks]

22 Orange juice and lemonade are mixed in the ratio 3 : 5 to make orangeade.

Orange juice costs £1.60 per litre.
Lemonade costs £1.20 per litre.

What is the cost of making 18 litres of orangeade?

£ ....

[Total 4 marks]

23 Make x the subject of the formula

$$y = \frac{x^2 - 2}{5}$$

....

[Total 2 marks]

24 The scatter graph shows the maximum power (in kW)
and the maximum speed (in km/h) of a sample of cars.

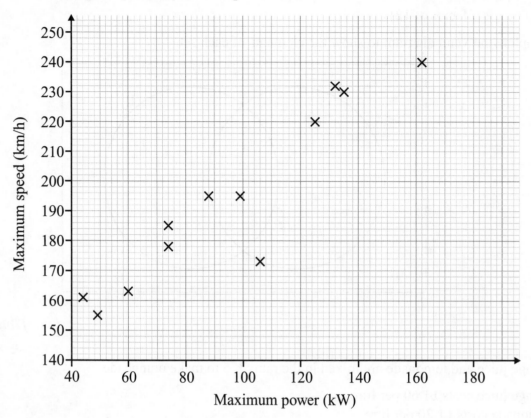

(a) One of the cars has a maximum speed of 220 km/h.
Write down the maximum power of this car.

.... kW

[1]

(b) One of the points is an outlier as it does not fit in with the trend.
Draw a ring around this point on the graph.

[1]

(c) Ignoring the outlier, describe the correlation shown on the scatter graph.

.... correlation

[1]

(d) A different car has a maximum power of 104 kW.
By drawing a suitable line on your scatter graph, estimate the maximum speed of this car.

.... km/h

[2]

(e) Explain why it may not be reliable to use the scatter graph to estimate
the maximum speed of a car with a maximum power of 190 kW.

....

....

[1]

[Total 6 marks]

25 Ollie and Amie each have an expression.

Ollie	Amie
$(x + 4)^2 - 1$	$(x + 5)(x + 3)$

Show clearly that Ollie's expression is equivalent to Amie's expression.

26 A company consists of 80 office assistants and a number of managers.

The pie chart shows how the 80 office assistants travel to work.

Office Assistants

(a) How many office assistants travel to work by car?

....

[2]

18 of the managers travel by car.
Overall, 40% of the people in the company travel by car.

(b) Work out how many people there are in the company.

....

[2]

[Total 4 marks]

27 The diagram shows a solid aluminium cylinder and a solid silver cube.

Cylinder (aluminium)   Cube (silver)

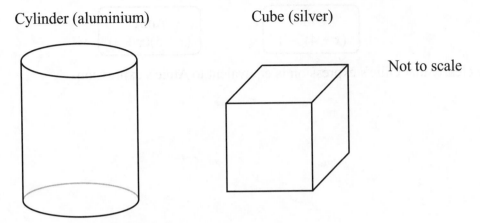

Not to scale

- The volume of the cylinder is 1180 cm³.
- The cylinder and the cube have the same mass.
- The density of aluminium is 2.7 g/cm³ and the density of silver is 10.5 g/cm³.

(a) Calculate the mass of the cylinder.

.... g

[2]

(b) Calculate the side length of the cube. Give your answer correct to two significant figures.

.... cm

[4]

[Total 6 marks]

28 The diagram shows a right-angled triangle.

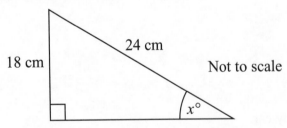

18 cm

24 cm

Not to scale

$x°$

Calculate the value of x. Give your answer correct to 1 decimal place.

$x =$ ....

[Total 2 marks]

[TOTAL FOR PAPER = 80 MARKS]

Practice Paper 3: Calculator
Finally, here's Practice Paper 3 — you'll be pleased to know that you can use your calculator for this one too. Take a look at the formulas page on p.244 if you need a reminder of which formulas you need to learn and which you'll be given in the exam.

Candidate Surname		Candidate Forename(s)

Centre Number	Candidate Number	Candidate Signature

GCSE

Mathematics
Paper 3 (Calculator)

Foundation Tier

Practice Paper
Time allowed: 1 hour 30 minutes

You must have:
Pen, pencil, eraser, ruler, protractor, pair of compasses.
You may use tracing paper.

You **may use** a calculator.

Instructions to candidates
- Use **black** ink to write your answers.
- Write your name and other details in the spaces provided above.
- Answer **all** questions in the spaces provided.
- In calculations, show clearly how you worked out your answers.
- Do all rough work on the paper.
- Unless a question tells you otherwise, take the value of π to be 3.142, or use the π button on your calculator.

Information for candidates
- The marks available are given in brackets at the end of each question.
- You may get marks for method, even if your answer is incorrect.
- There are 28 questions in this paper. There are no blank pages.
- There are 80 marks available for this paper.

Answer ALL the questions.

Write your answers in the spaces provided.

You must show all of your working.

1   Write one of the signs <, =, or > on each answer line to make a true statement.

$$0.4 \quad \text{............} \quad 0.34$$

$$\frac{3}{4} \quad \text{............} \quad 0.75$$

$$7\% \quad \text{............} \quad 0.7$$

[Total 2 marks]

2   The diagram shows part of a number line.

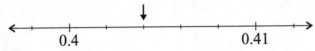

Circle the number the arrow points to.

0.42   0.44   0.402   0.404

[Total 1 mark]

3   Round 20 758 to the nearest 100.

....
[Total 1 mark]

4   What number is 12 less than −4.2?

....
[Total 1 mark]

5   Circle the number below that has exactly four factors.

2   3   5   8   9   12

[Total 1 mark]

6 24 pupils take a violin exam. Their marks are shown below.

110	103	115	134	121	98
128	112	107	112	125	132
114	102	125	93	120	120
106	111	99	98	127	115

The certificate each pupil receives depends upon their mark.

Result of exam	Mark
Fail	Under 100
Pass	100 – 119
Merit	120 – 129
Distinction	130 and above

(a) Complete the table to show the number of pupils achieving each result.
The first row has been filled in for you.

Result of exam	Tally	Frequency
Fail	I I I I	4
Pass		
Merit		
Distinction		
	Total:	24

[2]

(b) What fraction of the pupils failed the exam? Give your fraction in its simplest form.

....

[2]

(c) Draw on the grid a suitable diagram to show the number of pupils achieving each result.

[3]

[Total 7 marks]

2

7   A pencil case contains 10 coloured pencils.

  1 pencil is yellow.
  2 pencils are red.
  The other pencils are either green or blue.

Carla picks one coloured pencil at random.
She has the same chance of picking a green pencil as a red pencil.

Circle the word that describes the probability of picking:

(a)   a black pencil,

  impossible   unlikely   evens   likely

[1]

(b)   a blue pencil.

  impossible   unlikely   evens   likely

[1]

[Total 2 marks]

8   Here are the names of four types of quadrilateral.

  [Parallelogram]   [Square]   [Trapezium]   [Kite]

Choose from this list the quadrilateral that has:

(a)   exactly one pair of parallel sides,

  ....
[1]

(b)   no lines of symmetry, but rotational symmetry of order 2.

  ....
[1]

[Total 2 marks]

9   Circle the vector that translates a shape 5 units **left**.

  $\begin{pmatrix} -5 \\ 0 \end{pmatrix}$ $\begin{pmatrix} 5 \\ 0 \end{pmatrix}$ $\begin{pmatrix} 0 \\ 5 \end{pmatrix}$ $\begin{pmatrix} 0 \\ -5 \end{pmatrix}$

[Total 1 mark]

10 Rick multiplies three different numbers together and gets 90.
One of his numbers is a square number, and the other two are prime numbers.
What are the three numbers he uses?

....

[Total 3 marks]

11 Nigel sees this recipe for cupcakes.

> **Recipe for 12 cupcakes**
> 140 grams butter
> 140 grams flour
> 132 grams sugar
> 2 eggs
> 1 tablespoon milk

Nigel wants to make 30 cupcakes. How much sugar does he need?

.... g

[Total 2 marks]

12 Ajay buys some packets of ginger biscuits.
Jane buys some packets of shortbread biscuits.

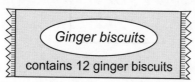
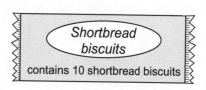

Ajay and Jane buy the same number of biscuits.

What is the smallest number of packets of shortbread biscuits Jane could have bought?

.... packets

[Total 3 marks]

13 Mary is preparing cream teas for 30 people.

Each person needs 2 scones, 1 tub of clotted cream and 1 small pot of jam.

She has £35 to buy everything.

> A pack of 10 scones costs £1.35
> A pack of 6 tubs of clotted cream costs £2.95
> Each small pot of jam costs 40p

Will she have enough money? Show how you work out your answer.

....

[Total 5 marks]

---

14 The grid shows part of two shapes, *A* and *B*.

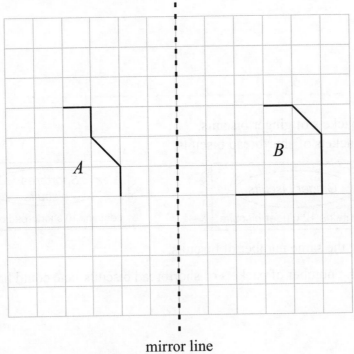

mirror line

B is the reflection of *A* in the mirror line.

Complete both shapes.

[Total 2 marks]

15 The diagram shows an object made from 8 centimetre cubes.

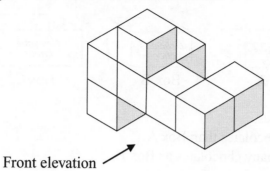

Front elevation

Draw on the grids below the plan view and the front elevation of the object.

Plan view

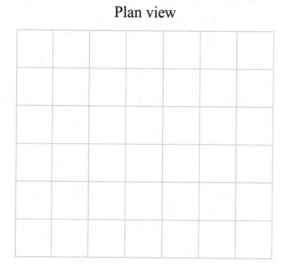

Front elevation

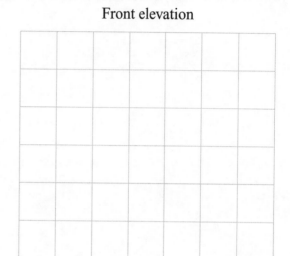

[Total 2 marks]

16 Two congruent trapeziums and two triangles fit inside a square of side 12 cm as shown.

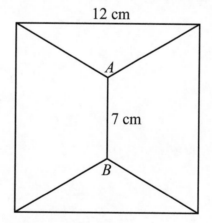

12 cm

Not to scale

7 cm

A

B

$AB = 7$ cm

Work out the area of each trapezium.

.... cm²

[Total 2 marks]

17 A chocolate manufacturer makes boxes of chocolates in three different sizes.

Box A   Box B   Box C

Box A contains c chocolates.
Box B contains 4 more chocolates than Box A.
Box C contains twice as many chocolates as Box B.
Altogether there are 60 chocolates.

Work out how many chocolates there are in each box.

Box A: ....

Box B: ....

Box C: ....

[Total 5 marks]

18 Simplify

(a) $y \times y \times y$

....
[1]

(b) $n^6 \div n^2$

....
[1]

(c) $(a^4)^3$

....
[1]

[Total 3 marks]

19 The diagram shows a ramp placed against two steps.

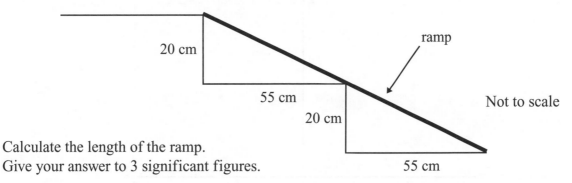

20 cm

ramp

55 cm

20 cm

Not to scale

Calculate the length of the ramp.
Give your answer to 3 significant figures.

55 cm

.... cm

[Total 3 marks]

20 A route between Guilford and Bath has a distance of 180 kilometres.
Dave drives from Guilford to Bath. He takes 3 hours.

Olivia drives the same route. Her average speed is 15 kilometres per hour faster than Dave's.

(a) How long does it take Olivia to drive from Guilford to Bath?
Give your answer in hours and minutes

.... hours .... minutes
[3]

(b) Why is it important to your calculation that Olivia drives the same route as Dave?

....

....
[1]

[Total 4 marks]

8

21 (a) Complete the table of values for $y = x^2 + x - 2$.

x	-3	-2	-1	0	1	2	3
y		0	-2	-2			10

[2]

(b) Draw on the grid the graph of $y = x^2 + x - 2$ for values of x between -3 and 3.

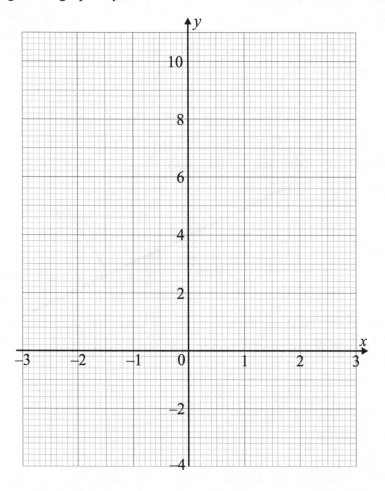

[2]

[Total 4 marks]

22 The ratio of angles in a triangle is $2:3:5$.
Show that this a right-angled triangle.

[Total 3 marks]

23 The values of four houses at the start of 2017 are shown.

| House 1 | House 2 | House 3 | House 4 |
| £120 000 | £144 000 | £145 000 | £150 000 |

(a) Which house has a value 25% higher than House 1?

House ....
[1]

(b) At the start of 2019, the value of House 2 is £161 280.
Find the percentage increase in the value of House 2.

.... %
[3]

[Total 4 marks]

---

24 Anna and Carl each think of a sequence of numbers.

Anna's sequence

4th term = 17

Term-to-term rule is
Add 3

Carl's sequence

Term-to-term rule is
Add 6

The 1st term of Anna's sequence is double the 1st term of Carl's sequence.

Work out the 5th term of Carl's sequence.

....

[Total 3 marks]

25 (a) Factorise $x^2 + 7x - 18$.

....
[2]

(b) Solve the equation $x^2 + 7x - 18 = 0$.

$x =$ .... or $x =$ ....
[1]

[Total 3 marks]

26 George has two fair spinners.

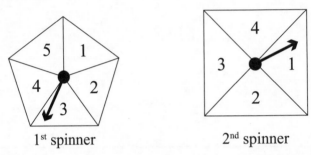

1ˢᵗ spinner   2ⁿᵈ spinner

He spins each spinner once and records whether the score is an odd or an even number.

(a) Complete the tree diagram to show the probabilities.

1ˢᵗ spinner   2ⁿᵈ spinner

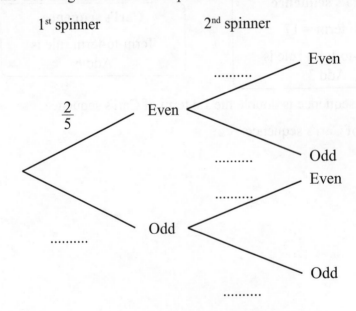

[2]

(b) Work out the probability that George spins two odd numbers.

....
[2]

[Total 4 marks]

27 The line L passes through the points $(-2, -7)$ and $(3, 8)$.
Find the equation of line L.

....

[Total 4 marks]

28 The grouped frequency table below shows the weights of 25 rabbits in a pet shop.

Weight (w g)	Frequency
$800 \leq w < 1000$	5
$1000 \leq w < 1200$	8
$1200 \leq w < 1400$	9
$1400 \leq w < 1600$	3

Estimate the mean weight.

.... g

[Total 3 marks]

[TOTAL FOR PAPER = 80 MARKS]

Answers

Section One — Number

Page 7 (Warm-up Questions)

1 20

2 £14.70

3 a) 957   b) 48

4 a) 0.245   b) 5

5 a) 387   b) 544   c) 121.8   d) 8.45

6 a) 13   b) 121   c) 62   d) 30

7 a) 12   b) −6   c) 9   d) −3

Page 8 (Exam Questions)

3 a) 81 *[1 mark]*
   b) 64 *[1 mark]*

4 E.g. 288 ÷ −3 = −96
   −96 ÷ 12 = −8
   So the third number is −8
   [3 marks available — 1 mark for a correct method, 1 mark for at least one correct calculation, 1 mark for the correct answer]
   You could have worked out −3 × 12 (= −36) and divided by this instead, but the division would be pretty tricky.

5 £200 − £5 = £195
   $15\overline{)1^19^45}$, so each ticket costs £13
   [3 marks available — 1 mark for subtracting £5 from £200, 1 mark for dividing £195 by 15, 1 mark for the correct final answer]

6 Total miles travelled = (30 × 2) + (28 × 2) + (39 × 2) + (40 × 2)
   = 60 + 56 + 78 + 80
   = 274 miles
   Expenses for miles travelled = 274 × 30p = 8220p = £82.20
   Expenses for food = 4 × £8 = £32
   Total expenses = £82.20 + £32 = £114.20
   [4 marks available — 1 mark for finding total miles, 1 mark for multiplying total miles by 30 or 0.3(0), 1 mark for finding food expenses, 1 mark for the correct final answer]

Page 13 (Warm-up Questions)

1 31, 37

2 27 ÷ 3 = 9. So 27 is not a prime number because it divides by 3 and 9.

3 1, 2, 4, 5, 8, 10, 20, 40

4 2 and 5

5 20 *(multiples of 4 are: 4, 8, 12, 16, 20, ...,*
   multiples of 5 are: 5, 10, 15, 20, ...)

6 8 *(factors of 32 are: 1, 2, 4, 8, 16, 32,*
   factors of 88 are: 1, 2, 4, 8, 11, 22, 44, 88)

Page 14 (Exam Questions)

3 Jasmine is incorrect as there are four prime numbers (101, 103, 107 and 109) between 100 and 110.
   [2 marks available — 1 mark for stating that Jasmine is incorrect, 1 mark for providing evidence]
   Writing one prime number between 100 and 110 is enough.

4 E.g. 37 (3 + 7 = 10, which is 1 more than 9, a square number)
   [2 marks available — 2 marks for a correct answer, otherwise 1 mark for a prime of two or more digits]

5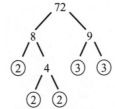
   72 = 2 × 2 × 2 × 3 × 3
   [2 marks available — 1 mark for a correct method, 1 mark for all prime factors correct]

6 a) LCM = $3^7 × 7^3 × 11^2$ *[1 mark]*
   b) HCF = $3^4 × 11$ *[1 mark]*

Page 20 (Warm-up Questions)

1 $\frac{3}{4}$

2 $\frac{2}{6}$ and $\frac{5}{15}$

3 a) $\frac{4}{15}$

   b) $\frac{2}{5} ÷ \frac{2}{3} = \frac{2}{5} × \frac{3}{2} = \frac{6}{10} = \frac{3}{5}$

   c) $\frac{2}{5} + \frac{2}{3} = \frac{6}{15} + \frac{10}{15} = \frac{16}{15} = 1\frac{1}{15}$

   d) $\frac{2}{3} - \frac{2}{5} = \frac{10}{15} - \frac{6}{15} = \frac{4}{15}$

4 0.7

5 66.6̇% (66.666...%) or 66$\frac{2}{3}$%

6 $\frac{2}{5}$

7 0.2̇85714̇

Page 21 (Exam Questions)

3 (12 400 ÷ 8) × 3 = 1550 × 3 = 4650
   [2 marks available — 1 mark for dividing by 8 or multiplying by 3, 1 mark for the correct answer]

4 65% = 0.65, $\frac{2}{3}$ = 0.666..., $\frac{33}{50}$ = 0.66
   So order is 0.065, 65%, $\frac{33}{50}$, $\frac{2}{3}$
   [2 marks available — 2 marks for all four numbers in the correct order, otherwise 1 mark for writing the numbers in the same form (either decimals, percentages or fractions)]

5 a) $1\frac{1}{8} × 2\frac{2}{5} = \frac{9}{8} × \frac{12}{5}$ *[1 mark]* $= \frac{108}{40}$ *[1 mark]*
       $= 2\frac{7}{10}$ *[1 mark]*
       [3 marks available in total — as above]
   b) $1\frac{3}{4} ÷ \frac{7}{9} = \frac{7}{4} × \frac{9}{7}$ *[1 mark]* $= \frac{63}{28}$ or $\frac{9}{4}$ *[1 mark]*
       $= 2\frac{1}{4}$ *[1 mark]*
       [3 marks available in total — as above]

6 $\frac{1}{4}$ = 25%, so Jenny pays 1 − 25% − 20% − 20%
   = 1 − 65% = 35% *[1 mark]*
   £17.50 = 35% *[1 mark]*, so 1% = £17.50 ÷ 35 = £0.50.
   The total bill was £0.50 × 100 *[1 mark]* = £50 *[1 mark]*.
   [4 marks available in total — as above]

Page 26 (Warm-up Questions)

1 a) 3.2   b) 1.8
   c) 2.3   d) 0.5
   e) 9.8

2 a) 3   b) 5
   c) 2   d) 7
   e) 3

3 a) 350 *(the decider is 2, so keep the 5, and fill the missing place with zero)*

   b) 500 *(the decider is 6, so round the 4 up to 5, and fill the missing places with zeros)*

   c) 12.4 *(the decider is 8, so round the 3 up to 4)*

   d) 0.036 *(the decider is 6, so round the 5 up to 6)*

4 a) 2900   b) 500

   c) 100

5 a) 100 *(This is approximately $(30 - 10) \times 5$)*

   b) Overestimate *(you rounded all the numbers up, so your estimate will be bigger than the actual answer)*

6 567.5 ml

7 a) $0.9145 \leq x < 0.9155$

   b) $1115 \leq y < 1125$

8 a) 37.9

   b) 2.1

Page 27 (Exam Questions)

2 a) 428.6 light years *[1 mark]*

   b) 430 light years *[1 mark]*

3 a) E.g. $(£4.95 \times 28) + (£11 \times 19) \approx (£5 \times 30) + (£10 \times 20)$
       $= £150 + £200 = £350$
       [2 marks available — 1 mark for rounding each value sensibly, 1 mark for a sensible estimate]

   b) E.g. This is a sensible estimate as it is very close to the actual value of £347.60 *[1 mark]*.

4 E.g. $\dfrac{12.2 \times 1.86}{0.19} \approx \dfrac{10 \times 2}{0.2} = \dfrac{20}{0.2} = 100$
   [2 marks available — 1 mark for rounding to suitable values, 1 mark for the correct final answer using your values]

5 Minimum weight = 56.5 kg *[1 mark]*
   Maximum weight = 57.5 kg *[1 mark]*
   [2 marks available in total — as above]

6 Smallest possible value of $a = 3.8 - 0.05 = 3.75$
   Largest possible value of $a = 3.8 + 0.05 = 3.85$
   So error interval is $3.75 \leq a < 3.85$
   [2 marks available — 1 mark for $3.75 \leq a$, 1 mark for $a < 3.85$]

Page 32 (Warm-up Questions)

1 a) 0.4096

   b) 49

   c) 10^6

2 a) $4^6 (= 4096)$ b) $5^6 (= 15\ 625)$

   c) x^6

3 a) 49   b) $\dfrac{1}{27}$

4 a) 15

   b) 19

   c) 6

5 10 cm

6 27.18411

7 a) 2.89×10^6

   b) 0.0000711

8 2.1×10^4

9 a) 1.2×10^2

   b) 1.43×10^{-6}

Page 33 (Exam Questions)

2 $\sqrt{6.25} = 2.5$ cm *[1 mark]*

3 a) $A = 4.834 \times 10^9 = 4\ 834\ 000\ 000$ *[1 mark]*

   b) C, B, A $(5.21 \times 10^3, 2.4 \times 10^5, 4.834 \times 10^9)$ *[1 mark]*

4 $\dfrac{3^4 \times 3^7}{3^6} = \dfrac{3^{(4+7)}}{3^6} = \dfrac{3^{11}}{3^6} = 3^{(11-6)} = 3^5$
   [2 marks available — 1 mark for a correct attempt at adding or subtracting powers, 1 mark for the correct final answer]

5 a) $6^{(5-3)} = 6^2 = 36$ *[1 mark]*

   b) $(2^4 \times 2^7) = 2^{(4+7)} = 2^{11}$
       $(2^3 \times 2^2) = 2^{(3+2)} = 2^5$, so $(2^3 \times 2^2)^2 = (2^5)^2 = 2^{10}$
       So $(2^4 \times 2^7) \div (2^3 \times 2^2)^2 = 2^{11} \div 2^{10} = 2^1 = 2$
       [2 marks available — 1 mark if each bracket has been correctly simplified, 1 mark for the correct answer]

6 time (s) = distance (miles) ÷ speed (miles/s)
   $= (9 \times 10^7) \div (2 \times 10^5)$ seconds *[1 mark]*
   = 450 seconds *[1 mark]*
   [2 marks available in total — as above]

Page 34 (Revision Questions)

1 A square number is a whole number multiplied by itself. The first ten are: 1, 4, 9, 16, 25, 36, 49, 64, 81 and 100.

2 0.1

3 £38

4 a) £120   b) £0.50 = 50p

5 a) 1377   b) 26

   c) 62.7   d) 0.35

6 a) −16   b) 7   c) 20

7 41, 43, 47, 53, 59

8 The multiples of a number are its times table.

   a) 10, 20, 30, 40, 50, 60

   b) 4, 8, 12, 16, 20, 24

9 a) $210 = 2 \times 3 \times 5 \times 7$

   b) $1050 = 2 \times 3 \times 5 \times 5 \times 7$
       $= 2 \times 3 \times 5^2 \times 7$

10 a) 14   b) 40

11 a) $\dfrac{25}{16}$ or $1\dfrac{9}{16}$ b) $\dfrac{44}{15}$ or $2\dfrac{14}{15}$

    c) $\dfrac{23}{8}$ or $2\dfrac{7}{8}$ d) $\dfrac{11}{21}$

12 a) 320   b) £60

13 Amy

14 a) i) $\dfrac{4}{100} = \dfrac{1}{25}$ ii) 4%

    b) i) $\dfrac{65}{100} = \dfrac{13}{20}$ ii) 0.65

15 a) Recurring decimals have a pattern of numbers which repeats forever.

    b) $0.\dot{2}$

16 a) 17.7

    b) 6700

    c) 4 000 000

17 a) 100

    b) 1400

18 $150 \leq x < 250$

19 7^5

20 $\dfrac{1}{25}$

21 a) 11   b) 4

    c) 56   d) 10^5

22 a) 421.875   b) 4.8

    c) 8   d) 11

23 1. The front number must always be between 1 and 10.

    2. The power of 10, n, is how far the decimal point moves.

    3. n is positive for big numbers, and negative for small numbers.

24 a) 3.56×10^9 b) 0.00000275

25 a) 2×10^3 b) 1.2×10^{12}

Section Two — Algebra

Page 39 (Warm-up Questions)

1. a) $-2a$ b) $7p - 10q$ c) $6 + 7\sqrt{7}$
2. a) $-24mn$ b) $-6r + 33$ c) $5x^2 - 35xy$
3. $3(x + 4) - 6(3 - 2x) = 3x + 12 - 18 + 12x = 15x - 6$
4. a) $x^2 - 3x - 18$ b) $5a^2 - 18a - 8$
   c) $x^2 + 16x + 64$ d) $4y^2 - 12y + 9$
5. a) $3(x - 3)$ b) $4y(1 + 5y)$
   c) $(x + 4)(x - 4)$ d) $(4x + 5y)(4x - 5y)$

Page 40 (Exam Questions)

3. a) $4p$ *[1 mark]*
   b) $2m$ *[1 mark]*
   c) $4p + 3r$
   [2 marks available — 1 mark for 4p and 1 mark for 3r]
4. $6x + 3 = (3 \times 2x) + (3 \times 1) = 3(2x + 1)$ *[1 mark]*
5. a) $(x + 2)(x + 4) = x^2 + 4x + 2x + 8 = x^2 + 6x + 8$
   [2 marks available — 1 mark for expanding the brackets correctly, 1 mark for simplifying]
   b) $(y + 3)(y - 3) = y^2 - 3y + 3y - 9 = y^2 - 9$
   [2 marks available — 1 mark for expanding the brackets correctly, 1 mark for simplifying]
   c) $(2z - 1)(z - 5) = 2z^2 - 10z - z + 5 = 2z^2 - 11z + 5$
   [2 marks available — 1 mark for expanding the brackets correctly, 1 mark for simplifying]
6. a) $x^2 - 49 = x^2 - 7^2 = (x + 7)(x - 7)$
   [2 marks available — 2 marks for the correct final answer, otherwise 1 mark for attempting to use the difference of two squares]
   b) $9x^2 - 100 = (3x)^2 - 10^2 = (3x + 10)(3x - 10)$
   [2 marks available — 2 marks for the correct final answer, otherwise 1 mark for attempting to use the difference of two squares]
   c) $y^2 - m^2 = (y + m)(y - m)$
   [2 marks available — 2 marks for the correct final answer, otherwise 1 mark for attempting to use the difference of two squares]

Page 47 (Warm-up Questions)

1. a) $x = 2$ b) $x = 11$ c) $x = 6$ d) $x = 20$
2. a) $x = 4$ b) $y = 11$
3. $s = 12$
4. a) $y = 25$ b) $x = 11$
5. Total sweets in jar = $7b + 10$ (where b = number of blue sweets)
6. 20
7. $x = 3$
8. $b = 5a - 4$
9. $q = \dfrac{p + 8}{3}$

Page 48 (Exam Questions)

2. a) $S = 4m^2 + 2.5n$
   $S = (4 \times 2 \times 2) + (2.5 \times 10)$
   $S = 16 + 25 = 41$
   [2 marks available — 1 mark for correct substitution of m and n, 1 mark for correct final answer]
   b) $S = 4m^2 + 2.5n$
   $S = (4 \times 6.5 \times 6.5) + (2.5 \times 4)$
   $S = 169 + 10 = 179$
   [2 marks available — 1 mark for correct substitution of m and n, 1 mark for correct final answer]
3. a) $40 - 3x = 17x$
   $40 = 20x$ *[1 mark]*
   $x = 40 \div 20 = 2$ *[1 mark]*
   [2 marks available in total — as above]

b) $2y - 5 = 3y - 12$
   $-5 + 12 = 3y - 2y$ *[1 mark]*
   $y = 7$ *[1 mark]*
   [2 marks available in total — as above]
4. The sides of an equilateral triangle are all the same length, so
   $4(x - 1) = 3x + 5$ *[1 mark]*
   $4x - 4 = 3x + 5$
   $x = 9$ *[1 mark]*
   So each side is $(3 \times 9) + 5 = 32$ cm long *[1 mark]*.
   [3 marks available in total — as above]
   To check your answer, put your value of x into the expression for the other side of the triangle — you should get the same answer.
5. $\dfrac{a + 2}{3} = b - 1$
   $a + 2 = 3b - 3$ *[1 mark]*
   $a = 3b - 5$ *[1 mark]*
   [2 marks available in total — as above]
6. Call the number of Whitewater fans f. Redwood fans = $3 \times f = 3f$.
   Difference = $3f - f = 2f$, so $2f = 7000$, so $f = 3500$.
   Total fans = $3f + f = 4f = 4 \times 3500 = 14\,000$.
   [3 marks available — 1 mark for the expressions for the number of fans for each team, 1 mark for forming and solving the equation to find f, 1 mark for the correct answer]

Page 52 (Warm-up Questions)

1. a) $18, 22$ b) $81, 243$ c) $17, 23$
2. a) Rule = square the number of the term
   b) $36, 49$
   c) Yes, because $100 = 10 \times 10 = 10^2$ so it is a square number.
3. a) Arithmetic — to get from one term to the next, you add the same number to the previous term each time.
   b) Geometric — to get from one term to the next, you multiply the previous term by the same number each time.
4. a) $-4n + 31$ b) -49
5. $n = -2, -1, 0, 1, 2, 3, 4$
6. a) $x < 5$ b) $x \geq 7$

Page 53 (Exam Questions)

2. $-3, -2, -1, 0, 1$
   [2 marks available — 2 marks for all 5 numbers correct, otherwise 1 mark for the correct answer with one number missing or one number incorrect]
3. a)

   [1 mark]
   b) The number of circles added increases by one each time, so the tenth triangle number is:
   $1 + 2 + 3 + 4 + 5 + 6 + 7 + 8 + 9 + 10 = 55$.
   [2 marks available — 1 mark for 55 and 1 mark for correct reasoning]
4. Second term = $7 - 3 = 4$
   Fourth term = $4 + 7 = 11$
   Fifth term = $7 + 11 = 18$
   [2 marks available — 2 marks for all three terms correct, otherwise 1 mark for at least one term correct]
5. $\underset{+4}{2} \quad \underset{+6}{6} \quad \underset{+8}{12} \quad 20$

   The difference is increasing by 2, so the next term is:
   $20 + 10 = 30$
   [2 marks available — 1 mark for spotting the pattern, 1 mark for the correct answer]
6. Largest possible value of $p = 45$
   Smallest possible value of $q = 26$ *[1 mark for both]*
   Largest possible value of $p - q = 45 - 26 = 19$ *[1 mark]*.
   [2 marks available in total — as above]

Page 57 (Warm-up Questions)

1 a) $(x-4)(x-2)$ b) $(x+1)(x-3)$
   c) $(x+4)(x+3)$

2 a) $x=-2$ or $x=-5$ b) $x=2$ or $x=-7$
   c) $x=2$ or $x=3$

3 $x=1, y=4$

4 $x=-1, y=3$

5 a) E.g. $2^2 \times 5^2 = 4 \times 25 = 100 \; (=10^2)$
   b) E.g. $2+7 = 9 \; (9 = 3 \times 3)$

6 LHS: $(x+2)^2 + (x-2)^2 = (x^2+4x+4) + (x^2-4x+4)$
                             $= 2x^2 + 8$
                             $= 2(x^2+4) =$ RHS

Page 58 (Exam Questions)

3 a) 16 is a factor of 48 *[1 mark]*
   b) E.g. $4+16 = 20$, which is even *[1 mark]*
   c) E.g. 38 is not a multiple of 4, 6 or 8 *[1 mark]*

4 $x+3y = 11 \;(1) \xrightarrow{\times 3} 3x+9y = 33 \;(3)$ *[1 mark]*
   $3x+y = 9 \;(2)$
   $(3)-(2)$:
   $\begin{aligned} 3x+9y &= 33 \\ -\underline{3x+\;y} &= \underline{9} \\ 8y &= 24 \\ y &= 3 \text{ *[1 mark]*} \end{aligned}$ $\begin{aligned} x+3y &= 11 \\ x+(3\times 3) &= 11 \\ x &= 11-9 \\ x &= 2 \text{ *[1 mark]*} \end{aligned}$
   [3 marks available in total — as above]

5 6 and 2 multiply to give 12 and subtract to give 4,
   so if $x^2+4x-12 = 0$,
   $(x+6)(x-2) = 0$
   [1 mark for correct numbers in brackets,
   1 mark for correct signs]
   $x+6 = 0$ or $x-2 = 0$
   $x = -6$ or $x = 2$
   [1 mark for both solutions]
   [3 marks available in total — as above]

6 $2(18+3q) + 3(3+q) = 36+6q+9+3q$
                            $= 9q + 45$
                            $= 9(q+5)$

   $2(18+3q) + 3(3+q)$ can be written as $9 \times$ a whole number
   (where the whole number is $(q+5)$), so it is a multiple of 9.
   [3 marks available — 1 mark for expanding brackets and
   simplifying, 1 mark for writing the expression as 9(q + 5),
   1 mark for explaining why this is a multiple of 9]

Page 59 (Revision Questions)

1 a) $3e$ b) $12f$
2 a) $7x-y$ b) $3a+9$
3 a) m^3 b) $7pq$ c) $18xy$
4 a) $6x+18$ b) $-9x+12$ c) $5x-x^2$
5 $6x$
6 a) $2x^2-x-10$ b) $25y^2+20y+4$
7 Putting in brackets (the opposite of multiplying out brackets).
8 a) $8(x+3)$ b) $9x(2x+3)$ c) $(6x+9y)(6x-9y)$
9 a) $x=7$ b) $x=16$ c) $x=3$
10 a) $x=4$ b) $x=2$ c) $x=3$
11 $Q=8$
12 14
13 37 marbles
14 $6x$ cm
15 $v = \dfrac{W-5}{4}$
16 a) 31, rule is add 7
   b) 256, rule is multiply by 4
   c) 19, rule is add previous two terms.
17 $6n-2$
18 Yes, it's the 5th term.

19 a) x is greater than minus seven.
   b) x is less than or equal to six.
20 $k = 1, 2, 3, 4, 5, 6, 7$
21 a) $x < 10$ b) $x \le 7$
22 a) $(x+2)(x+8)$ b) $(x+1)(x-7)$
23 $x = -6$ or $x = 3$
24 $x = 2, y = 5$
25 E.g. 19
26 $3(y+2) + 2(y+6)$
   $= 3y+6+2y+12$
   $= 5y+18 = 5(y+3) + 3$.
   $5(y+3)$ is a multiple of 5, so $5(y+3) + 3$ is not a multiple of 5.

Section Three — Graphs

Page 66 (Warm-up Questions)

1 a)
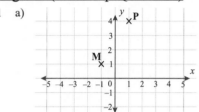
   b) Midpoint = $(0, 2.5)$

2 a) Yes b) No c) Yes d) Yes
   Try to rearrange each equation into the form y = mx + c —
   if you can do this then it's a straight line, if you can't it's not.

3
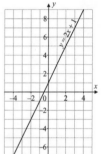

4
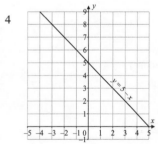

5 $\dfrac{15}{16}$
6 3
7 a) $y = -2x - 3$ b) $y = -2x + 9$

Page 67 (Exam Questions)

2 a) $\left(\dfrac{1+3}{2}, \dfrac{3+(-1)}{2}\right) = (2, 1)$

   [2 marks available — 1 mark for correct method and
   1 mark for correct final answer]
   A correct method here is to find the averages of the x- and
   y-coordinates. Or, you could identify the midpoint of AB on the
   graph to get your answer — but the first way is much safer.

   b) Comparing coordinates of point **C** and midpoint of **CD**:
   x-distance $= 2-0 = 2$
   y-distance $= 1 - -1 = 2$
   So to get from the midpoint to point **D**, move up 2 and right 2.
   So point **D** is $(2+2, 1+2) = (4, 3)$
   [2 marks available — 1 mark for each correct coordinate]

3 Find the gradient: $\frac{\text{change in } y}{\text{change in } x} = \frac{4-1}{1-0} = 3$

Line crosses y-axis at 1, so equation of line is $y = 3x + 1$.
[3 marks available — 3 marks for a fully correct answer, otherwise 2 marks for a correct gradient, or 1 mark for a correct method to find the gradient]

4 The lines are parallel, so their gradients are equal: m = 4 *[1 mark]*
When $x = -1$, $y = 0$, so put this into $y = 4x + c$
$0 = (4 \times -1) + c$, so c = 4 *[1 mark]*
So equation of line is $y = 4x + 4$ *[1 mark]*
[3 marks available in total — as above]

Page 74 (Warm-up Questions)

1 a)

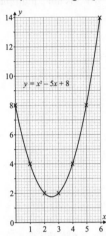

b) (2.5, 1.75)

2

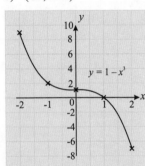

3 $x = 3$, $y = 1$

4 a) 36 litres (allow 35.5-36.5 litres)
   b) 4.4 gallons (allow 4.3-4.5 gallons)

5 a) 10 seconds   b) 4 m/s

6 Graph B

Pages 75-76 (Exam Questions)

2 a)

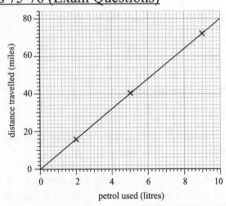

[2 marks available — 1 mark for all points plotted correctly, 1 mark for straight line joining points]

b) Gradient $= \frac{\text{change in } y}{\text{change in } x} = \frac{80-0}{10-0} = 8$

[2 marks available — 1 mark for correct method to find gradient, 1 mark for correct answer]

c) Distance travelled in miles per litre of petrol used *[1 mark]*

3 a) 0 *[1 mark]*
  b) −2, 0 *[1 mark]*
  c) (−1, −1) *[1 mark]*

4 a)

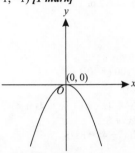

[2 marks available — 1 mark for correct shape, 1 mark for labelling (0, 0)]

b)

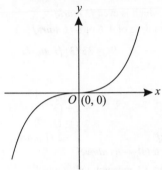

[2 marks available — 1 mark for correct shape, 1 mark for labelling (0, 0)]

5 a) $x = 1$ *[1 mark]*
  b)

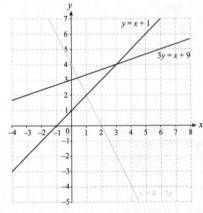

$x = 3$, $y = 4$
[3 marks available — 2 marks for correctly drawing the line $3y = x + 9$, 1 mark for the correct answer]

Page 77 (Revision Questions)

1 A(5, −3), B(4, 0), C(0, 3), D(−4, 5), E(−2, −3)

2 Midpoint = (2, 1.5)

3

4 E.g.

x	−2	0	2
y	6	−2	−10

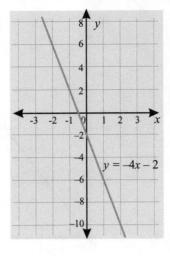

5 a) 2   b) $y = x + 15$

6 $y = 2x - 6$

7 $y = x - 9$

8 They are both "bucket shaped" graphs. $y = x^2 - 8$ is like a "u"
   whereas $y = -x^2 + 2$ is like an "n" (or an upturned bucket).

9 a)

x	−3	−2	−1	0	1
y	0	−2	−2	0	4

b)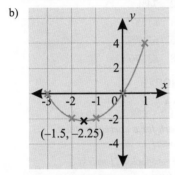

10 a) A graph with a "wiggle" in the middle. E.g.

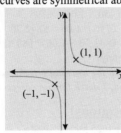

b) A graph made up of two curves in opposite corners.
   The curves are symmetrical about the lines $y = x$ and $y = -x$.
   E.g.

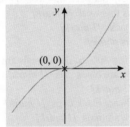

11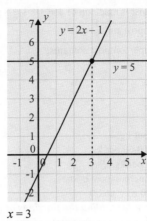

$x = 3$

12 The object has stopped.

13 a) Ben drove fastest on his way home.   b) 15 minutes

14 You would have to find the gradient, as the
    gradient = the rate of change.

15 a) 20 minutes   b) £20
    c) 26 minutes   d) 67p — allow between 65p and 69p

Section Four — Ratio, Proportion, and Rates of Change

Page 81 (Warm-up Questions)

1 a) 1:2   b) 4:9   c) 2:9   d) 16:7   e) 5:4

2 1:4.4

3 300 g ÷ 2 = 150 g; 150 g × 3 = 450 g of flour

4 a) 12:6 = 2:1   b) $\frac{12}{18} = \frac{2}{3}$

5 20

6 £1000:£1400

7 45, 60, 75
   (3 + 4 + 5 = 12 parts, so 180 ÷ 12 = 15 per part.)

Page 82 (Exam Questions)

2 a) Shortest side of shape A = 3 units
       Shortest side of shape B = 6 units
       Ratio of shortest sides = 3:6 = 1:2
       [2 marks available — 1 mark for finding the shortest sides of the triangles, 1 mark for the correct answer]

   b) Area of shape A = $\frac{1}{2} × 3 × 4$ = 6 square units *[1 mark]*
       Area of shape B = $\frac{1}{2} × 6 × 8$ = 24 square units *[1 mark]*
       Ratio of areas = 6:24 = 1:4 *[1 mark]*
       [3 marks available in total — as above]

3 Donations account for 14 parts = £21 000
   So 1 part = £21 000 ÷ 14 = £1500 *[1 mark]*
   Bills are 5 parts so cost £1500 × 5 = £7500 *[1 mark]*
   £21 000 − £7500 = £13 500 *[1 mark]*
   [3 marks available in total — as above]
   Careful here — you are given a part:whole ratio in the question.

4 Mr Appleseed's Supercompost is made up of $4 + 3 + 1 = 8$ parts,
so contains: $\frac{4}{8}$ soil, $\frac{3}{8}$ compost and $\frac{1}{8}$ grit.

16 kg of Mr Appleseed's Supercompost contains:

$\frac{4}{8} \times 16 = 8$ kg of soil

$\frac{3}{8} \times 16 = 6$ kg of compost

$\frac{1}{8} \times 16 = 2$ kg of grit

Soil costs £8 ÷ 40 = £0.20 per kg.
Compost costs £15 ÷ 25 = £0.60 per kg.
Grit costs £12 ÷ 15 = £0.80 per kg.
16 kg of Mr Appleseed's Supercompost costs:
$(8 \times 0.2) + (6 \times 0.6) + (2 \times 0.8) = £6.80$

[5 marks available — 1 mark for finding the fractions of each
material in the mix, 1 mark for the correct mass of one
material, 1 mark for the correct masses for the other two
materials, 1 mark for working out the price per kg for each
material, 1 mark for the correct answer]

Page 86 (Warm-up Questions)

1 £1.28

2 a) £12   b) 13

3 525 g

In the 250 g jar you get 250 g ÷ 125p = 2 g per p,
in the 350 g jar you get 350 g ÷ 210p = 1.666... g per p,
in the 525 g jar you get 525 g ÷ 250p = 2.1 g per p.

4 £210

5 Direct proportion graphs are straight lines and they go through
the origin.

6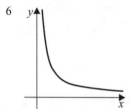

Page 87 (Exam Questions)

3 250 ml bottle: 250 ÷ 200 = 1.25 ml per penny
330 ml bottle: 330 ÷ 275 = 1.2 ml per penny
525 ml bottle: 525 ÷ 375 = 1.4 ml per penny
So the 525 ml bottle is the best value for money.

[3 marks available — 3 marks for finding the correct amounts
per penny for all three bottles and the correct answer, otherwise
2 marks for two correct amounts per penny or 1 mark for one
correct amount per penny]

You could also compare the cost per ml of each bottle.

4 1 bottle of water costs £52.50 ÷ 42 = £1.25 *[1 mark]*
There are £35 ÷ £1.25 = 28 girls in the club *[1 mark]*
[2 marks available in total — as above]

5 a) 250 people can be catered for 6 days
1 person can be catered for 6 × 250 = 1500 days
300 people can be catered for 1500 ÷ 300 = 5 days
[2 marks available — 1 mark for a correct method,
1 mark for the correct answer]

   b) For a 1-day cruise it could cater for 6 × 250 = 1500 people
For a 2-day cruise it could cater for 1500 ÷ 2 = 750 people
So it can cater for 750 – 250 = 500 more people
[3 marks available — 1 mark for a correct method to find
the number of people catered for on a 2-day cruise, 1 mark
for the correct number of people catered for on a 2-day
cruise, 1 mark for the correct final answer]

6 a)

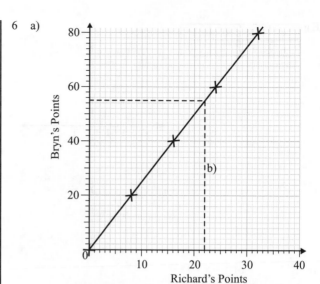

[2 marks available — 1 mark for two points marked
correctly, 1 mark for the correct straight line]

Use the ratio to work out the coordinates of a few points to plot.

E.g. If Richard scored 8 points, Bryn scored $8 \times \frac{5}{2} = 20$ points.

   b) 55 points (see graph) *[1 mark]*

Page 93 (Warm-up Questions)

1 £17   2 74%

3 9   4 £138

5 £205   6 62.5%

7 £3   8 £3376.53

Pages 94 (Exam Questions)

2 20% increase = 1 + 0.2 = 1.2
20% increase of £33.25 = 1.2 × £33.25 = £39.90
[2 marks available — 1 mark for a correct method,
1 mark for the correct answer]

3 He normally gets 240 ÷ 40 = 6 packs *[1 mark]*
40% cheaper = 1 – 0.4 = 0.6
So the stickers are 40p × 0.6 = 24p per pack this week *[1 mark]*
He can buy 240 ÷ 24 = 10 packs this week *[1 mark]*
So he can get 10 – 6 = 4 more packs *[1 mark]*
[4 marks available in total — as above]

4 A ratio of 3 : 7 means 3 out of 10 = 30% of the animals are cats
40% of 30% = 0.4 × 30% = 12% are black cats *[1 mark]*
100% – 30% = 70% are dogs *[1 mark]*
50% of 70% = 0.5 × 70% = 35% are black dogs *[1 mark]*
So, 35% + 12% = 47% are black animals *[1 mark]*
[4 marks available in total — as above]

5 Multiplier = 1 + 0.06 = 1.06
After 1 year she will owe: £750 × 1.06 = £795
After 2 years she will owe: £795 × 1.06 = £842.70
After 3 years she will owe: £842.70 × 1.06 = £893.262
= £893.26 (to the nearest penny)
[3 marks available — 1 mark for working out the multiplier,
1 mark for a correct method, 1 mark for the correct answer]

Page 100 (Warm-up Questions)

1 a) 65 mm   b) 0.25 kg

2 160 kg

3 3 feet 10 inches

4 a) 320 km   b) 4 feet

To do these conversions, find the conversion factor, then multiply and
divide by it. Then choose the most sensible answer.

5 a) 230 000 cm²   b) 3.45 m²

6 99 minutes

7 4.05 pm

8 0.16 m²

9   20 m/s

10 375 cm³

Pages 101 (Exam Questions)

2   4.30 pm till 5.00 pm is 30 minutes.
5.00 pm till 7.00 pm is 2 hours.
7.00 pm till 7.15 pm is 15 minutes.
So they spend:
2 hours + 30 minutes + 15 minutes = 2 hours 45 minutes
2 hours 45 minutes = 2.75 hours
2.75 × 12 = 33 hours
33 hours + 7 hours 10 minutes = 40 hours 10 minutes
[4 marks available — 1 mark for a correct method to find the time from 4.30 pm till 7.15 pm, 1 mark for finding the correct time from 4.30 pm till 7.15 pm, 1 mark for the correct total time for the first 12 days, 1 mark for the correct answer]

3   64 pints = 64 ÷ 8 = 8 gallons *[1 mark]*
8 gallons = 4 × 2 gallons ≈ 4 × 9 litres *[1 mark]*
= 36 litres *[1 mark]*
[3 marks available in total — as above]

4   One book weighs 0.55 lb so 8 books will weigh
8 × 0.55 lb = 4.4 lb *[1 mark]*
1 kg ≈ 2.2 lb
4.4 ÷ 2.2 = 2
So the eight books weigh 2 kg. *[1 mark]*
1 kg = 1000 g
2 × 1000 = 2000
So the books weigh 2000 g. *[1 mark]*
For 100 g postage is £0.50, so for 2000 g postage is
£0.50 × 20 = £10. *[1 mark]*
[4 marks available in total — as above]

5   Area of face A = 2 m × 4 m = 8 m² *[1 mark]*
Pressure = Force ÷ Area = 40 N ÷ 8 m² *[1 mark]*
= 5 N/m² *[1 mark]*
[3 marks available in total — as above]

Page 102 (Revision Questions)

1   a)   9 : 11   b)   3.5 : 1

2   80 blue scarves

3   $\frac{7}{2}$ or 3.5

4   a) $\frac{5}{25}$ or $\frac{1}{5}$ b)   384

5   51 ml olive oil, 1020 g tomatoes, 25.5 g garlic powder, 204 g onions

6   960 flowers

7   See p.84

8   The 500 ml tin

9   18

10 a)   19   b)   114   c)   21.05% (2 d.p.)   d)   475%

11 percentage change = (change ÷ original) × 100

12 35% decrease

13 17.6 m

14 2%

15 a)   £117.13 (to the nearest penny)   b)   6 years

16 a)   5600 cm³   b)   240 cm   c)   336 hours
d)   12 000 000 cm³   e)   12.8 cm²   f)   2750 mm³

17 9.48 pm

18 67.2 km/h

19 12 500 cm³

20 11 m²

Section Five — Shapes and Area

Page 110 (Warm-up Questions)

1   €   1 line of symmetry, rotational symmetry order 1
W   1 line of symmetry, rotational symmetry order 1
+   2 lines of symmetry, rotational symmetry order 2
-Đ   1 line of symmetry, rotational symmetry order 1
Q   0 lines of symmetry, rotational symmetry order 1

2   An equilateral triangle has 3 equal sides, 3 equal angles of 60°, 3 lines of symmetry and rotational symmetry of order 3.

3   A kite has 1 line of symmetry.

4   a)   **B** and **E** are similar.
b)   **A** and **D** are congruent.

5   A → B — rotation of 90° clockwise about the origin.
B → C — reflection in the line *y* = *x*.
C → A — reflection in the *y*-axis.
A → D — translation by the vector $\begin{pmatrix} -9 \\ -7 \end{pmatrix}$.

6   (9, –3)

Page 111 (Exam Questions)

2   *x* = 3 *[1 mark]*

3

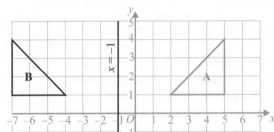

[2 marks available — 2 marks for correct reflection, otherwise 1 mark for triangle reflected but in wrong position]

4   a)   Scale factor from *EFGH* to *ABCD* = 9 ÷ 6 = 1.5 *[1 mark]*
EF = 6 ÷ 1.5 = 4 cm *[1 mark]*
[2 marks available in total — as above]
b)   *BC* = 4 × 1.5 = 6 cm *[1 mark]*

5

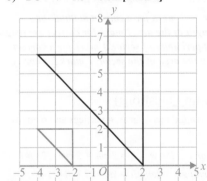

[3 marks available — 3 marks for correct enlargement, otherwise 2 marks for a correct triangle but in the wrong position or for an enlargement from the correct centre but of the wrong scale factor, or 1 mark for 2 lines enlarged by the correct scale factor anywhere on the grid]

Page 114 (Warm-up Questions)

1   42 cm

2   a)   area = length × width, A = l × w
b)   circumference = π × diameter, C = π × D (or C = 2πr)
c)   area = base × vertical height, A = b × h

3   10.5 m² *(Area = ½ × base × vertical height = 0.5 × 3 × 7)*

4   201.06 cm² to 2 d.p. (or 201.09 cm² to 2 d.p. using π = 3.142)
(Area = πr² = π × 8²)

5 a) A straight line that just touches the outside of a circle.

b)

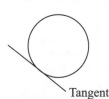

Tangent

Page 115 (Exam Questions)

3 a) Area of trapezium = ½(8 + 11) × 6
 = ½ × 19 × 6 = 57 cm²
Area of triangle = area of trapezium ÷ 3 = 57 ÷ 3 = 19 cm²
Total area of the shape = area of trapezium + area of triangle
 = 57 + 19 = 76 cm²
[3 marks available — 1 mark for the area of the trapezium, 1 mark for the area of the triangle, 1 mark for correct final answer]

b) Area of triangle = ½ × base × height
 19 = ½ × 8 × height *[1 mark]*
height = 19 ÷ 4 = 4.75 cm *[1 mark]*
[2 marks available in total — as above]

4 Area of rectangle = 6 × 8 = 48 cm² *[1 mark]*
Base of triangle = 8 cm – 5 cm = 3 cm
Height of triangle = 6 cm – 2 cm = 4 cm
 [1 mark for base and height]
Area of triangle = $\frac{1}{2}$ × 3 × 4 = 6 cm² *[1 mark]*
Area of shaded area = 48 – 6 = 42 cm² *[1 mark]*
[4 marks available in total — as above]

5 Circumference of full circle = 2 × π × 6 = 12π cm
Length of arc = $\frac{30}{360}$ × circumference of circle
 = $\frac{30}{360}$ × 12π = π cm
Perimeter of sector = π + 6 + 6 = 15.1415... = 15.1 cm (3 s.f.)
Area of full circle = π × 6² = 36π cm²
Area of sector = $\frac{30}{360}$ × area of circle
 = $\frac{30}{360}$ × 36π = 3π cm² = 9.4247... = 9.42 cm² (3 s.f.)
[5 marks available — 1 mark for a correct method for calculating the length of the arc, 1 mark for correct arc length, 1 mark for correct perimeter of sector, 1 mark for a correct method for finding the area of the sector, 1 mark for correct area of sector]

Page 122 (Warm-up Questions)

1 A triangle-based pyramid has 4 faces, 4 vertices and 6 edges.

2 4 cm

3 8 cm³ *(8 × 1 cm³, or v = l × w × h = 2 cm × 2 cm × 2 cm)*

4 672 cm³ *(area of triangle × length = ½ × 12 × 8 × 14)*

5 624π cm³

6 6 cm

7 a)   b)

c)

Pages 123-124 (Exam Questions)

2 Split the shape into two cuboids, looking at the front elevation. The bottom cuboid has 4 × 2 × 4 = 32 cubes in it. The cuboid at the top has 2 × 2 × 4 = 16 cubes in it. So there are 32 + 16 = 48 cubes in the shape.
[2 marks available — 1 mark for a correct calculation, 1 mark for the correct answer]
You might have split your shape up differently — as long as your working is correct and you get the correct answer, you'll get all the marks.

3

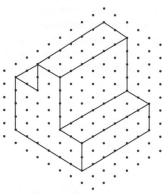

[2 marks available — 2 marks for a correct diagram, otherwise 1 mark for the correct cross-section but wrong length]

4 Volume of sphere = $\frac{4}{3}πr^3$ = $\frac{4}{3}$ × π × 15³ *[1 mark]* = 4500π cm³
 = 14 137.166... = 14 100 cm³ (3 s.f.) *[1 mark]*
[2 marks available in total — as above]

5 a) Volume = 90 × 40 × 30 *[1 mark]* = 108 000 cm³ *[1 mark]*
[2 marks available in total — as above]

b) Volume of cuboid = length × width × height
 108 000 = 120 × width × 18
 108 000 = 2160 × width
 width = 108 000 ÷ 2160 = 50 cm
[2 marks available — 1 mark for correctly rearranging the formula to find the width, 1 mark for the correct answer]

6 a) Volume of water in paddling pool = π × r² × h
 = π × 100² × 40 *[1 mark]* = 400 000π cm³ *[1 mark]*
[2 marks available in total — as above]

b) Time it will take to fill to 40 cm = 400 000π ÷ 300 *[1 mark[*
 = 4188.790... seconds
Convert to minutes = 4188.790... ÷ 60
 = 69.813... = 70 minutes (to the nearest minute) *[1 mark]*
[2 marks available in total — as above]

Page 125 (Revision Questions)

1 H: 2 lines of symmetry,
 rotational symmetry order 2
Z: 0 lines of symmetry,
 rotational symmetry order 2
T: 1 line of symmetry,
 rotational symmetry order 1
N: 0 lines of symmetry,
 rotational symmetry order 2
E: 1 line of symmetry,
 rotational symmetry order 1
✕: 4 lines of symmetry,
 rotational symmetry order 4
S: 0 lines of symmetry,
 rotational symmetry order 2

2 2 angles the same, 2 sides the same, 1 line of symmetry, no rotational symmetry.

3 2 lines of symmetry, rotational symmetry order 2

4 Congruent shapes are exactly the same size and same shape. Similar shapes are the same shape but different sizes.

5 a) D and G   b) C and F
6 $b = 89, y = 5$
7 a) Translation of $\binom{-2}{-4}$.
   b) Reflection in $x = 0$ (the y-axis).
8
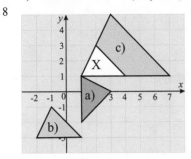
9 Area = ½(a + b) × h
10 36 cm²
11 52 cm²
12 Area = 153.94 cm² (2 d.p.)
    Circumference = 43.98 cm (2 d.p.)
13 E.g.
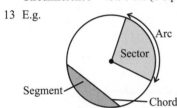
14 Area = 7.07 cm² (2 d.p.)
    Perimeter = 10.71 cm (2 d.p.)
15 a) faces = 5, edges = 8, vertices = 5
    b) faces = 2, edges = 1, vertices = 1
    c) faces = 5, edges = 9, vertices = 6
16 150 cm²
17 125.7 cm² (1 d.p.)
18 Volume = $\pi r^2 h$
19 360 cm³
20 a) 113.10 cm³ (2 d.p.)
    b) 4.5 s (1 d.p.)
21 Front: Side:

    Plan:

Section Six — Angles and Geometry

Page 131 (Warm-up Questions)
1 a) Any angle less than 90°
   b) Any angle greater than 90° and less than 180°
   c) Any angle greater than 180° and less than 360°
   d) 90°
2 a) 37°   b) 287°
   Accept answers within 2°

3 a)   b)   c)
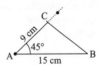
4 $x = 110°, y = 40°$
   Using angles in an isosceles triangle and angles on a straight line.
5 $a = 120°, b = 60°$
   Using the rule for allied angles (60° + a = 180°) and using the rule for corresponding angles (b = 60°).
6 540°

Page 132 (Exam Questions)
3 $a = 75°$ *[1 mark]*
   because vertically opposite angles are equal. *[1 mark]*
   [2 marks available in total — as above]
4 70° + 90° + 97° = 257°
   Angle $ADC = 360° − 257° = 103°$
   (angles in a quadrilateral add up to 360°)
   [2 marks available — 1 mark for a correct method, 1 mark for the correct answer]
5 Exterior angle = 180° − 150° = 30° *[1 mark]*
   Number of sides = 360° ÷ 30° *[1 mark]*
                   = 12 *[1 mark]*
   [3 marks available in total — as above]
6 Angle BCG = Angle $CGE = x$ (alternate angles)
   So 78° + x = 180° *[1 mark]*
   $x = 180° − 78°$
   $x = 102°$ *[1 mark]*
   [2 marks available in total — as above]
   There are other ways to find x. For instance angles ACB and CGF are corresponding angles. You can then use angles on a straight line to find x.
7 The polygon is split into 5 triangles.
   Angles in a triangle add up to 180°
   Angles in polygon = 5 × 180°
                     = 900°
   [3 marks available — 3 marks for correct explanation, otherwise 1 mark for stating angles in triangle add up to 180° and 1 mark for an attempt at adding to find angles in polygon]

Page 140 (Warm-up Questions)
1 a)
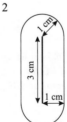
   b) 11 cm
2

3
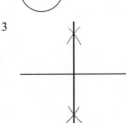
4 a) 1100 m (5.5 × 200)   b) 2.5 cm (500 ÷ 200)

5

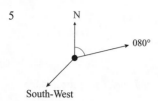

South-West

Pages 141-142 (Exam Questions)

3 a) Drawing of dining table is 4 cm long.
So 4 cm is equivalent to 2 m.
$2 \div 4 = 0.5$
Therefore scale is 1 cm to 0.5 m *[1 mark]*

b) On drawing, dining table is 3 cm from shelves.
So real distance = $3 \times 0.5 = 1.5$ m *[1 mark]*

c) The chair and the space around it would measure 4 cm × 5 cm on the diagram and there are no spaces that big, so no, it would not be possible.
[2 marks available — 1 mark for correct answer, 1 mark for reasoning referencing diagram or size of gaps available]

4 260° (allow 258°-262°) *[1 mark]*
It's easier to measure the 100° angle and subtract it from 360°.

5 $180° - 79° = 101°$ (allied angles) *[1 mark]*
$360° - 101° = 259°$
Ishita travels on a bearing of 259°. *[1 mark]*
[2 marks available in total — as above]

6 Using the scale 1 cm = 100 m:
400 m = 4 cm and 500 m = 5 cm

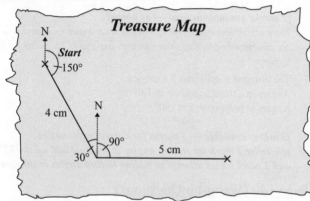

Treasure Map

[3 marks available — 1 mark for line on accurate bearing of 150°, 1 mark for line on accurate bearing of 090°, 1 mark for accurate 4 cm and 5 cm line lengths]

7

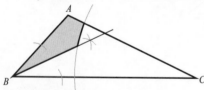

[4 marks available — 1 mark for arc with radius of 6.5 cm with centre at C, 1 mark for construction arcs on AB and BC for angle bisector at ABC, 1 mark for correct angle bisector at ABC, and 1 mark for the correct shading]
Remember to leave in your construction lines.

Page 149 (Warm-up Questions)

1 7.6 m

2 1.94 cm

3 $\dfrac{12}{\sqrt{3}}$

4 $\dfrac{1}{2}$

5 a) $\begin{pmatrix} -15 \\ 9 \end{pmatrix}$ b) $\begin{pmatrix} -2 \\ -12 \end{pmatrix}$ c) $\begin{pmatrix} 8 \\ 15 \end{pmatrix}$

6 $\mathbf{b} - \mathbf{a}$ (or $-\mathbf{a} + \mathbf{b}$)

Page 150 (Exam Questions)

3 The triangle can be split into two right-angled triangles.

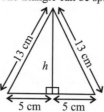

Let h be the height of the triangle:
$13^2 = 5^2 + h^2$ *[1 mark]*
$h^2 = 169 - 25 = 144$
$h = \sqrt{144}$ *[1 mark]*
$h = 12$ cm *[1 mark]*
[3 marks available in total — as above]

4 $\sin x = \dfrac{14}{18}$ *[1 mark]*

$x = \sin^{-1}\left(\dfrac{14}{18}\right)$

$x = 51.0575... = 51.1°$ (1 d.p) *[1 mark]*
[2 marks available in total — as above]

5 a) $\overrightarrow{AC} = \overrightarrow{AB} + \overrightarrow{BC}$ *[1 mark]*
$= 2\mathbf{c} + 2\mathbf{d}$ *[1 mark]*

[2 marks available in total — as above]

b) $\overrightarrow{AL} = \dfrac{1}{2} \times \overrightarrow{AC} = \dfrac{1}{2} \times 2\mathbf{c} + \dfrac{1}{2} \times 2\mathbf{d}$ *[1 mark]*
$= \mathbf{c} + \mathbf{d}$ *[1 mark]*

[2 marks available in total — as above]

c) $\overrightarrow{BL} = \overrightarrow{BA} + \overrightarrow{AL}$ *[1 mark]*
$= -2\mathbf{c} + \mathbf{c} + \mathbf{d}$
$= -\mathbf{c} + \mathbf{d}$ *[1 mark]*

[2 marks available in total — as above]

Pages 151-152 (Revision Questions)

1 An obtuse angle

2 360°

3 a) 154°   b) 112°   c) 58°

4 140°

5 60°

6 1080°

7 162°

8 (Not full size)

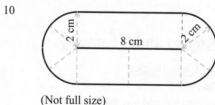

9 A circle

10

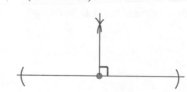

(Not full size)

11

12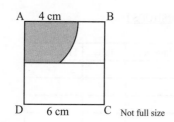

13 295°

14 280°

15 26 km

16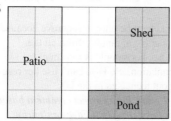

Patio
Shed
Pond

17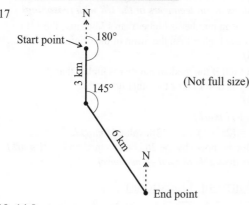

Start point
180°
3 km
145°
6 km
N
End point
(Not full size)

18 14.5 cm

19
$$\triangle \begin{array}{c} O \\ \hline S \times H \end{array} \quad \triangle \begin{array}{c} A \\ \hline C \times H \end{array} \quad \triangle \begin{array}{c} O \\ \hline T \times A \end{array}$$

20 $x = 33.4°$ (1 d.p.)

21 $x = 51.8°$ (1 d.p.)

22 $12\sqrt{3}$ cm

23 $\tan 45° + \sin 60° = 1 + \dfrac{\sqrt{3}}{2}$

$= \dfrac{2}{2} + \dfrac{\sqrt{3}}{2}$

$= \dfrac{2 + \sqrt{3}}{2}$

24 a) $\begin{pmatrix} -3 \\ -8 \end{pmatrix}$ b) $\begin{pmatrix} 20 \\ -10 \end{pmatrix}$

25 $2\mathbf{a} + 3\mathbf{b}$

26 $5\mathbf{a} - 7\mathbf{b}$

27 $-\mathbf{i} + \mathbf{j}$

Section Seven — Probability and Statistics

Page 157 (Warm-up Questions)

1 $\dfrac{1}{3}$

2 $\dfrac{5}{6}$

3 a) HH, HT, TH, TT

   b) $\dfrac{1}{2}$ or 0.5

4

Score	Relative frequency
1	0.14
2	0.137
3	0.138
4	0.259
5	0.161
6	0.165

5 $\dfrac{30}{120} = 0.25$

6 250

Pages 158-159 (Exam Questions)

3   $10 - 4 = 6$ red counters.

P(red) $= \dfrac{6}{10} = 0.6$

[2 marks available — 2 marks for correctly drawn arrow, otherwise 1 mark for finding the correct probability of picking a red counter]

You could also work out the probability of a blue counter (0.4) and subtract it from 1 to get the probability of a red counter.

4 a) (Hockey, Netball), (Hockey, Choir), (Hockey, Orienteering), (Orchestra, Netball), (Orchestra, Choir), (Orchestra, Orienteering), (Drama, Netball), (Drama, Choir), (Drama, Orienteering).

[2 marks available — 2 marks for listing all 9 correct combinations, otherwise 1 mark if at least 5 combinations are correct]

   b) There are 9 combinations and 1 of them is hockey and netball, so P(hockey and netball) $= \dfrac{1}{9}$ *[1 mark]*

   c) There are 9 combinations and 3 of them involve drama on Monday, so P(drama on Monday) $= \dfrac{3}{9} = \dfrac{1}{3}$ *[1 mark]*

You could also count the choices for Monday — there are 3, and 1 of them is drama.

5 a) EHM, EMH, HME, HEM, MEH, MHE

[2 marks available — 2 marks for listing all 6 correct combinations, otherwise 1 mark if at least 3 combinations are correct]

   b) There are 6 possible combinations and in 3 of them he does Maths before English (HME, MEH, MHE).

So P(Maths before English) $= \dfrac{3}{6} = \dfrac{1}{2}$ *[1 mark]*

6 a)

Prediction   Outcome

100
Heads 47
Tails 53
Heads 25
Tails 22
Heads 27
Tails 26

[2 marks available — 1 mark for the correct numbers for the predictions, 1 mark for the correct numbers for the outcomes]

   b) She predicted the flip correctly $25 + 26 = 51$ times out of 100

[1 mark], so relative frequency $= \dfrac{51}{100} = 0.51$ *[1 mark]*

[2 marks available in total — as above]

7 a) Relative frequency of hitting the target with a left-handed throw $= \dfrac{12}{20} = \dfrac{3}{5}$ or 0.6.

[2 marks available — 1 mark for a correct method, 1 mark for the correct answer]

   b) E.g. The estimated probability is more reliable for her right hand because she threw the ball more times with that hand. *[1 mark]*

Page 163 (Warm-up Questions)

1 $\dfrac{1}{6} \times \dfrac{1}{6} \times \dfrac{1}{6} = \dfrac{1}{216}$

2 $0.5 \times 0.7 = 0.35$

3 a) $0.2 \times 0.25 = 0.05$ b) $0.2 + 0.25 = 0.45$

4 $\dfrac{6}{10} \times \dfrac{6}{10} = \dfrac{36}{100} = \dfrac{9}{25}$

5 a)

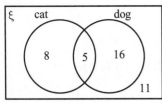

b) P(owns a cat but not a dog) = $\frac{8}{40} = \frac{1}{5}$

Page 164 (Exam Questions)

2 a) P(4 or 5) = P(4) + P(5)
= 0.25 + 0.1 *[1 mark]*
= 0.35 *[1 mark]*
[2 marks available in total — as above]

b) P(1 and 3) = P(1) × P(3)
= 0.3 × 0.2 *[1 mark]*
= 0.06 *[1 mark]*
[2 marks available in total — as above]

3 a) P(no prize) = 1 − 0.3 = 0.7 *[1 mark]*

b) P(no prize on either game) = P(no prize) × P(no prize)
= 0.7 × 0.7 *[1 mark]*
= 0.49 *[1 mark]*
[2 marks available in total — as above]

4 a) Number of students who only like apples = 70 − 20 = 50
Number of students who only like bananas = 40 − 20 = 20
Number of students who don't like either
= 100 − 50 − 20 − 20 = 10

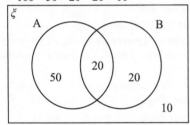

[3 marks available — 3 marks for a fully correct Venn diagram, lose 1 mark for each incorrect value]

b) 50 + 20 + 20 = 90 students out of 100 like apples or bananas,
so P(A ∪ B) = $\frac{90}{100} = \frac{9}{10}$ or 0.9.

[2 marks available — 1 mark for 90 students liking either fruit, 1 mark for the correct answer.]

Page 168 (Warm-up Questions)

1 Two from, e.g: sample too small, one city centre not representative of the whole of Britain, only done in one particular place.

2 Continuous data
E.g.

Weight (w kg)	Tally	Frequency
0 ≤ w < 10		
10 ≤ w < 20		
20 ≤ w < 30		
30 ≤ w < 40		
w ≥ 40		

3 a) This question is ambiguous. "A lot of television" can mean different things to different people.

b) This is a leading question, inviting the person to agree.

c) The answers to this question do not cover all possible options.

4 First, order the numbers:
−14, −12, −5, −5, 0, 1, 3, 6, 7, 8, 10, 14, 18, 23, 25
Mean = 5.27 (2 d.p.), Median = 6, Mode = −5, Range = 39

5 2, 4 and 6

Page 169 (Exam Questions)

2 a) E.g.

Number of chocolate bars	Tally	Frequency
0-2		
3-5		
6-8		
9-11		
12 or more		

[2 marks available — 1 mark for a suitable tally table, 1 mark for non-overlapping classes that cover all possible values]

b) E.g. Faye's results are likely to be unrepresentative because she hasn't selected her sample at random from all the teenagers in the UK. Also, her sample is too small to represent the whole population. So Faye can't use her results to draw conclusions about teenagers in the UK.
[2 marks available — 1 mark for a correct comment based on sample size, 1 mark for stating that Faye can't draw conclusions about teenagers in the UK with reasoning]

3 a) Yes, the mean number is higher than 17 because the 11th data value is higher than the mean of the original 10 values. *[1 mark]*

b) You can't tell if the median number is higher than 15, because you don't know the other data values. *[1 mark]*

4 a) Mode = 1 *[1 mark]*

b) Median = (25 + 1) ÷ 2 = 13th value *[1 mark]*.
13th value is shown by the 2nd bar, so median = 1 *[1 mark]*.
[2 marks available in total — as above]

Page 174 (Warm-up Questions)

1 a)

Red	●●●●●
Purple	●●
Blue	●●●●◖
Orange	●●●◖

b) No. According to the pictogram, there are only (4 × 8) + (½ × 8) = 32 + 4 = 36 blue balloons at the shop, and Ellen needs 37.

2

	Walk	Car	Bus	Total
Male	15	21	13	49
Female	18	11	22	51
Total	33	32	35	100

3 Giraffe = 31 × 4° = 124°
Penguin = 25 × 4° = 100°
Lemur = 34 × 4° = 136°

4 a) There is a strong positive correlation. The taller the student, the bigger their shoe size.

b) Approximately 7.5

c) The estimate should be reliable because **[either]** 1.75 m is within the range of the known data **[or]** the graph shows strong correlation.

d) Yes. If you plotted Amal's height and shoe size, it would be close to the other points on the graph, so it follows the trend.

Page 175 (Exam Questions)

2 E.g.

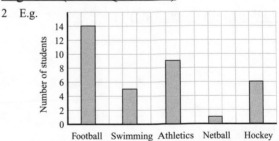

[4 marks available — 1 mark for a suitable scale starting from zero on the vertical axis, 1 mark for correctly labelling the vertical axis, 1 mark for bars of equal width and all bar heights correct, 1 mark for all bars correctly labelled]

3 a) $15:20 = 3:4$ *[1 mark]*

b) $\frac{20}{50} \times 100$ *[1 mark]* $= 40\%$ *[1 mark]*
[2 marks available in total — as above]

4 a)

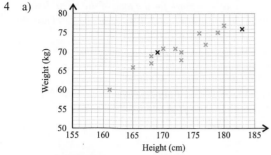

[1 mark for both points plotted correctly]

b) $\frac{5}{14}$ *[1 mark]*

c) E.g. In general, as the height increases, the weight also increases — there is a positive correlation.
[1 mark for any answer indicating a positive correlation]

Page 180 (Warm-up Questions)

1 a) Mode = 3   b) Median = 3

2 E.g.

Height (h cm)	Tally	Frequency
$150 < h \leq 160$	||	2
$160 < h \leq 170$	₩₩	5
$170 < h \leq 180$	|||	3
$180 < h \leq 190$	||	2

3 a) Estimated range = 185 − 145 = 40

b) Median is in the group containing the 40th value, so the median group is $155 \leq x < 165$.

c) Modal Group = $165 \leq x < 175$

4 The mode is 30°C but most of the temperatures are less than 20°C, so it's not representative of all the data.

Page 181 (Exam Questions)

2 a) Total number of people = 12 + 18 + 9 + 21 = 60
Multiplier = 360 ÷ 60 = 6
Plain: 12 × 6 = 72°
Salted: 18 × 6 = 108°
Sugared: 9 × 6 = 54°
Toffee: 21 × 6 = 126°

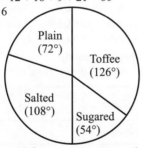

[4 marks available — 1 mark for one sector correctly drawn, 1 mark for a second sector correctly drawn, 1 mark for a complete pie chart with all angles correct, 1 mark for correct labels]

b) E.g. Kim is not right because there is no information about the number of people in the ice-cream survey. *[1 mark]*

3 a) Max value = 63 mm, min value = 8 mm *[1 mark for both]*, so range = 63 − 8 = 55 mm *[1 mark]*
E.g. a range of 55 mm isn't a good reflection of the spread of the data because most of the data is much closer together.
[1 mark for a correct comment]
[3 marks available in total — as above]
Or you could say that the single value of 63 mm has a big effect on increasing the value of the range so that it doesn't represent the spread of the rest of the data.

b) Median rainfall in June = (12 + 1) ÷ 2 = 6.5th value
= (29 + 30) ÷ 2 = 29.5 mm
E.g. The rainfall was generally higher in June, as the median was higher. The rainfall in June was much more varied than in November as the range was much bigger.
[3 marks available — 1 mark for calculating the median rainfall in June, 1 mark for a correct statement comparing the medians and 1 mark for a correct statement comparing the ranges]

Page 182 (Revision Questions)

1 $\frac{8}{50} = \frac{4}{25}$

2 0.7

3 a) HHH, HHT, HTH, THH, TTH, HTT, THT, TTT   b) $\frac{3}{8}$

4 a) See page 155   b) See page 156

5 a)

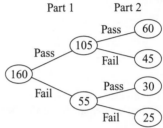

b) Relative frequency of:
pass, pass = $\frac{60}{160} = \frac{3}{8}$ or 0.375
pass, fail = $\frac{45}{160} = \frac{9}{32}$ or 0.28125
fail, pass = $\frac{30}{160} = \frac{3}{16}$ or 0.1875
fail, fail = $\frac{25}{160} = \frac{5}{32}$ or 0.15625

c) 300 × 0.375 = 113 people (to the nearest whole number)

6 0.5

7

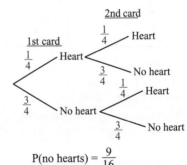

P(no hearts) = $\frac{9}{16}$

8 a)

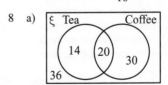

b) $\frac{64}{100} = \frac{16}{25}$

9 A sample is part of a population. Samples need to be representative so that conclusions drawn from sample data can be applied to the whole population.

10 Qualitative data

11

Pet	Tally	Frequency
Cat	₩₩ |||	8
Dog	₩₩ |	6
Rabbit	||||	4
Fish	||	2

12 Mode = 31, Median = 24, Mean = 22, Range = 39

13 Count the number of symbols, then use the key to work out what frequency they represent.

14 E.g.

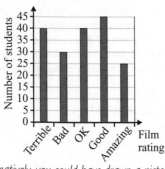

Alternatively, you could have drawn a pictogram.

15 a)

b) There is a seasonal pattern that repeats itself every 4 points. Sales are lowest in the first quarter and highest in the fourth quarter.

16 Draw a pie chart to show the proportions.

17 a) 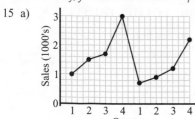 b) c)

18 a) Modal class is: $1.5 \leq y < 1.6$.

b) Class containing median is: $1.5 \leq y < 1.6$

c) Estimated mean = 1.58 m (to 2 d.p.)

19 Outliers can have a big effect on increasing or decreasing the value of the mean or range, so that it doesn't represent the rest of the data set very well.

20 Black cars were only owned by men and silver cars were only owned by women. So black cars were more popular amongst men and silver cars were more popular amongst women.
There are similar proportions of men and women owning blue and green cars. So blue and green cars are equally popular amongst men and women.
The proportion of men owning red cars was nearly double the proportion of women owning red cards. So red cars were almost twice as popular amongst men as women.

Practice Paper 1

1 $\frac{113}{1000}$ *[1 mark]*

2 $40 : 25 = 8 : 5$ *[1 mark]*

3 a) *F [1 mark]*

b) $x = 3$ *[1 mark]*

4 $3.97 \times 1000 = 3970$ m *[1 mark]*

5 a) $-12, -8, -6, 2, 6$ *[1 mark]*

b) $2 - -8 = 10$ *[1 mark]*

6 $5p \times 28 = 140p$
$10p \times 41 = 410p$
$140p + 410p = 550p$
$550p \div 50p = 11$, so she gets 11 50p coins.
[3 marks available — 1 mark for the total of the 5p or 10p coins, 1 mark for the overall total, 1 mark for the final answer]

7 $1.2 - 0.2 \times 4 = 1.2 - 0.8 = 0.4$ *[1 mark]*
So $\frac{1.2 - 0.2 \times 4}{0.05} = \frac{0.4}{0.05} = \frac{40}{5} = 8$ *[1 mark]*
[2 marks available in total — as above]

8 E.g. 6 (multiple of 3) + 6 (multiple of 6)
= 12 (not a multiple of 9) *[1 mark]*

9 a) $9a + 7b$ *[1 mark]*

b) $6a^2$ *[1 mark]*

10 1% of £300 = £3, so 2% = £3 × 2 = £6 *[1 mark]*
Interest for 4 years = £6 × 4 = £24 *[1 mark]*
£300 + £24 = £324 *[1 mark]*
[3 marks available in total — as above]

11 a) $3 + 6 + 5 + 2 + 6 + 1 + 3 = 26$ pupils
The frequency of the final bar should be $30 - 26 = 4$

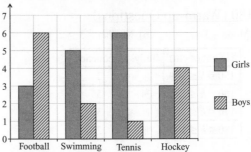

[2 marks available — 2 marks for correctly drawing missing bar, otherwise 1 mark for attempting to add the seven frequencies shown on the chart]

b) Number of children whose favourite sport is swimming is $5 + 2 = 7$. The probability is $\frac{7}{30}$
[2 marks available — 1 mark for the numerator (7) and 1 mark for the denominator (30)]

c) 2 boys chose swimming and 6 girls chose tennis, so the ratio is $2 : 6 = 1 : 3$ in its simplest form.
[2 marks available — 2 marks for the correct answer, otherwise 1 mark for 2 : 6]

12 Geometric *[1 mark]*
Rule: multiply the previous term by 4 *[1 mark]*

13 a)

Pattern	Number of triangles	Number of dots	Number of lines
Pattern 1	1	3	3
Pattern 2	2	4	5
Pattern 3	3	5	7
Pattern 4	4	6	9

[1 mark]

b) The number of lines column increases by 2 each time.
The column would continue 11, 13, 15, 17, 19, 21.
Pattern 10 has 21 lines.
[2 marks available — 1 mark for finding the sequence, 1 mark for the correct number of lines in Pattern 10]
You could also find an expression for the nth term (2n + 1) and work out the value when put n = 10, (2 × 10) + 1 = 21.

c) (i) The number of dots is two more than the pattern number, so $D = n + 2$
[2 marks available — 2 marks for D = n + 2, otherwise 1 mark for n + 2, D − n = 2, or '2 more than the pattern number']

(ii) Number of dots in pattern 200 = 200 + 2 = 202 *[1 mark]*

14 The number of tickets sold was:
Adults: $(8 \times 3) + 6 = 30$
Child: $(8 \times 5) + 2 = 42$
Senior: $(8 \times 2) + 4 = 20$
Adult tickets: $30 \times £9 = £270$
Child tickets: $42 \times £5 = £210$
Senior tickets: $20 \times £6.50 = £130$
Total sales $= 270 + 210 + 130 = £610$
[6 marks available — 1 mark for each correct number of tickets sold (adult, child, senior), 1 mark for multiplying number of tickets sold by cost, 1 mark for attempting to add up the total sales, 1 mark for correct answer]

15 a) 067° (Accept answer between 065° and 069°) *[1 mark]*

b) Distance on map = 4.3 cm
Actual distance = $4.3 \times 100 = 430$ metres
[2 marks available — 2 marks for an answer in the range 420 m-440 m, otherwise 1 mark for a measurement in the range 4.2 cm-4.4 cm]

c) Draw an arc of a circle with radius 4.5 cm from the house and 7 cm from the greenhouse.

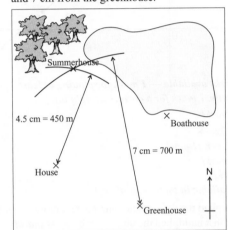

[2 marks available — 2 marks for summerhouse plotted in the correct position with construction arcs shown, otherwise 1 mark for one correct arc or for the summerhouse in the correct position but construction arcs not shown]

16 The top tier needs 50% of 800 g = 400 g of sultanas *[1 mark]*
The middle tier needs 75% of 800 g = 600 g of sultanas *[1 mark]*
One wedding cake needs $800 + 400 + 600 = 1800$ g of sultanas *[1 mark]*
Five wedding cakes need 1800 g $\times 5 = 9000$ g $= 9$ kg of sultanas *[1 mark]*, so Angie does not have enough sultanas. *[1 mark]*
[5 marks available in total — as above]

17 a) 69p rounds to 70p and 2.785 kg rounds to 3 kg to 1 s.f.
So estimate is 70p × 3 *[1 mark]*
= 210p *[1 mark]*
[2 marks available in total — as above]
If you've done 70p × 2.8 = 196p you'll still get the marks.

b) E.g. The estimate is bigger than the actual cost, as both numbers were rounded up. *[1 mark]*

18 a) Read off the graph: £300 = $540 *[1 mark]*

b) After spending $390, he is left with $150 *[1 mark]*
Convert to yuan: $150 \times 6 = 900$ yuan *[1 mark]*
[2 marks available in total — as above]

19 $3^{-2} = \frac{1}{9}$ *[1 mark]*
$k \times \frac{1}{9} = 4$, so $k = 4 \times 9 = 36$ *[1 mark]*
[2 marks available in total — as above]

20 Angles in a square are 90°.
There are three squares around O, so $90° \times 3 = 270°$. *[1 mark]*
Angles round a point add to 360°,
so angle $AOB = (360 - 270) \div 3 = 30°$ *[1 mark]*
The two base angles in an isosceles triangle are equal,
so angle $OAB = (180 - 30) \div 2$ *[1 mark]*
$= 75°$ *[1 mark]*
[4 marks available in total — as above]

21 $1\frac{2}{3} \times 1\frac{5}{8} = \frac{5}{3} \times \frac{13}{8} = \frac{65}{24} = 2\frac{17}{24}$
[3 marks available – 1 mark for converting both numbers to improper fractions, 1 mark for multiplying, 1 mark for the correct answer]

22 $594\,000\,000\,000 = 5.94 \times 10^{11}$ *[1 mark]*

23 Year 9 — $\frac{9}{20} = \frac{45}{100} = 45\%$
Year 10 — 49%
Year 11 — $\frac{12}{12+13} = \frac{12}{25} = \frac{48}{100} = 48\%$
So Year 10 has the largest proportion of girls.
[3 marks available — 2 marks for converting two proportions to the same form as the third, and 1 mark for the correct answer.]
You could convert any two proportions to the form of the third, e.g. convert Year 10 and Year 11 into fractions.

24 Shape A: Area $= \pi \times 4^2 = 16\pi$ cm²
Shape B: Area $= \frac{80}{360} \times \pi \times 6^2 = 8\pi$ cm²
$16\pi = 2 \times 8\pi$ so the area of A is twice the area of B.
[4 marks available — 1 mark for the area of shape A, 1 mark for the correct method to find the area of shape B, 1 mark for the area of shape B, 1 mark for showing that the area of shape A is twice the area of shape B]

25 a) $AC^2 = AD^2 + DC^2 = 3^2 + 4^2 = 9 + 16 = 25$
So $AC = \sqrt{25} = 5$ cm
$x^2 = AC^2 + AB^2 = 5^2 + 12^2 = 25 + 144 = 169$
So $x = \sqrt{169} = 13$ cm
[4 marks available — 1 mark for using Pythagoras' theorem to find the length of AC, 1 mark for the correct length of AC, 1 mark for using Pythagoras' theorem to find the length of x, 1 mark for the correct length of x]

b) Area of triangle $ACD = 0.5 \times 4 \times 3 = 6$ cm²
Area of triangle $ABC = 0.5 \times 5 \times 12 = 30$ cm²
Area of quadrilateral $ABCD = 6 + 30 = 36$ cm²
[2 marks available — 1 mark for finding the areas of triangles ACD and ABC, 1 mark for adding to find the area of the quadrilateral]

26 $2x + y = 10 \xrightarrow{\times 2} 4x + 2y = 20$ *[1 mark]*

$\begin{array}{r} 4x + 2y = 20 \\ -\ 3x + 2y = 17 \\ \hline x = 3 \end{array}$ *[1 mark]*

$4(3) + 2y = 20$
$2y = 20 - 12$
$2y = 8$
$y = 4$ *[1 mark]*

[3 marks available in total — as above]
You could have found the value of y first then used it to find x.

Practice Paper 2

1 $\frac{3}{5} = 0.6 = 60\%$ *[1 mark]*

2 $20 + 4 = 24$
$24 \div 2 = 12$ *[1 mark]*

3

Menu Item	Number Ordered	Cost per Item	Total
Tea	2	£1.25	£2.50
Coffee	6 *[1 mark]*	£1.60	£9.60
Cake	4	£1.30 *[1 mark]*	£5.20
Tip			£2.50
		Total cost	£19.80 *[1 mark]*

[3 marks available in total — as above]

4 a)
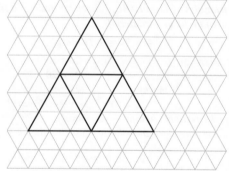

cone — 4
sphere — 3
cylinder — 2
— 1

[2 marks available — 2 marks for all lines correct, otherwise 1 mark for 2 lines correct]

   b) 6 *[1 mark]*

5 a) 107.3158498 *[1 mark]*
      Your calculator may display more or fewer digits than this.

   b) 107.32 *[1 mark]*
      If you got a) wrong but rounded it correctly, you'll still get the mark for part b).

6 The possible numbers are:

4356	4536
5346	5364
5436	5634
6354	6534

[2 marks available — 2 marks if all 8 possible numbers are given with no errors or repetitions, otherwise 1 mark if at least 5 of the possible numbers are listed]

7 64 (4^3 and 8^2) *[1 mark]*

8 a) $4(a + 2) = 4a + 8$ *[1 mark]*

   b) $y^2 + 5y = y(y + 5)$ *[1 mark]*

9 a) Mode is the most common value = 6 years *[1 mark]*

   b) Rewrite data in order: 5, 6, 6, 7, 9, 11, 12
      Median is the middle (4th) value = 7 years *[1 mark]*

   c) Mean = $\dfrac{6 + 12 + 9 + 6 + 5 + 7 + 11}{7}$ *[1 mark]*

      $= \dfrac{56}{7}$ = 8 years *[1 mark]*
      [2 marks available in total — as above]

10 a) Two equilateral triangles join together to form a rhombus.
      So 2 lines of symmetry. *[1 mark]*

   b) E.g.

[1 mark]

11 185% of £3500 = 1.85 × 3500 *[1 mark]*
      = £6475 *[1 mark]*
   [2 marks available in total — as above]
   You could also build up to 185%, by finding 50%, 5% etc. and adding these to the original value.

12 Method 1: 2 × 27 = 54 miles
            Expenses = 54 × 0.40 = £21.60 *[1 mark]*
   Method 2: Expenses = (8 × 0.40) + 17.60 = £20.80 *[1 mark]*
   She should travel by the cheaper method, which is Method 2 (by car and train). *[1 mark]*
   [3 marks available in total — as above]

13 There are $\dfrac{3}{4}$ × 28 = 21 red cars and
   $\dfrac{3}{8}$ × 16 = 6 red motorbikes *[1 mark for both]*.
   So there are 21 + 6 = 27 red vehicles in total *[1 mark]*.
   The probability of picking a car from the red vehicles
   is $\dfrac{21}{27} = \dfrac{7}{9}$ *[1 mark]*.
   [3 marks available in total — as above]

14 a)

x	−2	−1	0	1	2	3	4
y	11	9	7	5	3	1	−1

[2 marks available — 2 marks for all entries correct, otherwise 1 mark for at least 2 correct entries]

   b)
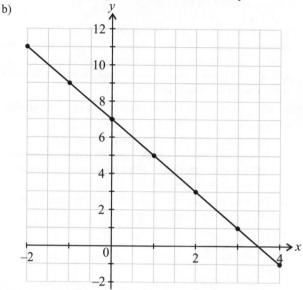

[2 marks available — 1 mark for plotting at least 3 points correctly, 1 mark for a correct straight line]

   c) −2 *[1 mark]*

15 $3(2x − 4) = 2x + 8$
   $6x − 12 = 2x + 8$ *[1 mark]*
   $4x = 20$ *[1 mark]*
   $x = 5$ *[1 mark]*
   [3 marks available in total — as above]

16 He has multiplied the denominator and numerator by 5, but he should have just multiplied the numerator by 5. *[1 mark]*

17 E.g. The vertical scale does not begin at 0 so the graph could be misinterpreted.
      The horizontal scale does not increase by even amounts.
      The graph is difficult to read due to the thickness of the line.
      [3 marks available — 1 mark for each correct comment]

18 Angle $EBF = 90°$ *[1 mark]*
   Angles on a straight line add up to 180°,
   so angle $ABE = 180 − 90 − 39 = 51°$ *[1 mark]*
   Angles ABE and DEH are corresponding angles,
   so angle $DEH = 51°$ *[1 mark]*
   [3 marks available in total – as above]

19 a) $L = 2(3x + 1) + 2(2x − 3) − 2$ *[1 mark]*
      $= 6x + 2 + 4x − 6 − 2 = 10x − 6$ *[1 mark]*
      [2 marks available in total — as above]

   b) $L = 10x − 6 = 2(5x − 3)$, so it is always even as it can be written as 2 × a whole number, where the whole number is $(5x − 3)$
      [2 marks available — 1 mark for writing the expression as $2(5x − 3)$ and 1 mark for explaining why this is always an even number.]

20

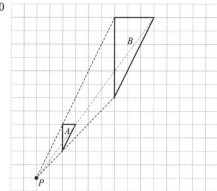

[2 marks available — 2 marks for image totally correct, otherwise 1 mark for 2 vertices in the correct position or for an image of the correct size but positioned incorrectly on the grid]

21 Elements of A are 3, 4, 5, 6
Elements of B are 1, 2, 3, 4, 6

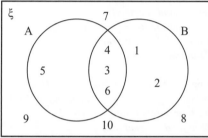

[3 marks available — 3 marks for a completely correct diagram, otherwise 1 mark for identifying the elements of sets A and B and 1 mark for correct elements in the intersection.]

22 8 litres of orangeade costs $(3 \times £1.60) + (5 \times £1.20) = £10.80$
So 1 litre of orangeade costs $£10.80 \div 8 = £1.35$
18 litres of orangeade cost $£1.35 \times 18 = £24.30$
[4 marks available — 1 mark for using the ratio to find the cost of 8 litres of orangeade, 1 mark for dividing by 8, 1 mark for multiplying by 18 and 1 mark for the correct final answer.]
There are several different methods you could use here. Any correct method with full working shown and a correct final answer would get 4 marks.

23 $y = \dfrac{x^2 - 2}{5}$
$5y = x^2 - 2$ *[1 mark]*
$5y + 2 = x^2$
$x = \pm \sqrt{5y + 2}$ *[1 mark]*
[2 marks available in total— as above]

24 a) 125 kW *[1 mark]*
b) See diagram in part d).
[1 mark for circling the point shown]
c) Strong positive correlation *[1 mark]*
d) Ignore the outlier when drawing a line of best fit.

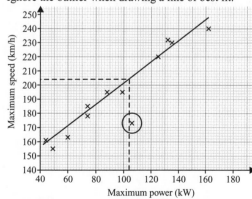

Maximum speed = 204 km/h (allow ± 2).
[2 marks available — 1 mark for drawing a line of best fit (ignoring the outlier), 1 mark for accurately reading from your graph the speed corresponding to a power of 104 kW]

e) 190 kW lies outside of the range of data plotted on the scatter graph. *[1 mark]*

25 Ollie's expression:
$(x + 4)^2 - 1 = (x + 4)(x + 4) - 1 = x^2 + 4x + 4x + 16 - 1$ *[1 mark]*
$= x^2 + 8x + 15$ *[1 mark]*
Amie's expression:
$(x + 3)(x + 5) = x^2 + 3x + 5x + 15 = x^2 + 8x + 15,$ *[1 mark]*
so the two expressions are equivalent.
[3 marks available in total — as above]

26 a) Angle for car = $360 - 162 - 36 - 45 = 117°$ *[1 mark]*
No. of office assistants that travel by car is = $\dfrac{117}{360} \times 80$
$= 26$ *[1 mark]*
[2 marks available in total — as above]
b) Total number of staff that travel by car
$= 26 + 18 = 44$ *[1 mark]*
44 represents 40% of the staff in the company, so the total number of staff (100%) is $44 \div 40 \times 100 = 110$ *[1 mark]*
[2 marks available in total — as above]

27 a) Mass of cylinder = volume × density
$= 1180 \times 2.7 = 3186$ g
[2 marks available — 1 mark for using the density formula correctly and 1 mark for the correct final answer.]
b) Mass of cube = mass of cylinder = 3186 g
Volume of cube = mass ÷ density
$= 3186 \div 10.5 = 303.428...$ cm³
Side length = $\sqrt[3]{303.428...}$
$= 6.719...$ cm = 6.7 cm (to 2 s.f.)
[4 marks available — 1 mark for using the density formula correctly, 1 mark for finding the volume of the cube, 1 mark for attempting to find the cube root of the volume and 1 mark for the correct final answer.]

28 $\sin x = \dfrac{18}{24}$ *[1 mark]*
$x = \sin^{-1}\left(\dfrac{18}{24}\right) = 48.590... = 48.6$ (to 1 d.p.) *[1 mark]*
[2 marks available in total — as above]

Practice Paper 3

1 $0.4 > 0.34$
$\dfrac{3}{4} = 0.75$
$7\% < 0.7$
[2 marks available — 2 marks for all correct signs, otherwise 1 mark for 2 signs correct]

2 0.404 *[1 mark]*

3 20 800 *[1 mark]*

4 −16.2 *[1 mark]*

5 8 *[1 mark]*

6 a)

Result of exam	Tally	Frequency
Fail	IIII	4
Pass	++++ ++++ I	11
Merit	++++ II	7
Distinction	II	2
	TOTAL:	**24**

[2 marks available — 1 mark for tally marks fully correct, 1 mark for correct frequencies]

b) $\dfrac{4}{24} = \dfrac{1}{6}$
[2 marks available — 2 marks for correct answer, otherwise 1 mark for $\dfrac{4}{24}$ or $\dfrac{2}{12}$]

c) E.g.

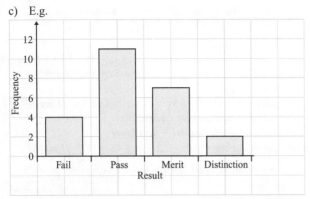

[3 marks available — 1 mark for correct vertical axis scale and labelling, 1 mark for 4 labelled bars of equal widths, 1 mark if the bars all have heights that agree with the frequencies found in (a)]

7 a) Impossible *[1 mark]*

b) There are 5 blue pencils, so evens. *[1 mark]*

8 a) Trapezium *[1 mark]*

b) Parallelogram *[1 mark]*

9 $\begin{pmatrix} -5 \\ 0 \end{pmatrix}$ *[1 mark]*

10 Square numbers: 1, 4, 9, 16, 25, 36...
Prime numbers: 2, 3, 5, 7, 11, 13, 17...
$2 \times 5 \times 9 = 90$, so Rick's numbers are 2, 5, and 9.
[3 marks available — 3 marks for correct answer, otherwise 1 mark for listing at least 2 square numbers or 2 prime numbers, 1 mark for 3 numbers which multiply to give 90, but which aren't 1 square number and 2 prime numbers.]
You could also answer this by using a factor tree to find that
$90 = 2 \times 3 \times 3 \times 5 = 2 \times 9 \times 5$

11 1 cupcake needs $132 \div 12 = 11$ g sugar.
So 30 cupcakes need $30 \times 11 = 330$ g sugar.
[2 marks available — 1 mark for a correct method, 1 mark for the correct answer]

12 Multiples of 12: 12, 24, 36, 48, 60 …
Multiples of 10: 10, 20, 30, 40, 50, 60, …
The smallest number they could each have bought is 60.
This is 6 packets of shortbread biscuits.
[3 marks available — 3 marks for the correct answer, otherwise 2 marks for finding that smallest number of biscuits they can buy is 60, or 1 mark for listing at least three multiples of 12 or 10]

13 Mary needs $2 \times 30 = 60$ scones, 30 tubs of clotted cream and 30 small pots of jam. *[1 mark]*
$60 \div 10 = 6$ packs of scones, costing $6 \times £1.35 = £8.10$ *[1 mark]*
$30 \div 6 = 5$ tubs of clotted cream,
costing $5 \times £2.95 = £14.75$ *[1 mark]*
30 pots of jam costing $30 \times £0.40 = £12$ *[1 mark]*
The total cost is $£8.10 + £14.75 + £12 = £34.85$,
so yes, she has enough money. *[1 mark]*
[5 marks available in total — as above]

14

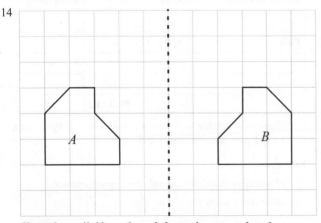

[2 marks available — 1 mark for each correct shape]

15

Plan view   Front elevation

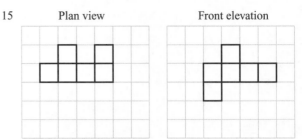

[2 marks available — 1 mark for each correct drawing]

16 Each trapezium has these dimensions:
Parallel sides: 12 cm and 7 cm
Height: 6 cm
So area $= \frac{1}{2}(12 + 7) \times 6$ *[1 mark]*
$= 9.5 \times 6 = 57$ cm² *[1 mark]*
[2 marks available in total — as above]

17 Box B contains $c + 4$ chocolates
Box C contains $2(c + 4) = 2c + 8$ chocolates
[1 mark for both expressions correct]
Total number of chocolates in Boxes A, B and C
$= c + c + 4 + 2c + 8 = 4c + 12$ *[1 mark]*
So $4c + 12 = 60$ *[1 mark]*
$4c = 48$
$c = 12$, so the number of chocolates in Box A is 12 *[1 mark]*,
the number in Box B is $12 + 4 = 16$ and the number in Box C is
$2 \times 16 = 32$. *[1 mark for boxes B and C correct]*
[5 marks available in total — as above]

18 a) $y \times y \times y = y^3$ *[1 mark]*

b) Subtract the powers: $n^6 \div n^2 = n^4$ *[1 mark]*

c) Multiply the powers: $(a^4)^3 = a^{12}$ *[1 mark]*

19 Use Pythagoras' theorem on the triangle formed by one step and the ramp. Let x be the length of the ramp.
$20^2 + 55^2 = x^2$ *[1 mark]*
$x^2 = 3425$
So, $x = \sqrt{3425}$ cm *[1 mark]*
Total length of the ramp $= 2 \times \sqrt{3425}$ cm
$= 117.046...$ cm
$= 117$ cm (3 s.f.) *[1 mark]*
[3 marks available in total — as above]

20 a) Dave's speed is $180 \div 3 = 60$ km/h *[1 mark]*
Olivia's speed is $60 + 15 = 75$ km/h
So it takes her $180 \div 75 = 2.4$ hours *[1 mark]*
$= 2$ hours 24 minutes *[1 mark]*
[3 marks available in total — as above]

b) E.g. If Olivia drove a different distance at the same average speed, her journey time would be different *[1 mark]*.

21 a)

x	−3	−2	−1	0	1	2	3
y	4	0	−2	−2	0	4	10

[2 marks available — 2 marks for all three values correct, otherwise 1 mark if one value is correct]

b)

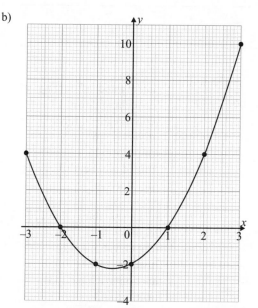

[2 marks available — 1 mark for plotting the points from your table and 1 mark for joining with a smooth curve to form a U-shaped curve]

22 $2 + 3 + 5 = 10$ 'parts' in the ratio. Angles in a triangle add to $180°$, so 10 parts = $180°$ and 1 part = $18°$.
So, the three angles in the triangle are $(2 × 18°) = 36°$, $(3 × 18°) = 54°$ and $(5 × 18°) = 90°$.
One angle is $90°$, so the triangle is a right-angled triangle.
[3 marks available — 1 mark for finding the size of one part of the ratio, 1 mark for finding the size of at least one angle in the triangle and 1 mark for showing that one angle is 90°.]

23 a) 25% higher than £120 000 = $1.25 × £120\,000$
= £150 000, so House 4 *[1 mark]*

b) £161 280 − £144 000 = £17 280 *[1 mark]*
% change = $\frac{17\,280}{144\,000} × 100$ *[1 mark]* = 12% *[1 mark]*

[3 marks available in total — as above]

24 Work back in Anna's sequence to find her 1st term:
$17 − 3 − 3 − 3 = 8$ *[1 mark]*
So the 1st term of Carl's sequence is $8 ÷ 2 = 4$ *[1 mark]*
So the first five terms of Carl's sequence are 4, 10, 16, 22, 28.
His 5th term is 28. *[1 mark]*
[3 marks available in total — as above]

25 a) $x^2 + 7x − 18 = (x + 9)(x − 2)$

[2 marks available — 2 marks for the correct factorisation, otherwise 1 mark for an answer of the form $(x ± a)(x ± b)$ where a and b are numbers that multiply to make 18]

b) $(x + 9)(x − 2) = 0$
$x = −9$ or $x = 2$
[1 mark for correct solutions using factorisation in (a)]

26 a)

1st spinner   2nd spinner

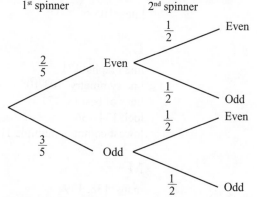

[2 marks available — 1 mark for the correct probabilities for the first spinner, 1 mark for the correct probabilities for the second spinner]

b) P(two odd numbers) = $\frac{3}{5} × \frac{1}{2}$ *[1 mark]*

= $\frac{3}{10}$ *[1 mark]*

[2 marks available in total — as above]

27 Change in $y = 8 − (−7) = 15$
Change in $x = 3 − (−2) = 5$
So gradient = $15 ÷ 5 = 3$
So $y = mx + c$ becomes $y = 3x + c$
Put in $x = 3$ and $y = 8$ to find the value of c:
$8 = 3(3) + c$, which means $c = 8 − 9 = −1$
The equation of the line is $y = 3x − 1$.
[4 marks available — 1 mark for a correct method for finding the gradient, 1 mark for the correct gradient, 1 mark for putting one point into the equation, 1 mark for the correct answer]

28

Weight (w g)	Frequency	Mid-interval value	Frequency × mid-interval value
$800 ≤ w < 1000$	5	900	4500
$1000 ≤ w < 1200$	8	1100	8800
$1200 ≤ w < 1400$	9	1300	11 700
$1400 ≤ w < 1600$	3	1500	4500
Total	25	—	29 500

Estimate of mean $29\,500 ÷ 25 = 1180$ g.
[3 marks available — 1 mark for attempting to find the mid-interval and frequency × mid-interval values, 1 mark for dividing the sum of the frequency × mid-interval values by 25, 1 mark for the correct answer.]